Remembering
Jack
Buck

By Rich Wolfe

ISBN: 0-9664912-5-4

Cover Photos: Courtesy of *The Sporting News*
Cover Design: Dick Fox
Photo Editor: Dick Fox
Cover Copywriter: Dick Fox
Interior Design: The Printed Page, Phoenix, AZ

Page Two. In 1941, the news director at a small radio station in Kalamazoo, Michigan hired Harry Caray away from a station in Joliet Illinois. The news director's name was Paul Harvey. Now you have the rest of the story............ ➡

DEDICATION

To Les Schepker, Jack Marlowe and Don Saforek

Three Great Guys, Three Great Cardinals Fans

In Memoriam

James Toomey
Jack Buck
Darryl Kile
Darrell Porter
Enos Slaughter

ACKNOWLEDGMENTS

Compiling the material for *Remembering Jack Buck* has been an experience I shall never forget. During this difficult time, his friends, co-workers, and loved ones have opened their hearts to recall their personal experiences—the fun, excitement, and interesting times spent with Jack Buck.

I am grateful to the hundreds of people who cooperated so willingly to make this tribute book special. There is no baseball family as close and wonderful as the Cardinal Family.

The author is personally responsible for all errors, misstatements, inaccuracies, omissions, commissions, communisms, fallacies...If it's wrong and it's in this book, it's my fault.

Sincere thanks to Special K, The Belle of Louisville, Jim Nuckols, Jim Meier and Bob Mayhall at *The Sporting News*, ESPN—The staff of ESPN.com and "Pardon The Interruption"; MLB.com and Mark Bowman and Jared Hoffman, Bill James, the baseball guru; the gorgeous Sheri Benoit; Dan Edson; Tom Langmyer and Jackie Paulus at KMOX, Dale Ratermann, Mr. Walter B. Planner and Tom McGivern, Allen Neuharth of *USA Today*, Curt Smith who wrote *The Story Tellers*, my over-qualified proof-readers Mike Roarty and John King, Jerald Andrews and the Missouri Sports Hall of Fame, Dan Caesar at the *St. Louis Post-Dispatch* for his Jack Buck Timeline and other considerable help, Tom Rohlfing, John Reheis, and the entire staff at Pinnacle Press.

This book would not be possible without the considerable efforts of Travis Seibert, Matt Fulks, and Swede Flodin. Muchas Gracias.

Because plagiarism is such an ugly word we give a tip of the Hatlo Hat and our appreciation to Diamond Publishing for use of limited material from The Mighty 'MOX a very interesting book and also to Rick Wolff and the folks at Warner Books for Jack Buck's entry in Curt Smith's terrific *What Baseball Means To Me*.

A sincere thank you to Rob and Sally Rains for all their wonderful input.

Thanks also must go to Lisa Liddy, The Printed Page, for her hard work at all hours of the day and night and her patience and professionalism in pulling the many pieces of this book together. Thanks also to Joe Liddy for proofing.

And most of all a very special thank you to the classy Carole Buck for her kindness and graciousness during a horrible period that saw her lose her husband and mother within a matter of a few weeks.

Chat Rooms

Preface

For many of us, baseball and Jack Buck defined our youth. Baseball is a game of memories, baseball is a game of sounds…the crack of the bat, the thud of a ball hitting a mitt, the roar of the crowd, the vendors hawking, the infielders chattering, but the sound the Cardinal fans came to cherish the most was the melodic voice of Jack Buck.

Jack and I go back a long time: We met when he was starting his first year announcing for the Cardinals and I was finishing my first decade on this planet. An intermediary named Philco introduced us one night in a granary on a farm in Iowa as I was practicing basketball. Once the chores were done, it was the same ritual every night: Start way on the left side of the radio dial. There was Earl Gillespie on WTMJ in Milwaukee covering Braves action for the team that had moved from Boston the year before…A little bit to the right was Detroit's WJR where Van Patrick, and later Ernie Harwell, sang the praises of Goebel's Beer and Harwell would tell stories about being baptized in the Jordan River or being Margaret Mitchell's paper boy in his Georgia youth…Slight twist of the dial towards the barn was WLW-700 AM—The Big One in Cincinnati where the Reds' Waite Hoyt talked about the taste of Hudepol Beer and the exploits of Klu…A little further south on the dial was **WGN**. Almost nightly, when the Cubs were on the road you could listen to Jack Quinlan, the Cubs talented, new young play-by-play man…Skip past the middle of the dial where the White Sox announcers were excruciatingly boring…A quarter twist more and you could listen to the Davenport Tigers in the Class B Three-I League. They were not as exciting as they had been in other years because their best player, Harvey Kuenn, and their announcer, Milo Hamilton, had gone to the big leagues the

> WGN and the Cubs are owned by the (Chicago) Tribune Company. WGN is an acronym for "World's Greatest Newspaper"…WLS—Chicago is an acronym for "World's Largest Store"— it was started by Marshall Field.

previous year…Just a smidgen further on the dial, towards town and there it was. Magic flowing through the air from St. Louis, Missouri. From the flagship station, KXOK (KMOX did not become the flagship station until the following year); excitement and enthusiasm from Harry Caray and Milo Hamilton and this new guy Jack Buck… Yup, that was the game to listen to tonight. It was going to be fun. It always was.

In those days when Elvis was the King, Little Richard was the Queen, and Springsteen wasn't even in middle management there were slide rules, but no major league team west of St. Louis, a Rapid Robert Feller but no batting helmets, a bazillion Wayne Terwilliger and Tommy Glaviano baseball cards but no Frank Lejas or Mickey Mantles, the Cubs were in the forty-sixth season of their first five-year plan, there were bomb shelters but no Mark McGwires, and there was the Cardinal announcing team and no one else. They brought their friends with them. They had neat names like Jabbo and Rip and Slats and Country, Vinegar Bend and the Kitten, but it was clear their best friend was Stan the Man.

Who needed to watch the pictures on that new Stromberg-Carlson thing my parents were watching in the farmhouse parlor when I could listen to Picassos. It was Christmas morning every broadcast; hopes sprung eternal every night. I was the perfect fan. The announcers were 154-0 managing from the booth. (Although it seemed like Harry did better than that). We never won a pennant but sometimes we felt like world champs…Then it was just a matter of time before one of my parents would yell from the front porch to bring the radio back into the house for their 10 o'clock news….but that was OK because we had the Kitten throwing in Brooklyn tomorrow night…. Eastern game, had to get the chores done earlier.

It was a great era in America. The people of my generation grew up during the very best time to be in sports: baseball cards were collected not for investments, but for the pure joy. You raced for the baseball diamond every free moment to play until you were called home for supper—without an adult being anywhere in sight. A trip to a major league baseball park, if it happened, was magical. Doubleheaders were plentiful. There were only eight teams in each baseball major league. A trade was a major deal. There were no free agents, there were no agents. There was no Astroturf, there was no designated hitter. It was speed and control, not velocity and location. There were no World Series night games. You waited impatiently each fall for the *Converse Basketball Yearbook* and every spring for the *Louisville Slugger Handbook*. It was a great time to grow up in the Midwest and the Cardinals and Jack Buck were a vital part of hundreds of thousands of childhoods.

There were two difficult obstacles in putting together this book. For openers, many close friends of Jack Buck would be in the middle of a wonderful story and suddenly break out in tears and choose not to continue. But the bigger problem by far was everyone—there were no exceptions—went off on long tangents about Jack Buck's kindness, his generosity, his quick wit, his helpful nature, and on and on with great testimonials about the type of person Jack Buck was. Sometimes repetition is good. For instance, in a book I did on Mike Ditka seven people described a run Ditka made in Pittsburgh the weekend of JFK's assassination as the greatest they have ever seen. Yet only one of those made the book. The editor didn't understand that when the reader was through with the book few would remember the importance or singularity of that catch and run, whereas if all seven had remained intact everyone would realize that one play summarized Ditka's persona and career.

So too, the repetition with Buck—except many times greater. It was overwhelming. More than 100 pages were deleted from this book because there were constant, similar and duplicate testimonials. Even so, many remained.

Another eerie happening was many fans talked about where they were or what they were doing when they heard of Jack's passing. It was like the JFK situation. Cardinal fans had a very special bond with Jack Buck. Jack Buck was an announcer and a man the way announcers and men used to be in an America that is not the way it used to be. He was really special.

Since the age of ten I've been a serious collector of sports books. During that time—for the sake of argument let's call it 30 years—my favorite book style is the eavesdropping type where the subject talks in his own words. In his own words, without the "then he said" or "the air was so thick you could cut it with a butter knife" waste of verbiage which makes it hard to get to the meat of the matter. Books such as Lawrence Ritter's *Glory of Their Times*, Donald Honig's *Baseball When the Grass was Real*, or any of my friend Pete Golenbock's books like *Go Gators* or *Amazin' (Mets)*. Thus I adopted that style when I started compiling oral histories of the Mike Ditkas and Harry Carays of the world. I'm a sports fan first and foremost, I don't even pretend to be an author. This book is designed solely for other sports fans. I really don't care what the publisher, editors or critics think. I'm only interested in the Cardinal fans having an enjoyable read and getting their money's worth. Sometimes a person being interviewed will drift off the subject but if the feeling is that baseball fans would enjoy their digression, it stays in the book. So if you feel there is too much material about Ireland, or ESPN, or midgets, or golfing, or Jack Buck's days at the racetrack, don't complain to the publisher... just jot your thoughts down on the back of a $20 bill and send it directly to me. Constructive criticism can be good for one's soul.

In an effort to get more material into the book, the editor decided to merge some of the paragraphs and omit some of the commas which will allow for the reader to receive an additional 20,000 words, the equivalent of 50 pages. More bang for your buck...more fodder for English teachers...fewer dead trees.

It's also interesting—as you will find in this book—how some people will view the same happening in completely different terms. Plus, with this format, you will usually find that the most interesting stories are from people you've never heard of before. There was a thought of omitting the attempts at humorous headlines (some of the headlines in this book prove that truly great comedy is not funny) and the factoids since this book was written shortly after Jack's death... but all of his friends questioned on this matter unanimously nixed that idea.

Every summer I make it back to my hometown to visit my parents' graves, followed by a trip to the family farm. No one lives there now, the granary burned down years ago, the other buildings have crashed on the jagged shores of modern farming realities, the house is history...but on each future visit—in my mind—I will lay my head on a pillow in my old bedroom and listen to Jack Buck on my transistor radio. It will be easy to do because memories, like heroes, never grow old.

Rich Wolfe
Scottsdale, Arizona

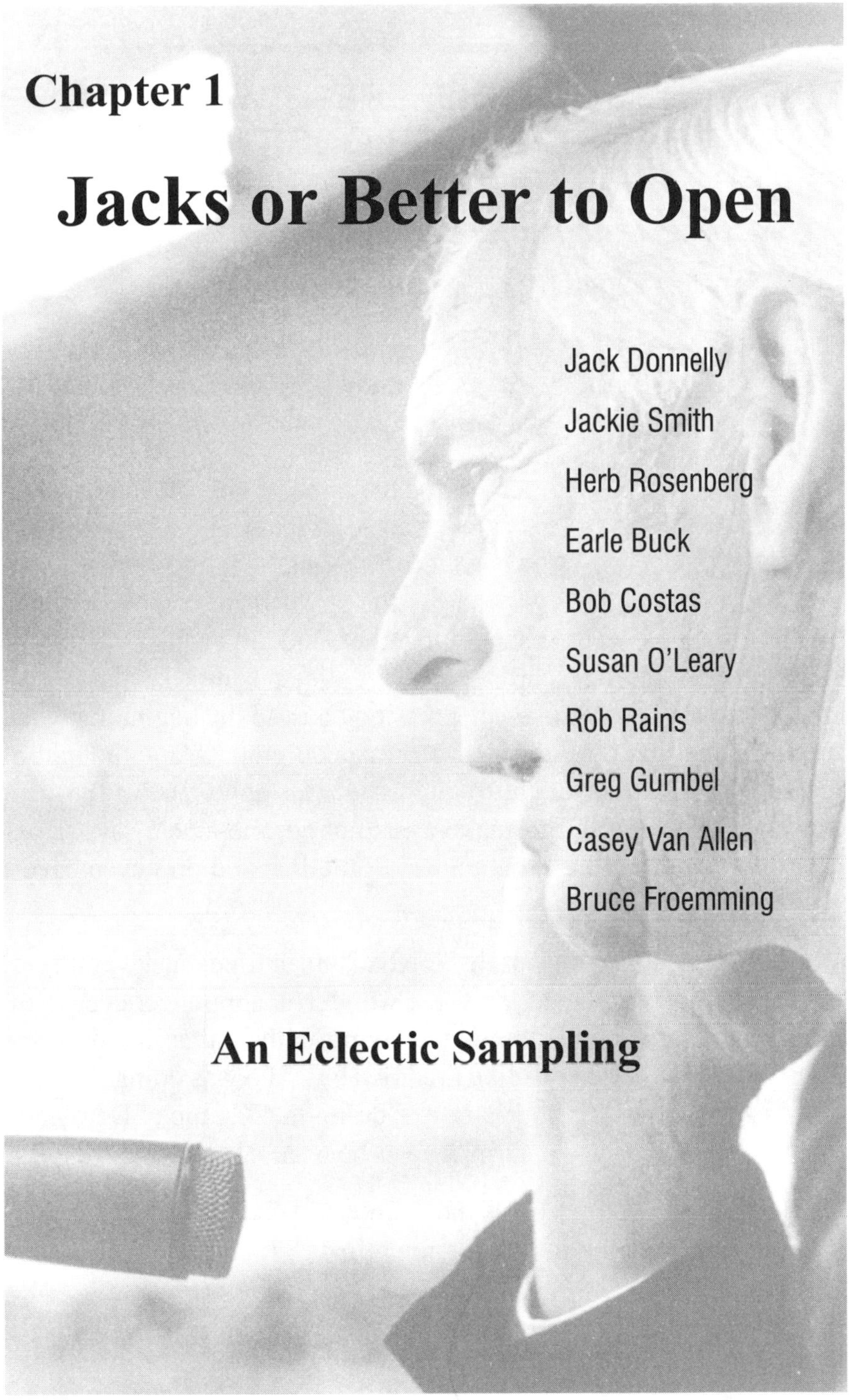

Chapter 1

Jacks or Better to Open

Jack Donnelly

Jackie Smith

Herb Rosenberg

Earle Buck

Bob Costas

Susan O'Leary

Rob Rains

Greg Gumbel

Casey Van Allen

Bruce Froemming

An Eclectic Sampling

THE WORLD WAS DIFFERENT WHEN JACK AND I WERE KIDS...FOR ONE THING IT WAS FLAT

JACK DONNELLY

Jack Donnelly was one of Jack Buck's closest childhood friends in Holyoke, Massachusetts. Donnelly is now in a nursing home in Tilton, New Hampshire.

Jack and I were best of friends when we were kids. I can remember when Jack's family moved in across the street from me. We became boyhood friends, went to school together, and did ordinary kid stuff. We collected baseball cards, and we collected milk bottles so we could go to the movies in the depression days. In the beginning when we played baseball, we didn't even have equipment. Jack thought of himself as a ballplayer; he thought he was going to be the next **Jimmy Foxx**. He used to make a joke about me—he'd say, "Donnelly, play right field and bat ninth." Sometimes I didn't even have a glove.

We played at Forestdale Park in Holyoke and at times Jack would call the game while we played. He was a wonderful announcer even then. He'd stand there and talk about the count on the batter and describe the game. He sounded just like Freddie Hoy, who was doing Red Sox games at the time. His specialty was doing the Kentucky Derby and other horse races—just making it up as he went. He really had a gift.

Our team was called the Highland Bombers. When Jack was inducted into the Hall of Fame in Cooperstown in 1987, all the old Highland

In Jimmy Foxx's last major league game (1945) he was the starting and winning pitcher. He pitched five innings throwing mainly a knuckleball.

Bombers went over to see him be inducted. Billy Williams and Catfish Hunter were inducted that day also.

When people ask me about Jack, I say he was just a regular guy. All the years he was the same to me as when we used to play after supper by throwing a tennis ball against the porch steps. We'd be out in the middle of the street, but there were very few cars in the '30s—he would even "announce" these two-person games.

Jack's father, Earle Buck, has the distinction of throwing the only perfect game in Holyoke High baseball history. It was in 1906 against West Springfield and Jack used to keep the clippings from that game in his scrapbook somewhere.

Although Buck is an English name, he has an Irish heritage from his roots on his mother's side. Her maiden name was Fox out of Dingle, County Kerry, Ireland. But as a kid we wouldn't call a Polish kid a Pole or an Irish kid an Irishman or a French kid a Frenchman. We all considered ourselves Yankees. If anyone asked us what we were, we'd always say Yankees.

Jack was a popular guy in school. I think when he left Holyoke, he was only about fifteen. He had an eye on the girls, like we all did. He came from a big family, three brothers and three sisters, seven in the family. Those were hard times in the depression. He and I always agreed that if we were poor, we never knew it. We always ate well. In later years we would talk and he'd say, "Donnelly, those were the days. Not much money, but a lot of fun." I always remember that. Every time we'd meet, he'd say it. That was one of his trademarks with me.

Every once in a while we would slip away, and hitchhike to New York or down to New Haven, Connecticut, and we used to hitchhike down to the Eastern League in Springfield to ball games. We never had the money to pay so I guess we'd go over a fence or under it or something, but we'd get in there.

Jack was about fifteen when his father was transferred by the Erie Railroad to Cleveland, and then Jack left. We would communicate with him from time to time thereafter. Holyoke was a great place to grow up. Jack and Herb Rosenberg and myself and some other guys—we were all like Huck Finn and Tom Sawyer. We were having a heck of a time with no money in our pockets. We have a lot of fond memories of growing up here. We would go swimming in the Connecticut River. We would explore underwater caves. We would dive for dinosaur tracks, showing them to friends and then we would throw them away. We would caddy over at Mount Tom **Golf** Club. We'd walk the railroad tracks to Springfield to watch professional baseball at Pynchon Park.

After Jack moved, we would hear what was going on with him through an aunt who still lived in Holyoke. His older brother Frank came back a couple of times so we still kept in contact. Then after the war, we got together again. Then the years went by so fast—I'm sitting here going to turn eighty. I thought when I was young—heck, when my uncle died, he was fifty, and I was in the service. I asked my mother how old he was and she told me he had just turned fifty—I thought that was ancient! Isn't that true how you think when you're young? When you're seventy, you think that's old, but then you look around and there's someone else who's eighty. Now, that's old. But seventy. Then all of a sudden you're going to turn eighty, and you say, "You know. Eighty's not bad at all."

During the war, he was in the Army in Europe, and I was in the Navy out in the Pacific. We met shortly after the war, 1945-46. He said, "What are you going to do, Donnelly?" I said, "I don't know. I'll look around a while and join that fifty-two/twenty club." That referred to the fact that after our discharge we got twenty dollars a week for fifty-two weeks. I said I'd join that and have a few Buds. I said, "What are you going to do?" He said, "I'm going to enroll at Ohio State under the GI bill." He was going to study journalism there, but anyway, he got into broadcasting while he was in college.

Sometimes I'd be with him in New York and after the game we'd go out to have a few Buds, or something, and it was just a natural thing with us. He was doing a hockey game at Boston Garden. He had two

> Geoff Long, a Cardinal in 1963-1964, once won golf's National Long-Drive Championship. Lon Hinkle is the only touring pro to win the same title.

others from his team with him, and we went to a nice restaurant in Boston. It's just automatic—he picks up the check. That was before he was making big money. His mother, a wonderful lady, had been a hard-working waitress in Holyoke at Gleason's Restaurant. When he was in town, we were eating there, and he said to the manager, "My mother was a waitress in this same restaurant." "Oh," she said, "that's nice." So he was just a regular guy.

Jack always used to like to joke that he made a heck of a lot more money than he thought when he was sleeping three in a bed in Holyoke here. He used to sleep with his brothers Earle and Frank as a kid. The family menu was oatmeal for breakfast, soup for lunch and leftovers for dinner. He used to come back here occasionally. He was back in about 1977 to show his wife Carole where he grew up. A few years before that he was back for a reunion of the Highland Bombers. Jack was a heck of a guy. If you told him you're from Holyoke, he'd treat you like a king. He was a big shot who didn't act like a big shot. He was easygoing and down to earth. That's why he lasted so long in the broadcasting business. People could identify with him. He knew what he was talking about and didn't try to make himself the show. That's why so many people, when Howard Cosell was on Monday Night Football, would turn off the sound on the TV and turn on the CBS Radio broadcast of the game so they could listen to Jack Buck and Hank Stram.

My mother was in a nursing home in Holyoke. I said, "If you think you've got time, we'll drop in and see her." He said, "Absolutely." She remembers when we were little kids eight and nine years old. When she saw him, she knew about his announcing games, and, by the way, up until she died, my mother was up on sports, and her mind was wonderful at almost ninety years old. When she saw Jack, she said, "Jack Buck. How does it feel to be rich?" He said, "Mrs. Donnelly, all we have are these plastic things." His credit cards, and she didn't even know what they were. That's just how kind he was.

I have a clipping from the *Boston Herald* during the 1986 World Series. A guy named Jim Baker of the *Boston Herald* was known for being extremely tough on media people. But he wrote, "Jack Buck has the right attitude about this World Series madness, or any major event, for that matter. He sits back, enjoys and communicates in a special way with his CBS radio audience. He low-keys it, he understates…he tells you what's happening in an authoritative yet simply stated manner. When his partner says the Red Sox are the least aggressive base running team he's ever seen in a Series, Buck sums it up with a phrase 'They call it station to station.'"

In 1970, he did TV baseball for ABC nationally so we got to see him all the time. Then in 1971 he returned as the "voice of the Cardinals." He also, of course, did the football Cardinals and the Chicago Bears, and he was the play-by-play man who broke in Pat Summerall, for a long time the top football announcer, into the broadcasting business. He also was the first voice of the St. Louis Blues in their early days in the National Hockey League.

We often talked about our memories—they were not of being poor at all, just a good childhood, a good place to grow up in.

The last time I saw Jack was up in Cooperstown, New York when he was inducted into the Baseball Hall of Fame as a broadcaster. I got together with Jack and Earle and Frank, his brothers. After his acceptance speech, they had a little party there at the hotel. That was about 1987.

My lasting memory of Jack is that he was the same guy when we were kids as when he got to the top of his profession. He just was a regular guy. He was a kind man, and caring, and he had great love for his family. He had a great love for people, the ordinary person and the more important ones. He loved people. I admired him for that.

On June 19, 2002, I had just gotten out of bed here at six o'clock in the morning. The first thing I do mornings is put the TV on. There looking at me was my best friend. He had passed away. Boy, that shook me up something terrible. It was on the news all day long that day. My sister lives in St. Louis, and she called and gave me the information. Also a nephew of mine called. I knew he had been sick for a long time. I wrote him get-well cards. Since then his wife Carole has written to me and filled me in on a lot of things. She said she and Jack had often talked about the good times we shared.

ALL IT TAKES IS ALL YA GOT

JACKIE SMITH

Former St. Louis Cardinal football great and member of Pro Football Hall of Fame, Jackie Smith currently holds an administrative position with a casino in the St. Louis area.

I first met Jack Buck when I was a rookie. My dad came to see me play. We walked up to him, and he said hello to my dad. Dad was very surprised to meet Jack Buck because he had listened to him on the radio a lot.

I don't think I was as much a personal friend of his as a lot of other guys were, but Jack was the type of guy who made you feel like that. He did a lot of football, and he and I talked about that. Outside of that we had a lot of occasions to run into each other at various functions we both went to over all the years.

Whenever a player gets nominated to the Hall of Fame, someone— usually a sportswriter from that player's city—is designated to speak to voters on behalf of the nominated player. Because of the great respect that everybody had for Jack, Dan Dierdorf and I probably had an edge on the other nominees. I think that went a long way toward our being elected to the Hall of Fame.

It is very hard to put a personality like his into focus. Jack was one of those people that you had to have been around to really appreciate because you can't believe that anybody can be quite that good and can have quite that impact on people and on a city as he did. He was just a special guy who lived what he was about and what he said he was about and what people would like to think he was about.

Sometimes, when you get to know a person in the public eye you discover they're really not the person they present themselves to be or that the media presents them to be. In Jack's case, he was much more than he ever presented himself to be. He was much more than people could discern about him by listening to him on the radio or seeing him on TV. He touched so many people in so many different ways, no matter who they were. He knew so many people all the way from Gene Autry to the President to whoever, and then there were so many people who were in the service industry, wait staff people and coat check girls who really felt a kinship with him and a friendship with him because he paid so much attention to them. He paid attention to everyone. You could be over in a corner and not part of the conversation and Jack would get you into the conversation by asking you questions about yourself. He was just an unusual guy like that because he would really go out of his way to do things for people. He really wanted people to like him, and they did, because he was so sincere about giving of himself.

He used to walk into a room and everybody's mood automatically perked up because Jack Buck had walked into the room, or because he was the master of ceremonies. You knew that as soon as he got to that microphone there was going to be a good time. Something was going to happen. He was going to be funny. He was going to be memorable. I never heard him ever get up to a microphone where he was just a normal, run of the mill deal. It was always a special treat to hear him talk. He was a motivator. When you listened to him, he made you think "How can I do things a little bit better myself?" And think better about people? Or about situations? Or about life?

I was playing with him in a golf tournament shortly after he got Parkinson's, and he really couldn't play so well. He would just go around the golf course and talk to the people. When he came to our green we had about a fifty-foot putt, and then he said, "Heck, I'll make that thing." He just walked up there and he made it. Then he got back in his cart and took off as if he did this every day. I played a round one time with him, Stan Musial, Dan Dierdorf and Red Schoendienst. It was quite a round of golf—it was very funny.

Another fun time with Jack was coming back from his installation as a Missouri Legend down in Springfield. I rode down and back with him and Charlie Spoonhour, Bob Broeg, Mike Roarty; all good friends and all great story tellers. It would have been okay with me if the plane had circled for a couple of days. In fact I would even go without food; we had enough beer, and we could have made it.

Jack was the kind of guy who always did this thing for a big Catholic church right before Christmas. He'd ask different players from different sports and everybody always came. If Jack asked you to do something, you came. You didn't even look at your schedule. If Jack asked you to do something, you just showed up. I remember all the parishioners were in there just trying to raise money and some guy was up trying to be the master of ceremonies. Jack stood up beside him and was just one-lining him back and forth. That was just Jack.

He had such a wonderful way of writing and presenting things. As a master of ceremonies, you hardly ever heard the same material repeated because he was so clever and witty and creative that he could put together something that fit every situation. He'd remember an old joke that would fit in there somewhere, and he'd just make the presentation delightful and very appropriate for that situation. He was always funny.

Jack handled his illness from Parkinson's with class and with his signature good humor. I was sitting next to him at a function once, and he had a piece of paper that had a word here and a word there. He had Parkinson's at the time so he couldn't write very clearly. I guess he was trying to write something and couldn't get it all written down because he'd have one word here and one word to the right of that, another word under it, another word down the page somewhere, then an underline mark, then some other kind of scribbly deal. He picked up that piece of paper when he was asked to get up and speak and read the most beautiful poem. It just came right out of the top of his head.

Two weeks before Jack went into the hospital, he asked Dan Dierdorf, **Stan Musial**, Mike Roarty and me to get together with him at a restaurant to talk about a project he wanted to do. We used to have an old

> Stan Musial hit 19 home runs as a grandfather in 1962. When he retired in 1963, he had every Cardinal batting record but one—highest single-season average. That was set by Rogers Hornsby.

stadium here, Sportsman's Park, which had been torn down a long time ago, back in 1967. That's where the other guys and I started playing. He wanted to have an artist create a painting or drawing of Sportsman's Park and have pictures of all the guys who played there superimposed on the painting. He then planned to have each player sign it so that the painting could be auctioned as a fundraiser for victims of the September 11th tragedy. That's the last time I saw him. He gave me a book of his poems and signed it over to me.

When Jack Buck died, the city of St. Louis lost a real treasure. He was as much a symbol of the city as the Gateway Arch. For all the people who knew Jack and were close to him or had any kind of association with him or knew about him at all, it was like the Gateway Arch just being taken away from St. Louis. He will never be replaced.

I rode to the cemetery and got in the line and headed out. It's the first time I've ever seen them stop the cars on an Interstate. We had to go through some semi-residential areas on the way to the Interstates, and there were people all along that route holding up signs or just standing there. You just really got a sense then of what an impact he had on the people of St. Louis.

Jack Buck's childhood home

IF YOUTH KNEW, IF AGE COULD DO

HERB ROSENBERG

Herb Rosenberg still lives in the same house in the same neighborhood where he and Jack Buck cavorted in their youth in Holyoke, Massachusetts.

Jack Buck was a real super guy. We grew up together and played ball. As a youngster, Jack knew all the players in the league and could give you their batting averages—there were only eight teams in each league.

He was not outstanding then. In those days we had nine different guys, and we didn't have enough gloves to go around. We used to have what was called "pickup games." We used to tape the bat with black tape. Sometimes when we would be playing ball, Jack would sort of announce to himself, "Here's so and so." When guys would bat in those days, and we'd be playing, we'd pretend we were some of the major league players and say, "**Ted Williams** at bat." Next guy up would announce himself as somebody else.

When we were kids, he was always interested in baseball. In those days all we did was buy these baseball cards. I wish I'd have saved them. We used to sail them against the wall in the winter and whoever would get the closest would pick them up. I had a whole room full of them.

I've kept in touch with him over the years. In fact, in his book, in the front, he's got a bunch of names. He's got "Herb Rosenberg, link-to-home man." In other words, when I see articles in the New York papers about his son or about him, I always send it to him. I figured

> Former astronaut and Senator John Glenn was Ted Williams' squadron leader in Korea. Ted Williams was John Glenn's wing man.

he wouldn't see these articles since they were in the New York papers. He was just the nicest guy.

One of our childhood friends was Jack Donnelly—his sister lives in St. Louis. Every once in a while when they would have a nice write-up about him in the different papers, she would send it to us. We've got one, *The Spirit of St. Louis*. I guess one of the headlines was "The Greatest Cardinal of Them All."

Jack was always very generous and went out of his way to make you feel like a king. When we went out to the '67 World Series, he introduced us to all the ball players. I've got a picture of Jack, myself, Stan Musial and Red Schoendienst.

We used to take trips with the Legion, bring the kids and go to **Shea Stadium**. Jack would always make sure to make it on the bus and say hello to all the guys. He'd bring a couple of baseballs, and every once in a while, he'd bring one of the ballplayers out to say hello.

Jack was a big sport—always picking up the checks. One time a guy admired his necktie, he took it off and gave it to the guy. Carole said she'd had to buy him more neckties! Little things like that.

My lasting memory of Jack is the time we went up to Cooperstown, New York, when he was inducted into the Baseball Hall of Fame. He didn't even know we were there. After the ceremony, we went by the hotel and couldn't even get near the place. They had guards all over, and you couldn't get in. Some guy was going through, and I just said, "Tell Jack that Rosenberg and Donnelly are down here waiting." Sure enough, he came down and got us, and took us up. We met all the ballplayers. When he got inducted, he just treated you like a king wherever you went.

I was at his seventy-fifth birthday two years ago. That was the last time I saw him. They had a party at one of his daughter's homes. He knew everybody was coming, but the surprise was that I was there

> During a 1979 Patriots vs. New York Jets game at Shea Stadium, a remote control model airplane crashed into the stands at half-time, hit a Patriots fan and killed him.

with my wife. There were five or six of us there that he hadn't known were coming. Jack Donnelly, who had lived across the street when we were kids, couldn't make it for health reasons. His brother Earle, in Cleveland, and his sister Mary came to the party. Musial and Schoendienst were the only ballplayers there. Most of the rest were family. The next day they picked us up, and we went over to his house. You should see his cellar. He's got things from all the years—Jackie Robinson and baseballs, you could spend a couple of hours there and never even see it all. We had a great time out there for two days.

Stan Musial was his best buddy. Earle Buck, Jack's brother, said to me once, "Of all the players, and I've met millions of them, by far Stan was probably the nicest one of them all."

During Jack's seventy-fifth birthday party I told the following story to one of his daughters and she roared with laughter. About thirty years ago, Jack was very busy doing several things. He was always a hit announcer. One time we called him up and said, "Do you think you could come and speak at a banquet?" Our high school had won the football championship and wondered if he would come as a guest speaker. He said he would come. The budget was zero, and we didn't have anything to give him. He came on his own, paying his own way. In those days in the Midwest he was considered the finest after-dinner speaker going. We had to pick him up at the airport. A few guys wanted to go with us so there were five guys there. There's an American Legion Post down the street a couple of blocks away from where we lived. We had about thirty or forty guys who were all excited because he was a celebrity. They were waiting to see him. We said, "Well when he comes in, maybe we'll bring him down there." So when we picked him up, we got in the car and we stopped in front of Jack Donnelly's house, which was across the street from where Jack had lived. We said, "You're going to stay here tonight." He said, "No, no." We said, "There's one other thing. If you don't mind, when we put your luggage away and get set, will you come down to Legion for about an hour? There are a bunch of guys there who want to meet you." He said, "Yeah, but wait a minute. I want to ask you guys one question. Be honest. What the heck am I doing here?"

BROTHERHOOD
EARLE BUCK

Earle Buck, Jack's brother, was almost two years older than Jack. They both graduated from Lakewood, Ohio High School and served in World War II. Earle is retired and lives in Avon Lake, Ohio.

I was almost two years older than Jack. We were both born in Holyoke, Massachusetts and we were very close as kids. In 1939, we moved to Lakewood, a suburb of Cleveland, Ohio. We both finished high school at Lakewood High School. I went into the Army in 1943 and Jack went in the following year. I stayed in the Army after the war was over. Jack went to Ohio State and, when he graduated, he got into the broadcasting business. We stayed in fairly close touch over the years.

I was traveling around, and he was down in Columbus, and then he moved to St. Louis. When I retired, we got more in touch with each other and remained very close until he died.

During the war, Jack was wounded in March of 1945 at Remagen Bridge. Lindsey Nelson was also wounded at Remagen Bridge at the same time. Then in April 1945, I was wounded in Germany also. We were both wounded badly but we came out of it okay. Our older brother, Frank was also in the Army, but he was not wounded.

I think Jack subscribed more to the personality of our mother than our father. Our father was a very quiet-spoken man with a great interest in baseball. Jack also had a great interest in baseball particularly when he was a kid—much more so than the rest of us. In later years, after we had moved to Ohio, he used to "broadcast" what was happening as we were playing sandlot ball. He just kept talking and talking and talking. "So and so hits a line drive. So and so hits a ball to the shortstop." We used to yell to him to shut up already, but he was practicing doing that. That's all he ever wanted to be, either a baseball player or a broadcaster. He followed through on the latter because he wasn't very good at the former.

He was my brother, but he also was my friend, and we remained friends. I never looked upon him as a celebrity, or whatever. I recognized him for what he did. I know that he lived and worked in an atmosphere that I'm not really in on. But I was proud of him for the recognition and the stature he received. I have to say that he never started out to attain stature or celebrity. He just wanted to broadcast ball games and whatever stature or recognition or celebrity he achieved just came to him. He didn't seek it, but when it came he used it wisely. He was a very, very generous person in giving of his time. He always had a kind word for someone. He never, ever turned his back on anyone. Naturally, we're all very proud of him and his achievements.

The last time I talked to him was about three weeks before he died. It was mostly one-way because he couldn't speak, but he knew what I was saying. He didn't have the words but I knew what he was saying. I knew when I left he told me he loved me, and I knew that was it. Jack was a good guy—a really good guy.

I was at home when Carole called me and told me about his passing. I felt a loss, but my own observation was that the thing that kept him living was his inner strength, not his physical strength. I mentally composed a letter, and this is going to shake me up. I was astounded at the size of the memorials and the tributes that he received. To me, the Cardinals front office management, ownership and the ball team just went overboard. It was a first class organization, and they did everything to help the Buck family and the fans of St. Louis celebrate Jack's life. Words can't describe it.

THE POISE THAT REFRESHES

BOB COSTAS

Perhaps the busiest man in sports, Bob Costas is like a young Jack Buck in the manner in which he cooperates with other people. He is outstanding in returning calls promptly and giving of his time.

The first time I met Jack, the people at KMOX took me for an audience with him. They decided to hire me, but they said I had to get the approval of Buck. He's got to sign off on it. So they brought me to the barbershop where he was getting his hair cut, and I actually talked to him through the mirror. I'm standing behind him, and they're snipping that white mane of hair, and he looks me up and down in the mirror and says, "How old are you, kid?" I looked like I was eleven—I was twenty-two. I said, "I'm twenty two." He said, "Well, I've got ties older than you, but I guess you'll be okay." That was the greeting. He was a wonderful guy.

I was in awe of him and was very much aware of who he was on a national basis because of all the big football games he'd done for CBS and because I was one of those kids who used to play with the radio dial and try to pull in out-of-town broadcasts. I often listened if the reception was good enough, even though it was a thousand miles away. I would listen to Jack and Harry Caray call Cardinal games on KMOX. It would come in sometimes on Long Island or Syracuse when I was going to college there. I was awed to meet him. I think I treated him not just respectfully, but almost reverently.

It took a while for Jack to warm to me. As time went on, I'd like to think that I proved not only worthy as a broadcaster, but that he saw that I was a well-intended person. We probably were more comfortable around each other as time went on.

Jack Buck was endeared to the people of St. Louis because he had the whole combination. I think you only got about seventy five percent of it on national radio or television, but day in, day out, in St. Louis, you got all the qualities. He had the commanding voice, especially in his prime. He had the glibness and the ability to describe plays, of course. He had a charismatic personal presence. He was unbelievable in person—in a banquet situation, or giving a speech. He had honest sentimentality, not some manipulative thing just designed to get a response. He could capture a moment, whether it was exciting or poignant or tragic, and he could speak for the audience as well as to the audience about that moment and really personify what the Cardinal fans and his listeners wanted to hear. Then on top of it, he had a tremendous dry sense of humor, often a self-deprecating sense of humor that pulled it all together.

I remember there was some dispute going on in a Saturday afternoon baseball game in the early nineties. It was a Game of the Week and he was doing the game with Tim McCarver. There was a camera person whose first name was Dena, I don't know her last name—who still works for NBC. He said something like, "If such and such ever occurred, I'll give you a thousand dollars." Something like that, and he said it on the air. Dena said it occurred, and she was right so he wrote this woman a check for a thousand dollars. He was known as a big tipper. He was known as a generous man. Obviously the greatest form of generosity is giving of his time to be at charity events. He was an excellent master of ceremonies, always had good, prepared material, and more important, he could react to the situation and respond to what was happening. Someone would get up to speak or something would happen, and he'd have a good line.

Jack had a presence in the life of anyone who was around St. Louis for any period of time. There were highlights—Ozzie Smith's home run, Jack Clark's home run, and the reading of the poem when baseball returned after the September 11th tragedy. There are individual highlights, but I don't know that any of them trumps the rest. He's just a presence, a combination of good naturedness and generosity in every sense—generosity of spirit, generosity with money, and generosity with time.

I think someday I will go back and broadcast locally when the cir-cumstance presents itself, but no matter how good a broadcaster may be, on a national level, they cannot be admired and respected and appreciated in a way you can with a local audience. Baseball allows that more than any other sport because you play a hundred and sixty two games, and it's day-in, day-out. The announcer is a guy describ-ing an event, but he's also a companion, someone you're just passing time with. It is a pastime. I don't think it's as possible, even on local radio now, to have the kind of connection that Vin Scully has had or Ernie Harwell or Jack Buck had or Mel Allen or Red Barber because the world has changed. So even if you root for the Cardinals, you're still bombarded by everything that's on cable TV and all the highlight shows, and the pace of the world is different. But there's still a differ-ent relationship. And it used to be a wonderful relationship in the fifties and sixties before the broadcasting world changed—a differ-ent relationship between a local announcer and his audience.

You know one of today's great voices is Jack's son, Joe. Joe has the whole package. I think, and I say this with great respect for both of them. He's every bit as talented as a broadcaster as his dad was, and he has that package of humor, knowledge of the game, good voice, everything else, but Joe's career essentially is going to be on national television. He's going to be great at it. He's the best play-by-play man of his generation, and he's only in his early thirties. But the circum-stances just won't allow him to have the same connection where people feel that the soundtrack of their life was Jack Buck's voice, or at least a huge part of the soundtrack of their life. That won't happen for Joe. It's not his fault. He's painting on a different canvas.

Jack's disease was very, very apparent, but he just persevered through it. It wasn't that he didn't let it show, he didn't try to hide it at all. He didn't go to any great lengths. If he was self-conscious about it, he wouldn't have gone out on the field to read the poem. The person who went out on the field to read the poem was an aging and afflicted Jack Buck, and that's one of the things that endeared him to people. They remember him when he was at his peak, and yet they saw in him the same worthwhile qualities toward the end of his life. To the end he retained his sense of humor. One of his best lines ever was "I've given the Cardinals some of the best years of my life, and now I'm gonna give them some of the worst." I thought that was simultaneously very witty and very endearing.

Jack's death is a great loss. There are circumstances that are unique to St. Louis. During Jack Buck's entire career, since he arrived in 1954, the Cardinals were the only team in St. Louis—not the dominant team—the only team. You've got a combination of factors. The diversity of talent that wasn't confined to just calling baseball games. He did interview shows, he was a tremendous emcee, he did countless charity events and he was an amazing presence around town. Many people in St. Louis had some personal contact with him even if it was only being in the audience when he emceed an event. Or they had some personal recollection of him in addition to all the memories of the games that he called. And then you have the reach and power of KMOX. You know, Ernie Harwell is rightly beloved in Detroit, but baseball in Detroit is not the same thing as baseball in St. Louis. St. Louis is the number one baseball city in America, according to most objective observers. So you've got tremendous passion. Football was absent here for a while. Until the recent success of the Rams, it never came close to baseball. In terms of roots and generational significance, it just doesn't compare to baseball. Jack was a great announcer that had the team and the stage to enhance his unique ability. It mattered that the team was often very good. It had Musial and Brock and Gibson and McGwire and everybody in between. So you've got a little bit of everything. There are some announcers that are in Jack's class in terms of greatness, but I don't know that anybody ever pulled in as many different elements for his audience as Jack did.

> **One of his best lines ever was "I've given the Cardinals some of the best years of my life, and now I'm gonna give them some of the worst."**

As far as naming a new stadium after Jack, it would be nice to see it happen. It would certainly be an appropriate thing. I think there would be broad public support for it happening.

I thought the Cardinals handled his death perfectly. There is some conflict involved over the financing of the new stadium. They have had, in everything that has to do with their history, and their relationship to their fans, almost perfect pitch—the present Cardinal administration. From 1996 on, every touch is just right, the statues, the retired uniform numbers, the display of the past pennant winners and world champions, changing from artificial turf to grass, the way they made the stadium look like a ballpark even though by design it's a cookie-cutter place like Cincinnati, Pittsburgh, and Philadelphia, but they've made it feel like something other than that. In that sense, they have a perfect understanding of what the team means to the region, what it's history means, and the way they handled everything—the ceremony regarding Jack and then the ceremony for Darryl Kile. It's all been classy.

Bust of Jack Buck, Missouri Sports Hall of Fame

Jack came
self out
to the
to

...S GOD'S WAY OF BEING
...NAL FANS

*...ry of St. Louis is the mother of
...hn O'Leary who was badly burned in a
home accident in 1987. Many people credit
Jack Buck with inspiring young John to fight
for his life.*

Our son John, who is soon going to be twenty-five, was badly burned on January 17, 1987. It was about nine o'clock on a Saturday morning, and there was a fire burning in our fireplace in the family room. John, at age nine, had the curiosity as to what would happen if you took some paper and lit it and poured gasoline on it. He went out into the garage, poured gasoline on this piece of lit paper, the Saturday comic strip. Of course, before the gasoline even hit the paper, the fumes ignited and just exploded spewing gasoline all over John. Immediately he was inflamed completely. He ran into the house, screaming, and our son Jim threw him down on the rug and burned his own hands trying to put the flames out on John. John was at that time burned on a hundred percent of his body, eighty-five percent were third-degree burns, and fifteen percent were second degree burns, so he was burned all over. They didn't expect John to survive the two-minute ambulance ride from our house to St. John's Hospital.

That night there was some kind of big sports dinner. A friend of mine, Colleen, who is Red Schoendienst's daughter, told her mother about it that day. That night Mary Schoendienst told Jack what had happened. Then on Monday or Tuesday, Jack appeared at John's room in the burn unit at St. John's. At that time you had to put on a mask, and hat, and gloves, and booties just to come into the room. He came in, and John had swollen to about twice his usual size. The only thing that could be seen on John were his eyelids and his lips. He was on a pirator so he couldn't talk—he was not in a coma. But , and just talked to him, "John, you know when you get you of here, and you're feeling up to it, I want you to come down ballpark, and I want you and your dad to come up, and I want yo sit next to me in the broadcast booth." We found out years later, tha when he left John's little cubicle, he walked up to the main station, and said to the nurse, "That kid's not gonna make it. He's really messed up, isn't he?" The nurse said, "Yeah. John is going to die. He's not going to make it." Jack just grabbed a towel and put his head down on it and sobbed, not knowing us, not knowing John, just having driven out there. He came out another two or three times to the hospital. He brought Ozzie Smith. He brought Larry Stallings of the football Cardinals. His wife Carole came out a couple of times to deliver a tee shirt to John or something else from Jack.

Before John was able to go down to one of the games, he started getting baseballs in the mail. We knew they were from Jack Buck; although, he claims he didn't send them. We knew that Jack was doing it. He would say to John, "All you have to do is write a thank-you note to the person who sent you the ball, and you'll get another one." The burns were terrible, and John lost all of his fingers, but he would write those thank-you notes and three or four days later, he would get another autographed ball.

We took him down to the ball field, and the first night he just was there in the booth. Then there were other occasions when he went down early with his dad. He and his dad and Jack Buck and Red Schoendienst, and maybe Ozzie Smith, sat and watched batting practice, just the five of them. John periodically would go up and visit in the booth throughout the years, just say "hi" to him.

At Jack's induction into the Hall of Fame, Jack said something to the effect that "I have been called a hero. But I'm not a hero. The real hero is John O'Leary who's back in St. Louis and encountered massive burns and is overcoming them." Can you believe that Jack Buck made reference to John at his induction into the Hall of Fame? When John graduated from St. Louis University, three years ago, Jack and Carole were invited to a dinner for John at Busch's Grove restaurant, which they couldn't attend because he was broadcasting a game that night. When we got to the little hut at Busch's Grove, there was this present on the table. The maitre'd said, "Mrs. Buck brought this over about an hour ago for John." When John opened it later, he found that Jack had given him the Waterford cut-glass baseball that he received when he was inducted into the Hall of Fame. It was incredible. He's just an absolutely incredible, amazing person. There is no doubt in my mind. I just wrote his wife a note and told her how that it had been a privilege and a joy and a thrill and a blessing to have had the relationship we had with her husband, and that there was no doubt in my mind that Jack was most definitely a part of John's mastering his comeback from a terrible, terrible accident with the incredible burns. John is the most seriously burned patient that has ever survived at St. John's Hospital. They've got that in his record. I have talked to people, and they have said that there is no one else. A doctor said there may have been two since who have come back but that neither of them have the mobility and have the life that John has. I told Carole that there's no doubt in my mind that Jack's goodness and his interest in John was one of those parts of the puzzle that helped John come through and ultimately live the life he is living right now. John was in the hospital four months and Jack was very faithful to him throughout that time, whether it was a phone call or coming out, by himself or bringing someone else with him, to visit John.

In a local story recently, John simply said that Jack Buck had been to him like a grandparent who lived out of town, who you loved very much, but didn't get to see, when he died, it really hurt. John said what Jack Buck really did, "he visited me, and he sent me balls, but his interest in me changed so many things in my life and made me realize what I could do for other people." After John's party that Jack couldn't attend, the next day we were having Sunday brunch in our house, and the phone rang. It was Jack and he wanted to know how John's party was, if you can imagine.

All of us, like all of St. Louis and so much of the world, has just been saddened and so touched by the passing of this man who was so good to people he had never met before. That was the amazing thing—his compassion for people that he had never even known before.

There is no doubt that we all feel like he's a part of our family. We would talk about how unusual it was for someone to have an interest in someone they didn't even know. I remember saying to John's doctor, "Why are you letting somebody come in here?" We had found out right before he got there that he was coming in. I said, "How can you let Jack Buck come in here when you're telling me that John might die. Any little germ could cause the end of him in hours. How can you let someone else come in?" Doctor Vatche Ayvazian, Burn Specialist, said, "You never know when just that one moment, that one visit, that one person, is going to add a spark that will just contribute to someone's ability and their decision to keep fighting." Really we feel so strongly that he did that for John. We were "family from afar." There's no doubt about it. They were certainly always in our hearts.

I'm thankful that my son is the person that he is, and to just be able to attribute a great portion of that to the encouragement and the interest that Jack took in John. He had him on the radio his first time when he sat by his side. It was the summer after the accident and he and his dad sat in the booth. We were in the Anheuser-Busch booth looking over there constantly. I think it went into fifteen innings, and John was by Jack Buck's side the whole time. I think he was on the radio at one time talking about his dad saying that he had beat him a footrace a week before, or that he'd had a footrace with him, and I can remember John saying, "We did have a footrace, and I won." So for a little boy nine years old who had been through all that, Jack Buck was very perceptive and like in everything else, he was able to get into the heart of where John was and say something pertinent like that. John would go down and visit him periodically in the booth after he was out of the hospital. Jack would mention John, "My friend, John O'Leary, back in St. Louis," or "I wonder if my friend, John O'Leary, is listening to this game." So he was just very sweet with him all the way through. That was fifteen years ago.

It's almost like Jack Buck was an angel.

OUTSIDE OF A DOG, A BOOK IS MAN'S BEST FRIEND; INSIDE A DOG, IT'S TOO DARK TO READ
ROB RAINS

Rob Rains grew up in Springfield, Missouri listening to Jack Buck. After graduating from Kickapoo High, he earned a degree from the University of Kansas. He has written books on Ozzie Smith and Whitey Herzog, and The Cardinal Nation, among others. His best seller by far has been That's a Winner *with Jack Buck in 1997. Rains' wife, Sally, is also an accomplished writer.*

In the early '90s I was working for *Baseball Weekly* covering the National League. I saw Jack off and on whenever I would come into town to do Cardinal stories. At some point in there I said, "Have you thought about doing a book?" He said, "No, I don't want to do a book." In the spring of 1995, I was in Washington and was talking to Jack on the telephone. I said, "I'm never going to ask you again to do a book, but if you ever decide that you want to do a book, you know that I'd love to do it." Then I went to teach at Arizona State for the 1995-96 school year. We moved back to St. Louis in May of 1996, Memorial Day weekend. The Cardinals were playing so I went down to the ballpark. I had just gotten to the ballpark and walked into the club house, and the first person I saw in the club house when I walked in was Jack. The first thing he said to me was, "When are we going to do that book?"

I talked to a couple of different people that I knew within publishing circles and realized our choices were to either go with a large publishing firm, perhaps in New York City, and they would want us to criticize CBS and other people and they would treat it just like any other book and it would not get the attention we wanted. Or we could go with somebody like Sports Publishing, Inc in Champaign,

Illinois, and they didn't really care what he said about people. In other words, it didn't have to be controversial. They were really excited about the book and they promised to treat it well and make it their number one book.

We did the book over the course of about six months from May of 1996, till I turned in the final manuscript in December. When Jack was in town and had some time, we would go over the thing. Mostly it was at his house, and we would work two or three hours doing taped interviews. Then it came out in April of 1997.

When people asked me what is the favorite book that I have done, I always say it's Jack's book simply because it was so much more than anybody expected it to be. He talked about so many things other than just baseball. I think people thought he would just talk about baseball and that was it. I did not know until I started getting involved with the project and doing the research and talking to him that he has had so many unique life experiences. That's what made the book so special, and why I enjoyed it so much. We ended up with twenty-eight hours of tapes. The manuscript ended up a little over three hundred pages, single-spaced.

At the time the book came out, it may have been the biggest-selling book on the market. We did some signings and Jack did some radio interviews. He'd promote it. Jack was more involved in the editing and rewriting phases of the book than anybody I'd ever been involved with. He really reviewed the manuscript and made suggestions and changed some words. He was really a hands-on person more than anybody I've ever dealt with. He really wanted the book to be good. He wanted it to be accurate. He wanted it to be a good portrayal of his life. What made me the proudest is that I think he was happy with it. He worked hard making sure it was good.

I saw Jack the night before he went into the hospital. He was the emcee at a banquet that I was in charge of at the Missouri Athletic Club. He had told me a week or so ahead of time that he wasn't feeling well and to get somebody else to be available as a back-up in case he wasn't able to come. I knew he was supposed to be going into the hospital that weekend to have a battery in his pacemaker changed. I called him the day before the banquet just to make sure he was home and see what was going on. He said he hadn't gone into the hospital yet, but that he was going to leave from the banquet, which was on a Wednesday night, and go straight into the hospital from there. I thought that he was just going in for the pacemaker operation. We were sitting in my office about an hour before the banquet was going to start and he told me about the cancer and that's why he was going into the hospital to have surgery. He stayed for about half, maybe three-quarters of the banquet and then left.

Jack was a wonderful person—a wonderful announcer. People in St. Louis didn't realize how big a part of this community he was and how beloved he was. Everybody thought that when Jack died, it would be a big deal, but I don't think anybody in their wildest imagination realized how big it would be and what the public response would be. *The Post* didn't intend to do a special section. They were going to do a couple of pages. Then advertisers just started calling asking how they could get an ad in the paper for Jack. It ended up being a special section for about three days in a row.

Some people said that it wasn't that big of a deal in Chicago when Harry Caray died. Of course, it was. Harry Caray was a very popular broadcaster—and obviously it was a very big deal when he died. But it was not like losing an icon in a town the size of St. Louis. Jack was Mr. St. Louis. He was so much more than just a baseball broadcaster. Everybody in St. Louis knew who Jack Buck was—you didn't have to be a baseball fan. I can't begin to tell you how many people on the radio and fans on the street that had their own story about a time when they met Jack.

EVEN GREG'S CHILDHOOD PICTURES WERE HAND-ME-DOWNS FROM HIS BROTHER, BRYANT

GREG GUMBEL

Greg Gumbel was the first network broadcaster to host and call the play-by-play at the Super Bowl. For five years, he hosted CBS Radio's coverage of Monday Night Football. Currently, Gumbel is the main play-by-play announcer for the NFL on CBS. He is a graduate of Loras College, Dubuque, Iowa.

Credit: CBS Photo Archive

I remember Jack as being, first and foremost, maybe one of the funniest human beings I've ever encountered in my life. Secondly, I thought that he exuded class. People say that a lot about him, but it's tough to overemphasize just how classy a guy he was. It's a rare broadcaster who's very secure. Jack never had any inhibitions whatsoever. He knew how good he was, and it showed. Jack was very easygoing. He went about his work as easily as anybody I've ever seen.

The one Jack Buck call I remember the most is the Kirk Gibson home run. The magnitude of the home run, to me, kind of drowned out the fact that here's Kirk Gibson with a bad leg, who looked horrible on the fastball that **Dennis Eckersley** threw him, so why does Eckersley throw him a breaking ball? Nobody ever mentioned that. Not that

> Late in his career, Dennis Eckersley was second among all active Major League pitchers, in complete games—even though he hadn't thrown a complete game in eleven years…Eckersley once had 21 consecutive hitless innings…one year he had more saves than base runners allowed.

Kirk Gibson couldn't hit a fastball, but he was clearly injured at the time. If you throw him anything but a fastball in that situation, you're doing him a favor. Nobody ever seemed to bring up that point.

Jack had his fair share of great calls. Some of that is due to longevity, but some of them he probably made famous just by his style and his ability to do it.

I read an article recently that showed that style, that Jack sense of humor, from a game when the Cardinals were playing in San Diego. At this particular point in the game, the next three hitters for the Padres had German names. Jack said something to the effect of, "Did a U-boat just surface off the San Diego coast?" That's amazing to me because it's so funny and it was so quick.

Unfortunately, there are some who walk into a broadcast with a script. They wait for a particular moment to happen, and then they "read" their script. That, to me, is not what you consider the true measure of a broadcaster. Just about any announcer could sit at home and try to write something for every single occasion, then when it happens, you go flipping through your notepad. If you sat down and talked to Jack, and realized how incredibly funny he was, you realized that his lines weren't scripted.

I was in Tampa with Jack and Hank Stram for Super Bowl XXV, for CBS Radio, when the New York Giants beat the Buffalo Bills. During the game, Jack said, "Thurman Thomas around the right side, and a heck of a lick put on Thomas by Lawrence Taylor." There was about 10 seconds of silence before Hank said, "I don't know who made that tackle, Jack, but it was a heck of a tackle."

After the game we were walking through the parking lot. Jack was about 15-20 feet behind me. He called my name and nodded for me to drop back, so I did. As we were walking he said, "If I ask you a question, will you be straight with me?" "Sure." He said, "Do you think Stram listens to 20 percent of what I say?" It was so typical of Jack.

Without question, Jack and Hank were a great broadcasting team. I don't care how much **Howard Cosell** tried to deny it or downplay it, people didn't tune in to Monday Night Football to listen to him. ABC really didn't care whether you tuned in to love Cosell or hate him; they just cared that you tuned in. I didn't care enough to tune in to hate him (and I certainly didn't love him). I thought that Jack and Hank were a much better listen.

I hosted Monday Night Football on radio for five years. We would talk on the radio during the pregame. It would be Jack, Hank, John Madden and me in this discussion. John Madden always wanted to know what Hank thought about the game coming up that night. Always. However much anybody would joke about Hank Stram, John wanted to know what Hank thought about the game. There's no question that Hank had one of the brilliant football minds of his day.

I never had the pleasure to hear him emcee an event, but I have heard he was one of the best. The best speaker I have ever seen at an event is Terry Bradshaw. He's far and away the best speaker I have ever seen. He is completely entertaining. But I have heard stories about how Jack could emcee an event every night of the week and never tell the story twice. He's a great storyteller in the way that I consider Pat Summerall to be a great storyteller. He is incredibly funny. Pat could sit and tell you jokes for two hours, and his delivery is as funny as the story. Jack was the same way. They both have that deadpan approach with the deep, serious voice right through the punch line.

To be able to have gotten to know Jack Buck, and be on personal terms with him, to know that when he sees me he says, "Hi, Greg, how are you doing?"; to know he's gone so far as to invite me to his home; and we've had dinners together, is one of those huge thrills in life that you never expect, but for which you're very grateful when it comes along.

Dinner with Jack was incredible. He would sit there, then all of a sudden he'd nudge me and whisper, "Watch Stram." He loved Hank.

John Lennon's death was first reported to the nation by Howard Cosell on Monday Night Football. In 1999, Monday Night Football became the longest-running prime-time entertainment series ever, breaking a tie with Walt Disney at 29 years.

He really loved Hank, but we were sitting together out in Honolulu by the pool, when they kicked Hank out of the swimming pool because he was leaving a layer of suntan lotion on the surface of the water. So, they asked him to get out of the pool, because it looked like the Exxon Valdez had gone through there.

I thought they were one of the terrific broadcast teams. Cosell was popular, and Jack and Hank were popular, but Jack and Hank were popular for all the right reasons. For all of the shouting and screaming that was made over Dennis Miller, I'll tell anybody who will listen, Dennis Miller knew more football than Howard Cosell ever did.

There are people who ask me if it's important that a broadcasting team gets along off the air. I've had great partners in my career. I have a great one now in Phil Simms. I have a great one in the studio during the Final Four in Clark Kellogg. Terry Bradshaw and I were partners for four years on the NFL Today, and he is terrific. I also worked with Quinn Buckner on basketball broadcasts, and Ken Stabler on football. Both of those guys are great. I cannot **fathom** how difficult it would be to do what is a difficult job, if you didn't get along with your partner.

It's not absolutely necessary that you get along with your partner in order to deliver a good broadcast. There have been plenty of people who wouldn't fall into that category. Having said that, it's a lot easier on the announcers, and it's easier on everyone who has to work with the announcers. Hank and Jack were almost inseparable.

I can't imagine anyone not getting along with Jack. You may have a real problem finding someone to say a negative word about him. Even for the sake of balance in a book, it would be difficult to accomplish finding someone to talk negatively about Jack. I don't know of anybody who disliked him.

> During the Seattle Mariners first year in 1977, they measured their distance to the fences in fathoms. A fathom is 6 feet. For instance, where a park may have a sign that denotes 360 feet, the Kingdome would have the number 60.

CALLING MR. HYLAND "BOB" IS LIKE CALLING ATTILA THE HUN "TILLY"

CASEY VAN ALLEN

Casey Van Allen (real name Dennis Klautzer) owns KRMS-AM and KRMS-FM of Osage Beach, Missouri in the heart of the Lake of the Ozarks. At the age of 16, he lucked into a disc jockey job with a St. Louis station and hosted a live show from Teen Town, a "hot" youth scene. One of the house bands was Michael McDonald. Upon joining KMOX, his on-air name was Casey Van Allen, which was a take-off on popular St. Louis DJ and Program Director, Al Casey.

I worked at just about every St. Louis radio station throughout my career and there was only one left to conquer. That was the number one mamma-jamma, and that was KMOX of course. I got close. I got to work for KMOX's FM, which was KMOX-FM at the time. Then in 1980 we changed the call letters to KHTR and made it a **top forty station**. We went from the bottom of the heap in the music ratings to the top in just two rating periods. I had Mr. Hyland's attention at the big Mighty 'Mox. His office was down on the third floor. We never went on the third floor, by the way. You didn't go down on the third floor unless you were in trouble. That's where Mr. Hyland was.

I was working the seven to midnight shift and my ratings just kept getting bigger and bigger and bigger. Finally I had a third of the St. Louis audience on my show. That was hurting KMOX, and nobody

> The band, Pearl Jam, was originally named Mookie Blaylock, after the NBA player, and they recorded their first album, "Ten" under that name. In 1992, the band Mookie Blaylock changed their name to Pearl Jam after a hallucinogenic concoction made by lead singer Eddie Vedder's great-grandmother, Pearl.

hurts Mr. Hyland's mighty station. So the offer was made for me to go to work for KMOX. I went down there to KMOX and Mr. Hyland wanted me to do commercials and be the imaging director for the station and control the image of KMOX. Mr. Hyland came in at midnight and didn't leave until five o'clock in the afternoon the next day. I came down real early in the morning and met with him. He takes me into the studio and tells me this is where I would be working. I looked around and the equipment was like from the Marconi era. I said, "Thanks Mr. Hyland. I really wanted to work for the number one station in St. Louis, but I think I'm just going to pass." He said, "No, no, no. Make me a list of what you need." I really did want to work there but I was afraid I was going to get short-changed somewhere down the line and not get the proper tools to do the job. So I made this outrageous list of equipment—I mean it was outrageous—wanted a whole new studio. I think the total tab came to five to six hundred thousand dollars. I took it in to him the next day. He looked at it, turned the page over, and he said, "Okay, when do you want to start?" I said, "Holy Toledo. I can't say no to that."

I ended up being the production and imaging director for KMOX in 1982. At that time Dan Dierdorf and Bob Costas and Jack Buck made up the sports department. It was a real thrill—more than a thrill, it was an honor to work with those guys. I produced all of Bob Costas's syndicated shows that were on two hundred radio stations around the country. I produced his *Sporting News Flashback*, *The Sporting News Report*, daily three-minute shows, for the entire run. I also did *John Madden's Sports Quiz*. I created that show and produced it.

Jack was the director of sports at KMOX so I worked pretty closely with him throughout the years and I'd only been the imaging guy at KMOX for a short period of time when the Cardinals went to the World Series. I thought this was really the time to make Jack Buck shine because he was such a talent. He was really at the top of his game at that time. He was so interesting to listen to. He adopted the attitude that "I know I'm good, and I don't have to prove it to anybody." He got to that confidence level and that he was just so overwhelming to me. I decided I was going to put something together that would really make the Cardinals shine during the Series and make Jack shine. That was when I did a song called, *The Heat is On*. I produced it. It was a **Glenn Frey** song. Then I interjected a whole bunch of highlights of Jack, making calls, in between the lyrics of the song. The lyrics of the song tended to talk to Jack. It was the first time that had ever been done. Now anytime anybody gets in the World Series, you hear somebody putting a song together with highlights in it. Nobody really had, and none of the songs that I've ever heard have really had the flair that our song had. It's not because of my talent by any stretch—it was because of Jack. Jack had an unusual way of leaving the story of baseball in your ear, and throughout the game, and he caused you to listen to the whole game. I used clips from a whole game. The song became extremely popular in the city. That was the one thing that bonded Jack and me together. He would come in, and I would say, "Hey, Jack, I need you to say this during the game for the song. Do this in a call." He would say whatever it was that I wanted him to say—I can't remember now what these were, but he did them. And I had to record the whole game because you never knew when it was going to happen. He would say it for the song, sometime during the game.

I was going for the big home run. In 1998, I did another song similar to *The Heat Is On*, and I was in the process of putting it together. I went to Jack and said, "Jack, is there any chance you could grab Sammy Sosa before the game tonight and have him say, 'Mark McGwire, he's de man.'?" He says, "Yeah, I can get him to do that." So he went down there with a tape recorder and got Sosa to say it. Sosa said, "I don't know if I should say it." "Oh, go ahead, say it," Jack said. Everybody trusted Jack Buck. Sosa knew he would never cross the line and do something that was not right, and that's why he did it.

He had a couple of other stories. He was always the Master of Ceremonies of every sporting event or any sports talk thing that was going

Phil Rizzuto is the only baseball person to earn a Gold Record…his game calling was in the background of Meatloaf's *Paradise by the Dashboard Lights*.

on in the town. *St. Louis was famous for the 'Cauliflower Ear' all these different kinds of shows.* Jack would be sitting at the head table, and I would be there with the engineer recording it or whatever, or in the audience looking at it. You would see the waiter or waitress running behind the head table there and filling up their water glasses or getting them something. Jack was always famous for this. One night, Dan Dierdorf was up at the podium talking and Jack leaned his chair back from the table, as one of the waiters ran behind him. He motioned his finger to slow him down and flipped him a hundred dollar bill. The waiter goes, "No s—t." That broke everybody up at the table.

> The wrong picture is on the hundred dollar bill. It should be a picture of Jack Buck.

But that's the kind of guy Jack was. The wrong picture is on the hundred dollar bill. It should be a picture of Jack Buck. He was without a doubt one of the most generous people at the radio station. I can't tell you how many times we would have interns in the radio station and how many times he would flip one of those interns a hundred dollar bill. One of the interns would produce *Sports Open Line* some night, and maybe it was a night that Jack was on. Jack would take a kindly flair to one of these young college kids, and he'd flip them a hundred dollar bill, "Go out and have a good time tonight on me. You've got a career here." He always encouraged the young people around the radio station to be the best they could be. There were so many people who went through that radio station during Jack Buck's reign. Jack never asked to be put on a pedestal. He never asked to be thought of as anything more than just another worker at the radio station. Even during the times that he was on CBS football, and he was really riding high there in the Eighties, and he was on national television all the time. He was on national radio all the time.

St. Louis was so proud to have him as an ambassador. That's the funny thing about it. St. Louis will never, ever have another person like Jack Buck because he was not just a person of personality in the city—he was an ambassador. There never will be another person like him. I don't see it ever happening. When the mayor needed to impress some out-of-town corporation or something to try and lure them to St. Louis, the mayor would call Mr. Hyland. Mr. Hyland would ask Jack Buck, and Jack Buck would show up. He very seldom ever said no to anyone.

I can't tell you how many times he flipped me a hundred dollar bill. I would be responsible for recording all of his commercials, and he was probably one of the most saleable properties on KMOX. You had to pay extra money to get Jack Buck to read your commercial. And Jack was selective with who he would do commercials for. He wanted to make sure that it wasn't just anybody.

One time we had this client on who was selling some product, and I can't remember what it was. In this product was eucalyptus mint. You've got to understand that the first time I met Jack Buck, and we would sit down and do commercials, this man would sit down and read thirty sixty-second commercials one right after another. Every one of them would come out to be exactly sixty seconds. He would never, ever make a mistake. Never. At least not up until 1995 or so. In his later years, he wasn't quite as good, but in the beginning there I was absolutely amazed at how we could go through thirty commercials, and he could read them, and he would just keep his eye on the clock, and he would stop talking when that second hand got up to sixty. He did it every single time.

Except this one time. We had a product that had eucalyptus mint in it. For the first time, Jack broke up reading a commercial. He could not say "eucalyptamint" at all. He laughed so hard. We must have done fifty tries on it. He could not say it. He was crying so hard that tears were coming out of his eyes because he couldn't say eucalyptamint. Every time I would run into him, I would say, "Say eucalypta-mint for me." He could say it any other time after that, but he never could say it when we were in the recording studio.

Jack was such a gentleman. He was the kind of guy that you couldn't invoke into station gossip. You could not invoke him into saying anything negative. Negativity never really came out of his mouth. He would never say anything bad about anybody—except Mike Shannon. You never knew if he was serious about it or whether or not he was just joking. He loved to kid Mike Shannon. I never saw Jack Buck get irate. I did hear him get mad one time, and that's when he was reading commercials with Joe Buck, his son. I was not in the studio but I had a link from the ballpark over to my studio. I was recording them in my studio, and Jack said to Joe, "You've got a bad attitude." He was being a little father to him at that point, but really that was the only time I ever, ever heard him mad. Joe has a great attitude every day now, but he was really young at the time.

Jack got mad the day I quit, and he was the first person I called. I turned in my resignation to the program director, and I was expecting to hear at least a goodbye from the general manager, but the general manager didn't want to even talk to me. I called Jack and I said, "Jack, I gotta tell you. I had to quit." "Yeah, boy, why is that?" I said, "Well, I own these radio stations down at the lake, and it's really time for me to move on and run my own stations and master my own destinies." I think he was upset about that.

I know that after Hyland retired, Jack had to take a pay decrease. Rod Zimmerman was the hatchet man. Rod Zimmerman came in after Hyland and he went to Jack, and Jack met with him, and he says to Zimmerman, "I guess you're a little upset with all the money I make here." Zimmerman said, "Well, Jack, no I'm not upset about it. But we're going to have to change things a little bit." He gave Jack a pretty good cut from what I understand. But Jack was devoted to KMOX. He was devoted to the listeners of KMOX. You know I really think deep down inside that Jack would have worked at KMOX if he didn't get a single penny, didn't get any money.

You see, Hyland and he were best friends. I don't know where that friendship started, but I know that Hyland was a great humanitarian. Jack and he were very, very tight. I think he was bound and determined to live out his usefulness at that radio station that Hyland built. One day I was in the studio and tensions were really high. It was going through a lot of changes. It was tough. We were seeing things change—some things needed to be changed, but other things, part of the heritage of the station were being ripped. It affected us. Jack was in the studio, and I said, "Jack, sometimes I really miss Mr. Hyland." He said, "You know, strange thing," and I think this was right after his book came out, "the other day I was at a book signing. This person was in the line that came up to me and had a picture that was an oil painting of some picture that was taken of Robert Hyland and me together and said 'I think you should have this.'" He was touched so easily. Just telling that story to me he started crying. That's the kind of guy he was. He was so sensitive to other people's feelings and just to other people. That's part of the reason why the ball players liked him so much because he just was one of those kinds of guys that everybody trusted. Everybody trusted him. He would just reach out and touch their soul. I don't know. It was remarkable. He was just such a remarkable man. He was just great.

Everybody loved Jack so much that they just naturally wrapped their arms around Joe. As far as I knew, there was never any resentment of Joe, and they wanted Joe to do good. When Joe really started developing and really being something, they actually wanted to hear Joe, more than Jack. There at the end Jack's voice was breaking up so bad that it was getting hard to listen to especially right at the very onset of the Parkinson's. His voice was really, really bad. It cleared up later.

Oddly, Jack and I very seldom ever talked about baseball. We really didn't talk about baseball much. I would say, "What do you think we're going to do this year?" It was just in general terms. We never really talked specifically about players. We never really talked about managers. I know he liked Whitey. Jack was different to me than that. I'm sure back in the sports department that's all they talked about. It's unusual that a sports guy would talk about things other than sports, but that just shows you what a global person Jack was.

He talked a lot about being in the war. As a matter of fact, when he went to Normandy, he actually was in **D-Day** and jumped onto those shores. Then he went to see all the graves that were there. I think that was 1999 or 2000. He really was affected by it.

> The first American to jump off the boats at the D-Day invasion was James Arness of "Gunsmoke" fame. At 6' 7", he was the tallest man on the first ship and the ship's captain wanted to test how deep the water was.

Jack loved to write poetry—absolutely loved to write poetry. He loved to bring the poetry in to me and have me record it. He knew that I would always produce it. And I would produce it with music and sound effects. He told this story about walking through the graves and seeing the different tombstones and crosses. It was really compelling. Some people at the station said, "Boy, why did he write that?" It was a perfect piece that we could play on Veterans' Day. It was a perfect piece that we could play on any national holiday or the Fourth of July. It was great. It was Jack Buck at his finest. He could reach outside the box of baseball and be whatever he wanted to be—whether he was the one who was interviewing the mayor or whether he was the one that was talking to someone outside of sports. He was a natural conversationalist. He could carry on a conversation with anyone. Also, he would be in my studio, and let's say somebody would walk in my studio who was a sponsor or maybe it was just somebody visiting me. He was always the first to stand up in the room and introduce himself and shake their hands and sit there and talk to those people as if they were really important. When Jack would leave the room, they'd go, "My God, what a guy he is. He went out of his way to make me feel like I was the important one." That's the kind of guy he was.

Jack was very proud of his country and he was very proud to serve in the armed forces. He enjoyed his poetry and he was real good at it. It was just another part of his entertainment persona. He was a heck of a singer, too. He used to go into the studio, and before we'd record, he'd be singing some song. I'd turn up a little reverb on him and he was singing like he was singing in a big auditorium. He'd really get a kick out of that.

Jack Buck was truly a great guy and a great American.

THE BEST UMPIRE IN THE COUNTRY
THE COUNTRY IS CHINA

BRUCE FROEMMING

Bruce Froemming has been a Major League baseball umpire for four decades. He lives in Milwaukee and is the owner of the Brink-man-Froemming Umpiring School where about one in thirteen students obtains a professional baseball umpiring job.

The first time I met Jack Buck was in 1971 with Al Barlick, who was my crew chief. When we went to St. Louis, Jack came in to visit with the umpires and at that time I was working with Barlick, Eddie Vargas and Harry Wendelstedt. It was a nice meeting. Barlick told me that this guy, Jack Buck, was a great guy.

The next year after Al had left and I was working with Eddie Vargas, Buck started doing interviews with me. It just seemed like every time I came to town, we did something with Buck and Mike, on whatever the show was. That carried on until last year, 2001. We had one during the playoffs last year when St. Louis was playing Arizona. There were a lot of gifts that went with the show, and the relationship grew to where when I was on the road, he would come and see me. Once in a while we would go to dinner, and in one case, in San Francisco, he asked my partner, John Kibler, and me to go out to dinner. We went to a great place. Later we went out to places he knew, and we just had a great time.

Jack had the crew to his home with his wife Carole one Saturday afternoon in St. Louis. We were sitting by the pool but it was so hot we went inside and ate snacks. He just did things that weren't done by other people. Jack really became a super friend. I started playing a lot of golf with him out at Algonquin and another course out by where he lived. I played a lot of golf at the country clubs with Jack.

As a matter of fact, one of the funniest stories that involved Jack was a **golf** story. One Saturday morning in the early Eighties, Jack invited my partner, Dick Stello, and me out to Algonquin. When we got there, we had coffee and a donut or whatever and Jack said, "I've got a partner. He'll be here." The guy came, and when we went to the first tee, Jack was very nonchalant about everything. He said, "Well, do we want to have a game?" I said, "Whatever you want to do Jack." He said, "Well, I'll take my partner; you play with your partner, and we'll make up a game."

So we hit off the first tee, and everybody just hit the ball—no big deal. His partner popped it up maybe a hundred and seventy-five yards down the middle. We didn't think anything of it. The next shot was about two twenty-five uphill on the first hole there. The guy hit the green, but still it could have been a lucky shot. You're not thinking anything. Anyway, we're going around the first nine holes, and we're playing a five dollar Nassau and presses when you were two down—normal golf thing. When we made the turn, we were three or four down. I said to Dick, "What do you want to do?" He said, "Well, we've got to press." I said, "Sure." So we pressed the bets on the back side. We're going along, and we're getting killed. This guy, Jack's partner, is really playing golf now. He's hitting some unbelievable shots off every tee, down the middle, like two forty—two fifty.

When we get to the eighteenth hole, we're going up the hill. Jack was way on the other side of the fairway. I had hit one of my very few good drives on that hole, and I was going to my ball on the right side of the fairway. Jack came over in his cart, and he said, "And, how was your day today?" I said, "Well, Jack, you kicked our butt. But it was fun." He said, "I would like you to know that the player I'm playing with is the five-time amateur state champ from Missouri." He brought a ringer along and set us up! Dick Stello was in on it from about the twelfth hole on and Dick was egging me on. He said, "On the thirteenth and fourteenth and fifteenth holes, we've got to keep pressing." I said, "Absolutely." We just got killed. Jack had really set us up.

> Michael Jordan was given his first set of golf clubs
> by fellow University of North Carolina classmate
> Davis Love, Davis Love, Davis Love.

Another time, in San Francisco, we were in the airport getting our bags, and Jack's group was getting their bags off the same baggage area. Jack and I talked a little bit, and he said, "I'll see you at the ballpark." We had to go right out to the park. We'd had a night game in San Diego, with a one o'clock game in San Francisco. We were going right from the airport to the ballpark to work. When I get to the ballpark, and we go through the security there with our car, the guy stopped me and asked me for ID. They'd never asked me before, ever. I said, "Well, you've got to be kidding. I've been coming here forever." He said, "I've got to see ID." Jack told the guard that a short little round guy will be coming here, and he's gonna tell you he's an umpire. "Check his ID." This guy, not knowing me, gave me all kinds of trouble getting into the ballpark. So when we got to the dressing room, Buck came down and said, "How was your trip from the airport?" Then I knew what he had done. He then admitted he had told the guy, "Don't let the guy in. He's gonna tell you he's an umpire."

I called during the holidays and Carole told me he wasn't feeling well and that he had gone into the hospital just before Christmas. I continued to call after that, and there were highs and lows. Carole thought he was getting out—he was getting better. Then he had staph infection and everything else that he had, and he just was there forever, and he never got out of the hospital. So the last moment that I had with him was an interview that was done right outside our dressing room.

Once in St. Louis my wife was with me, and we were eating at Al's restaurant on First Street. We were alone in a corner having dinner. There was a big party in the back, and I didn't know who was back there. All of a sudden, Jack came out from that party. Anheuser-Busch was having a big dinner back there. Jack came over all by himself, and he said, "And I'd like to meet Mrs. Froemming." I said, "Jack, this is my wife." He stood around maybe five, six, seven minutes talking and doing a little teasing or whatever. Then he went back. I thought it was real nice that he came over to our table. When the guy came with the check, I don't have to tell you what happened—There was no check! I'd known Jack at that time maybe four or five years. Al came over and he said, "Your check is taken care of."

Through the years, all the things I ever did with him, Jack was such a generous guy. They used to have a dinner after an afternoon game with the Cardinals. The guy who put it on was his friend, Bob Hyland. Seems like it was called the "Cabbage Dinner," or whatever—it was a funny name. All the players with the Cardinals attended. Jack came in the dressing room and said, "What are you doing tonight?" I said, "Really, nothing." He said, "Would you like to make fifteen hundred dollars?" I said, "How do I do that?" He said, "You just show up to dinner, and you'll be one of the speakers." So I showed up, and he gave me fifteen hundred bucks, and then a couple of years later, he asked me to come again. So I did it twice, and I had a super time there. Of course, Jack was the emcee. He had a big time introducing me. There was an episode where when he introduced me to all the Cardinals, they had white handkerchiefs and they all started waving them, and I played off them. To get back at them, I said, "That's all right. I'll be there tomorrow on the field. I'll remember all the faces waving those hankies." We just had a great time.

Jack included me in so many different things. I felt in many ways, that I was part of his family because of the way he treated me. He treated me like a son, and yet he treated me like a great friend. He was a mentor in many ways. He told me things early on in my career that "maybe you could have done this," or whatever, during an argument or something that he saw.

Jack was just a complete person. He was a people person. How could you ever get cross with the guy? He was always beaming and happy and he was so professional, and yet he put so much humor into his work that it was just a pleasure to be around him. I thank the Lord that my time on earth included him because he was really a star in the sky for me.

Chapter 2

St. Louis Blues

It's Hard To Cheer With A Broken Heart

When I heard that Jack had died, my feeling was that I had lost a true mentor and a friend without ever getting real close. I found out on that Monday that I had cancer. I'm too young to have cancer. I know that Buck always said, "If you ever die, you go up there, and you just shake the hand of the Man and say, 'Man, why were you so good to me?'" That's the way I feel. When I heard that he died, I cried for a minute, not because I lost a friend, but just because he couldn't win the battle himself. That's one battle you don't control. I felt like I had lost someone, even though he's many miles away, who was very close to me. He knows what role he played in my career, and I owe a great debt to him. He was just a world-class individual.

——GEORGE MICHAEL, The Sports Machine

I was at home when I heard about his death. I was not surprised, frankly, because you knew he'd been going downhill. And by all the reports, through Joe Buck and some others, I knew it wasn't progressing. If it was progressing at all, it was in the wrong direction. Logic told me that when you've been in the hospital almost six months, you're really pushing the panic button. So I wasn't surprised actually. I attended the daytime ceremony for Jack that was held at the ballpark. The ceremony was an end-of-the-line with your thinking and your sorrow and your regrets—your long-time friendship with Jack Buck. Here it was. This is it. It's all over. That's a very sad moment, whether it's a member of the family or a good friend or for that matter, almost anybody when you have the interest and take the time to go to some kind of a ceremony like that.

——BING DEVINE, Retired Cardinal Executive

My lasting memory would be that I knew he was a friend. Somebody one time said you don't have that many friends in life. Well, I knew Jack was a friend. And he knew I was one. He had so many. I knew if I had anything I had to discuss with anybody, I could get an honest answer from Jack Buck.

I flew into St. Louis on Tuesday. I called his wife, Carole, because I didn't know Tuesday was going to be *the* day. I had told Carole a month before that when I got to St. Louis, I was hoping that I could come up and see Jack in the hospital. I didn't know how frail he had become. She told me that Jack was not in good shape, and she thought it was coming to the end.

That was the first words on the phone that day at Lambert Field. At the airport while I was waiting for my bag, I called. I was taken back by that. Carole said, "When you get to the ballpark tonight, look up Joe, and talk to Joe." She said, "I don't want to talk anymore about it." I said, "Thanks." So when I got to the ballpark that night, I went in C. J. Cherre's room and Red Schoendienst and Joe Buck were in there, and the air was extremely heavy. Everybody was very somber. Joe said, "He's not going to make it tonight. I wanted to tell you." I couldn't stay in the room long because I choked up. I looked at Red's eyes, and probably the most solid guy in the room was Joe. Buddy Bates, the equipment guy, was in the room, and Red and Joe and C. J. and everybody was upset. So I went to the dressing room with the knowledge that Joe had said that he wouldn't get through the night. They had taken all the equipment off of him, even the dialysis, everything that goes with being very sick. So I went in the dressing room and had my moment of thinking and thinking good things and, I guess, feeling sorry for myself, that I was going to lose such a good friend. The game ended. As soon as the game ended, and we were sitting in the dressing room just relaxing, we had the TV on, and the report came over the TV that Jack had passed on. I knew it was coming because of what Joe said, but you still feel bad to lose the guy.

I stayed for the funeral on Friday. I was scheduled to go on to Philadelphia. I called the league office and told them that I wanted to go to the funeral, and my supervisor, Ralph Nelson, said, "By all means, go to the funeral. We'll get another umpire." I went and if Jack could have come back for a moment and seen everything I saw there, he would have said, "My, what an operation this is." It was huge and the church was full. There were so many people feeling so bad. The family really handled it well. I was just happy I could be there to say the last goodbye.

——BRUCE FROEMMING, Long-time National League Umpire

My lasting memory of Jack Buck will be that he was genuinely interested in everyone, and that he made everyone feel special.

I just felt awful when I heard that he had died. I had been at the baseball game that Sunday before, Fathers' Day. I was with a friend who had also worked with him. At some point, we said, "Gosh, I wonder how he is. We haven't heard anything lately." I said, "I never want to hear the news, and I wonder how I'm going to find out—how

I'm going to hear it?" Every morning I walk my dog at five-thirty. That morning I was walking my dog, and I saw it when I passed the newspaper stand. It was in the box, and there his picture was with the headline that said, "The Soul of St. Louis."
——NANCY HIGGINS, St. Louis, Her mother was Harry Caray's Secretary

On June 19, My husband was down at work, and I hadn't had the news on or read the paper and he told me about Jack's death. It was just a sense of disbelief and a sense that the world as we've known it will never quite be the same. This is just a little part of the world that will never be the same, that part that Jack Buck played in our lives.

We went to the memorial service down at the stadium. There was just such a sadness in your heart. I didn't stop listening to KMOX for about fifty-two hours. Like everyone else, I guess, I was crying along with everyone else in hearing stories because you knew that it was real. So often in life, you hear stories of people that you may know, and you think, "Do they really know who they're talking about?" But in knowing Jack Buck as well as we did, for what he did for our child, and you know when someone does something for your child, they're doing it a hundredfold for you. And even more so in the circumstance John was in. It was just so sad. We have six children, three out of town and three in town, and we called them all. Each of the girls was just so touched and moved because they are so well aware of the part that Jack Buck played in John's life and what he meant to him. It was a tremendous sadness. We just took pride in having known the man and having been honored and privileged to have had the relationship, which we wouldn't have chosen certainly by any means—with our child going through what he had to go through and continues to, but what a gift he was to John and to all of us. He was just wonderful.
——SUSAN O'LEARY, Mother of burn victim befriended by Jack Buck

The night he died, I had left the ballpark early. There was a sense of foreboding that night. When I got home and had gone to bed, and I woke up in the morning his death had been made official overnight. So I was at home in the morning with my kids when I learned it, and it was heavy. The reason it was heavier than just a normal situation where you say, "Oh, whoever, a movie star, well-known person, somebody you liked, had died." It was more like a member of your family had died. I have a theory that for all of us who grew up in the fifties, sixties, seventies, eighties, and nineties the Cardinal baseball stories, as told to you by Jack Buck six months out of the year, were our bedtime stories. Jack Buck read me my bedtime stories every night; he just happened to be on the radio and the stories were about the Cardinals. So it's more than just—here's a guy, he's a broadcaster, wasn't he great? Yeah. You really felt like you were part of his radio family. I wrote a note to his daughter, Christine, who I've worked with previously, and said, "You know how I felt about your dad. I wanted to thank you and your siblings for sharing your dad with the community all these years." They really did, and he really was a part of our radio family. Or we were his radio children.

——BOB RAMSEY, KFNS Radio

When I heard that Jack had died, I was in my bedroom at home. I was watching ESPN, and I saw it come up at the bottom of the screen. There was a rumor that night at the ballpark that Jack Buck had passed away earlier in the day. I was hoping it was wrong, and certainly I did not go on the air with it because I had not heard any confirmation at all. So I had a little bit of a warning because of the rumors going around the ballpark, but it still came as kind of a shock and was a very sad moment.

Somebody, right after he died, had a great line. They said, "Every time you walked away from Jack Buck, you were almost always smiling, or you always felt better than you did before you saw him." I thought that was a great, great thing to say.

——PAT HUGHES, Chicago Cubs Broadcaster

I just felt lousy when I heard he had passed away. I remember making a note of the fact that he waited until they, the Cardinals, got in first place. The next morning, I do a morning thing here in LA, I went to work. I've been doing this for a long time so I don't let it affect my work, it just affected my innards. I made mention throughout the morning and talked about Jack and what people here think of Vin Scully, that's what people back in the Midwest think of Jack Buck. Then I told the story about the Monday Night Football thing, and made reference to the fact that had he given me a thumbs down, I might have ended up in a car wash. I was very much affected by his death. I thought the world of that man. I thought the world of him as a fan, never imagining that I would have the pleasure of sitting in a room with him. And not only sitting in the room, but know that I "passed muster." And it was very important to me to pass muster with him. It was very important.

——SCOTT ST. JAMES, Los Angeles Radio Personality

The last time I saw Jack would have been the last series that the Marlins played last year against the Cardinals in St. Louis. I saw him at that time and sat and talked with him for a while. The year before Jack and I had had several occasions to do some things together because the Cardinals and the Expos share a spring training facility in Jupiter. For example, I hosted the groundbreaking ceremony with Jack's son, Joe. Then when the stadium opened, Jack and I co-emceed the opening game and the on-field ceremonies. I remember talking to Jack and saying, "I'm not a collector of autographs and baseball things, but I've started a collection of Hall of Fame broadcaster autographs, and, Jack, would you sign a ball for me?" Jack was sitting in a booth at Busch Stadium at the time. Of course Parkinson's had set in. Jack said to me, "Sit down, Dave, this is going to take a while." He took the ball and signed it for me.

I had kept in touch with Joe Buck. I had called him a couple of times during this past winter to check on his dad. I knew that Jack was having a very difficult, long and tough, battle in the hospital. I know that the thought of him returning to the broadcast booth was one of the things that kept him going, other than his great love of life. I also knew from talking to Joe, and I could tell by the tone of Joe's voice, that it was a very grave situation for Jack throughout the winter and into the spring and the early part of the season. Of course, he was on the minds of everyone in the business. When the news came, it wasn't a shock, but it was just as devastating knowing that it had finally come to that end. I was as deeply saddened by it as was everyone who knew Jack.

——DAVE VAN HORNE, Florida Marlins Broadcaster

On June 19, I was home at my computer and got e-mail that linked me to a newspaper. Here on the East Coast there hadn't been a lot of talk about Jack being in a deteriorating condition so I was not aware that he had taken a turn for the worse. I was very sad. One of the things I did is call a friend here who does sports talk. I called Scott on the air and said, "A lot of people are talking today about what a great guy Jack is. When people pass away, a lot of people will remember good things about people. I just have to call you today to say that this isn't ritual or respect or doing the right thing that people are saying these things about Jack Buck. I can tell you first-hand and want your listeners to know that what you're hearing is really the truth about Jack Buck. I was there. I know first-hand, and I'll never forget it."

We were talking about Jack's great calls. Two in particular are when Lou Brock broke Maury Wills' base-stealing record, Jack said something along the lines, "I told myself I wasn't going to cry." I know the Mark McGwire call. I know the Kirk Gibson call. When I tried to repeat one of them on the air as we were talking about some of these lasting calls of Jack, I couldn't get the words out. It just stopped me dead in my tracks.

———JOHN MARTIN, Providence, Rhode Island

When I heard that Jack had died, I was here in my office in Pasadena, California doing some work and looking at the Internet. There I saw the news that he had passed away. The reaction you have is the reaction of any friend or someone you've known. It's just such a sense of loss. As we know, in knowing Jack, a life lived exactly the way that he wanted to live it.

———FRED CLAIRE, ex-Dodger General Manager 1987-98

The day Jack died, I was in Milwaukee. We were on a couple of Fox shows. The Fox regional here is based in Dallas. They do a studio show there every night after our telecast. We're usually on the air with them. They wanted a piece on Jack and wanted to get as many people who knew him as possible so Milo Hamilton, who is our lead radio broadcaster and had worked with Jack in St. Louis, came over, and he was very eloquent. Then they had me talk about Jack. I told them the story about listening to Harry Caray and preferring Jack when I was a kid. I really welcomed the opportunity to talk about Jack because I felt very strongly about him, about his personality and his style, and the way he was so helpful to young broadcasters, and just to young professionals in general. It was nice to be able to get that therapy of talking about Jack on the air.

One of the radio stations in St. Louis called as well. We talked a few days later about him. I appreciated that chance to sum up my feelings about him. It was obviously a very sad time, but I had talked with Joe the last time we were in St. Louis. Jack was in the hospital, and he told me things were not going well. My prayers were that he would not be in long-term pain and that the suffering be over. I think there was a sense of relief there that the long suffering the family had gone through was over.

I don't know that the ceremony the Cardinals put on in Busch Stadium could have been any better. The idea of having the casket there was something I had to get used to a little bit because it had been so many years since that had been done in baseball. But that was the appropriate way to give the fans a chance to honor him. That's what it was all about. There were so many fans who wanted to pay their respects. I thought that was extremely appropriate. I thought the way they did it was absolutely perfect.

———**BILL BROWN**, Astros' Play-By-Play Voice for TV for Fifteen Years

I'd been expecting Jack's death. I had talked to Carole and to Joe. Joe told a close friend of ours the day before that he didn't think his dad was going to last much longer. You're never completely ready, but he'd been in the hospital nearly six months, and the last two months had really been rough. My wife told me. My first thought was, "Well, he's a lot better off than lying down there with that respirator, and it certainly was time for him to go." Then over the next few hours, a lot of thoughts flooded your mind. People were calling and wanting me to say something. Most of us who were close to him said about the same thing. That's why I was thrilled to come up with something that nobody had really mentioned in the fact that he never complained. You don't meet many people who don't complain about something once in a while. I never heard him complain about anything.

I thought the ceremony the Cardinals did was outstanding. My wife, Sue, and I went to the memorial service, and it was beautifully handled. Then the church service—the music was just marvelous and very inspirational and uplifting. I thought the outpouring from the whole nation, not only The Cardinal Nation and this area, but all over the nation, was magnificent. I thought all the networks, Trey Wingo's piece on ESPN especially moved me because I know Trey so well. Trey worked here in St. Louis for me. I brought him to St. Louis to work at KSD for a while before he went to ESPN. I thought it was a very wonderful, wonderful two days of celebration of his life.

That's what it was, and that's what he would have liked. He wouldn't have wanted anybody to be maudlin or mourning him at that point in the proceedings. There's not a thing that I would have changed.

———JAY RANDOLPH, Fellow Broadcaster and Friend

I was down at the Lake of the Ozarks and was in bed when the announcement of his death was made. My wife was in St. Louis, and she called about four o'clock in the morning. When I heard about it, I immediately flipped on the television. I just had this empty feeling in my stomach. I know he went through a lot of really tough times fighting off the disease he had. Even though he made jokes about having Parkinson's all the time, he always used to say, "I shook hands with another guy the other day that had Parkinson's. We never let go."

———DENNIS KLAUTZER, Former Imaging Director, KMOX

On June 19, I was called at twelve-thirty in the morning. They woke me up to tell me that he had died. We had a plan in place here. One of my responsibilities was to come in and host our coverage for several hours. That's what I did. I got here about two in the morning and was on the air for most of the next twelve or thirteen hours. It was very difficult. Even though we knew the inevitable, we knew what was going to happen, it was tough because all these great memories would come back.

———RON JACOBER, Sports Operations, KMOX Radio

In June, I was in Atlanta for a Tigers' series. I believe there is some sort of telepathy that if something happens that means something to you, even if you're not directly aware of it, somehow your emotions are aware of it. I just didn't really feel like myself that entire day. I was edgy and tired. I couldn't sleep that night and got up at two in the morning in my hotel room. I went to look at my e-mail. A friend of mine had sent me a message that said, "I'm very sorry to hear of Jack Buck's passing, and I know you had said what you had thought of him. You'd said you could hear his voice only a few days before when you were covering a game." That was true. I regularly hear his voice when I'm sitting in a ballpark. There'd be a situation, and I'd hear his voice describing it.

———JOHN LOWE, *Detroit Free Press*

I had seen Joe, Jack's son, in early June at Yankee Stadium. He was there doing the Giants-Yankees game for Fox. We all asked how his dad was doing, and he told us not good. It was real sad to hear because a lot of those things we'd heard over those months, one of the dispatches, was that he was still coming on, that the surgeries had corrected some things and they had high hopes, and so it was kind of a downer. At the same time, we all realized that, the way Joe was talking about it, the family knew that it was about at the end.

So when I heard that he had died, I was kind of prepared for it. It wasn't as big a shock, but it had been kind of a shock just to hear what Joe said that day. Then they had the funeral on Friday and I flew to Chicago for a Cardinals-Cubs game the next day. When I landed, I got the news that Darryl Kile had just died, which was more sadness heaped upon sadness.

Even then Joe, I thought, was right there to say the right thing. His father had a rich full life and lived every moment of it. It wasn't anything at all related to the tragedy of a young man with a young family suddenly dying. I don't know how Joe made it through that week. That was just one of the saddest weeks there ever was in St. Louis.

In the ballpark the next night, I know for me and for Joe Morgan, when they decided to play that game and we all had to work that game, I don't know how the team made it through. It was not a happy night.

———JON MILLER, ESPN and Giants Play-By-Play Announcer

I had watched the Cardinal game the night before and listened to Joe call the game. Then I got to the office the next morning, and the first thing I always do is I pull up the Cardinal page to kind of look over the stats and everything from the previous night's game. I read about his death on the page. I was just in complete and utter shock. I just sat there and stared at the computer screen in disbelief I called my wife and told her. For a person who is not a friend, per se, I didn't hang out with him, but to just feel the way I felt over losing somebody that I'd only met two times was kind of odd. Jack was the kind of person that even though you didn't know him, you still felt like you knew him. That's just the kind of person he was. He projected himself as being an everyday guy, just like everybody else. When to everyone in St. Louis, he wasn't an everyday guy. He was Jack Buck.

———TOM MULLANEY, Cardinal fan, Conway, Arkansas

I thought the way the Cardinals handled the services at Busch Stadium was first-rate. He would have been embarrassed—"What's all the fuss about?" he would have said. It's not so much St. Louis, it's the St. Louis Cardinal fans all across the country. That station is picked up in some forty states. A lot of people went to sleep listening to him at night. That transcended him being in St. Louis where he was very active in charities and did all kind of banquets and all kinds of visits, and he lived here.

——RICK HUMMEL, *St. Louis Post-Dispatch*

I went to the ball game on Tuesday night, and I saw Joe Buck and asked him, "How's Jack?" I used to call Carole all the time to see how he was doing. Joe said, "It doesn't look very good now." And I got depressed then. The next day he lost his battle. It was very depressing.

I never saw a funeral like that before—as many people mourning somebody like they did Jack. He meant everything to them evidently. I've never in my life seen such mass depression about a guy. Everybody felt like they knew him.

He was a wonderful guy. And, away from the sports—forget the sports part. He was a greater guy than he was a sports guy.

——UNCLE JOE ARNDT, Close Friend of Jack Buck

When I heard about his death, I was very upset. It was like part of your childhood was dying. Like, "Golly, you're no longer that kid listening to that transistor radio underneath your pillow and hearing Jack doing the play-by-plays." He brought tears to your eyes, and even to my wife, too—things we would read in the paper. You had a feeling he wasn't going to come out of the hospital after being there so long, but even then, it was a shock. Part of your childhood died.

——MARK G. BECK, St. Louis Cardinal Fan

I heard about Jack's death at the bar. The word came in there, and Charlie Spoonhour was in there and some other people, and the word came there. We knew he hadn't been doing good that day. A rumor had spread through the restaurant but it wasn't announced yet, so we took it as a rumor. We didn't want to put it through our mind that maybe we wouldn't see Jack again. We sent him a couple of books. He liked to read.

Last fall when Jack missed a wedding (Michael Roarty's daughter), I felt, "Wow, he must really be sick." He would have been there. He never liked to miss a party.

He was my friend. I just can't believe I'm not going to see him anymore. Every time he would see me at a banquet or at a public function, he always had some wisecrack. To the biggest people and the littlest people—he made them all feel like they were special.

———**VINCE BOMMARITO**, Tony's Restaurant, St. Louis

I did the game with Joe that night and Joe told me before the game that his father was going to pass away. I immediately said Joe you don't have to do the game, Dan's here, we can do the game without you. Why don't you go to the hospital? And he said no, my Dad would want me here. That evening, Joe was—as always—brilliant. We won and went into first place by defeating the Anaheim Angels, with—by the way—Darryl Kile's last victory and the last time he pitched. And then remembering what Joe told me before the game, I said, well what happens now? And he said, well, they took him off the respirator and he's not supposed to breathe but he is. But it's just a matter of time. So, I went home that night and while watching television they broke in with the announcement that Jack had passed away. And I can remember sitting there, just tearing up and just remembering how incredible Jack's life was. I also thought of the brilliance he passed on to Joe Buck and the family.

———**AL HRABOSKY**, Cardinals broadcaster

Our third baseman, Joe Crede and I are both Missouri boys, and Jack wanted to interview us about being young guys, being in the big leagues, what it was like pitching in the big leagues. For me it was just an honor. I grew up a half hour from St. Louis, and anytime you hear his voice, it reminds you of baseball. Baseball is what you hear of in the off-season, and you know Spring Training is right around the corner. We had no idea that we would be the last players Jack Buck would ever interview.

It was just an honor being able to sit down with him because I grew up listening to him on radio and on TV all the time. That was the first time I met him, and I was kind of in shock. When you listen to him on the radio or TV, I knew he had some health problems, but I didn't know how severe it was. At the interview I was kind of in shock to see how bad he was doing. When you listened to him on TV, you didn't think anything was wrong with him—he sounded fine. I had known he was ill, but didn't know exactly what all was wrong with him, and it just kind of surprised me.

We were playing in Atlanta when everybody heard the news of his death. Everybody said they thought he was doing all right and wasn't getting worse, so it just got to you. I just sat down and thought of all the good times I'd had listening to him on TV. My memory of him will be just listening to him do the games as I was growing up.

——MARK BUEHRLE, St. Charles, Missouri, White Sox Pitcher

Jack had something like seven major hospital events there in a series. He was in Intensive Care for seven months. At each step of the way, I kept saying, "No, he's gonna come back because he's fought so hard." He tried hard to hang onto life and to lose him at the end was tough.

Jack was one of my closest friends. I don't know of anybody that was closer. Carole called me and asked me to come over a day or two before Jack died so we were kind of anticipating. Then I got a call that night that he had passed away about eleven-thirty in the evening. She called and told us.

At the memorial service in the stadium, there were eight eulogists. Joe, his son, handled the emcee role and did it extremely well. In my piece of it, I said, "Jack firmly believed in the Richard Rodgers' words, 'A bell is no bell till you ring it. A song is no song till you sing it. And love in your heart cannot stay. Love isn't love till you give it away.' Jack Buck gave away a lot of love to this community and to the people in it."

——MIKE ROARTY, Close friend of the Buck family

Chapter 3

Say What You Want About Chicago... Frankly, "Losers" Comes to Mind

Chip Caray

Pat Hughes

John Rooney

George Castle

Joe Rios

Steve Rousey

Welcome to Chicago Where the Local Time is Always 1908

THE REASON MANY PEOPLE ARE CUB FANS IS BECAUSE THEY CAN'T AFFORD WORLD SERIES TICKETS

CHIP CARAY

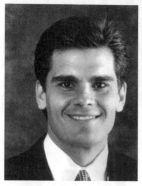

Chip Caray, a native of St. Louis, is a third-generation baseball announcer. He is the grandson of Jack Buck's former partner Harry Caray, and the son of Atlanta Braves play-by-play man Skip Caray. Chip joined the Chicago Cubs broadcasting crew in 1998. Chip attended Pierremont Elementary in Ballwin, Missouri and graduated from Parkway West High School in St. Louis.

The first thing that comes to mind when I think of Jack Buck is a cool, dry sense of humor. He was one of the funniest men I've ever had a chance to get to know. He had a tremendous self-deprecating sense of humor. For me at least, since I do the same thing he does, he's a guy who personified what St. Louis Cardinals baseball has meant for the last fifty years. The greatest thing I can say about him is that he was an incredible professional. The man saw everything there was to see in the world of sports, and had the unique and wonderfully innate ability to broadcast everything with such grace, such demeanor, and with such excitement, that you couldn't believe how easily it came to him. All of us who do this job are certainly envious of that ability that he had.

Like most kids who grew up in St. Louis, I went to bed at 9 o'clock at night with my transistor radio tucked under my pillow. I listened to the Cardinals playing the Padres, or the Giants or the Dodgers out on the West Coast with Jack Buck and, at that time, Ron Jacober, Jay Randolph, Bob Starr and Mike Shannon. Those were my heroes. I knew I wasn't going to be a baseball player. And if I couldn't be Ted Simmons, I wanted to be Harry Caray, Jack Buck or Skip Caray.

Listening to those games as a kid, and listening to the heroics of Ozzie Smith and Jack Clark and Ted Simmons, those were the memories that I'll never forget. It's like people in **Chicago** who listened to Jack Brickhouse or Harry Caray; or people in Atlanta who listened to Ernie Johnson or my dad; or people in Houston who listened to Gene Elston, hearing that voice of Jack Buck takes me back twenty or thirty years in time and makes me feel like a kid again.

My parents were divorced. My mom and dad obviously knew Jack Buck from when my grandfather, Harry Caray, and Jack worked together. I remember going to a baseball clinic in suburban St. Louis. There was Jack Buck with Al Hrabosky and Ted Simmons. In the middle of talking at this seminar, Jack Buck sees me, my sister, and my mom, and says, "Excuse me, folks, for a second." He walked over to us and said hello, and commented on how much I had grown, and all that kind of stuff.

The first time I met Jack was probably at that baseball clinic. It was one of those things where you think, "Man, is that *really* him?" As a kid, everyone who is involved in sports, is a larger than life hero. I could not believe that it was really Jack Buck coming over to say hello to me. He was so nice, so kind, and seemingly so interested in what we were doing.

Not only did he come up to me, he did so in front of my friends and other kids my age. I got my baseball glove signed, plus Ted Simmons and Al Hrabosky came over. What was neat for me is that it's such a thrill when you're part of the group, finally.

Then he saw me twelve years later. I was auditioning for one of the jobs with the Cardinals doing a fill-in radio game. I was reading the newspaper in the lobby of a Pittsburgh hotel. All of a sudden, this quarter comes flying out of the air and hits me square in the sports page. I looked up and there was Jack and his wife, Carole, walking down the stairs. He said, "Good luck; I know you're nervous." I said, "Yes, I'm very nervous." He told me, "You're going to do great. Just go out there and have a good time. I know you can do the job." I

> When the Cubs won their last World Series in 1908—any team can have a bad century—there was no radio coverage…because radio had not yet been invented.

thanked him for his support and wished them good-bye. As he was walking out the revolving door, he leaned back and said, "By the way, don't blow it." That's a typical personification of Jack Buck; he just had this unbelievably, incredible way of making a person feel at ease, relaxed, and like you were part of the group. He always managed to do that for everyone in my family, and for that we'll always be grateful.

> **As he was walking out the revolving door, he leaned back and said, "By the way, don't blow it."**

My first major-league baseball broadcast was in Atlanta against the Dodgers. Vin Scully came over and knocked on the Plexiglas between our booths at Atlanta's old stadium. I was getting ready to go on the air for the first time. Vin Scully, who knew who I was, walked over to me and said, "Welcome to the club." You can imagine what that means to a young broadcaster. Whether I was Skip Caray's kid and Harry Caray's grandson or not, the fact that Vin Scully did that for me is the lead in my life's story. Jack Buck did the same type of thing. Every time I went to St. Louis, he made a point to say hello, and ask about my mom and my grandparents. He would interview me on the broadcasts and always talk about my high school, my friends and my family. For a kid who grew up in St. Louis, to have Jack Buck consider you worthy of being able to talk to, again that's an incredible honor and an incredible thrill.

The great thing about our job is that the broadcasters come and go, the players come and go, the days on the calendar come and go, but the legend of the people who call the games live on because the memories and the highlights bring back such incredibly vivid lifelike memories for the people who were so lucky to listen to those calls.

Jack, and others from his generation, was a pure radio guy. The ability to draw an audience in by storytelling is a lost art in our sport, especially with those who are either blessed or cursed—depending on your outlook—with working in television. We really get in the way of the broadcast. Producers have to put up graphics and promotional items, and we don't have an opportunity to tell stories about things because you always have to shoot one of those things in. Baseball is a radio game. It's paced by the game itself. The broadcaster tells stories, spins yarns, and talks to his color man about how he used to play certain situations or remembering when something similar happened. Obviously the longer you're there, the more people assume you're the local expert on the team. That's the beauty of our jobs. That's the immortality aspect, which is part of the lure of our jobs. Jack was a great storyteller. He knew how to work with his color man. He knew how to zing people, and he knew how to get zinged in return. He had the ability to do that on radio, which is a real benefit for those who have had that break. If you asked every broadcaster in baseball which he'd rather do, they'd say that they would rather get paid like they're doing TV, but they'd rather perform like they're doing radio. Unfortunately, that doesn't happen.

This man was such a great family man, yet he gave so much of himself to the city of St. Louis. He did it because he loved the town. He was a part of that community. When you talk about someone who was selfless throughout his life with his money, with his time, with his wit, with his presence, I don't know if there's another broadcaster anywhere else that could come close to what Jack Buck meant, not just to the Cardinal franchise, but to the city of St. Louis. He was a civic treasure.

I know Joe is so proud of his dad, and he should be. I know Jack was awfully proud of Joe. They're a great family, and I wish Joe and his family all the best as these years go on.

I'm sure if Joe's around for thirty or forty years in St. Louis, he'll end up in the Hall of Fame. This is a business of longevity. If you can stick it out, if your family can make it, if you can get your children raised, if you can love and honor your wife, if you can enjoy the ride and love the place where you work, you have a chance to have a wonderfully long and successful run. Certainly all of those things applied to Jack Buck. When you think of guys who are deserving of the praise that is heaped upon us, Jack Buck is that guy.

The story about the night Mark McGwire broke **Roger Maris'** single season home run record is one of my favorite Jack Buck stories because it reveals his self-deprecating sense of humor. Steve Stone and I were doing the game on WGN. When McGwire hit the home run, we watched Jack Buck stand up and applaud in his booth, with tears rolling down his face. We asked if he would be kind enough to come over and do an interview with us in the next half inning. He very graciously appeared. Jack, who was suffering from Parkinson's at the time, came in, put on the headphones, sat down, looked at Steve, looked at me, and then said, "So guys, what's shaking besides me?" We were sitting there stunned. Did he really just say that? All of a sudden, he started laughing at our reaction, but that was Jack. He was just a great, great man.

When I got the Cubs job back in 1998, Jack was one of the first ones to come over and say how sorry he was about my grandfather's passing. He admitted that they didn't always get along so well, but I thanked him for not judging me by what my grandfather did or didn't do. Every time we were in St. Louis, he was there with a smile on his face. He was just great. I know that when the Cubs go there to Busch Stadium, the first time after Jack's passing, it's going to be a very bittersweet day for me. I'll be laying some flowers by the statue, and patting the statue while I think of him. Again, he was so instrumental for not only me but a lot of people in my family as a good man, a good friend, a guy who did things his way, and certainly reaped the rewards that have come his way.

When you're around guys like Jack Buck, you're in the presence of greatness. As a broadcaster, you think, "I'm doing the same thing they're doing, and people think I can do as good of a job as they can?" It's very humbling. All of us in this sport need that humbler. These guys are in the Hall of Fame for a reason. They're the kind of guys who you can't really call colleagues because there is such an age difference and such an entire life experience difference. The fact that they'll talk to you like a colleague is mind numbing. It'd be like Leonardo DaVinci walking up to you and talking about helicopters or art,

Roger Maris once held the national high school record for most kick returns for a touchdown in one game—five, at Bishop Shanley High School in Fargo, North Dakota. Maris received a full scholarship to play for Bud Wilkinson at the University of Oklahoma, but quit after two weeks.

or Michelangelo talking to you about painting your room. You cannot believe that these guys, who are such luminaries in your sport or in your craft, are going to take time and say hello.

Jack symbolized humility. For all that he did in the community, oftentimes giving speeches free of charge, or helping others who were less fortunate than he...that's humility. The fact that he could poke fun at himself. The fact that he was color blind, and would walk into a room and everybody would just cringe, then he'd start laughing because he knew that whatever he put on somehow didn't quite work out right. When you can poke fun at yourself, it makes it easier for everyone else to poke fun at you. There's an old saying in baseball: if they don't mess with you, they don't like you. Certainly, Jack was willing to mess with a lot of people, and have fun with a lot of people. I think he loved people. He loved meeting new and interesting or unique people. He loved life. Our lives certainly were better for having the brief opportunities we had to get to know him and talk to him.

"A lot of us think he's the greatest Cardinal of all time. When you got to know him, he was exactly the great and special man we thought he is...If we keep Jack in our heads and in our hearts, he'll always be with us—like today."
Cardinals manager, Tony LaRussa

WRIGLEY FIELD: THE LAST REFUGE OF SCOUNDRELS

PAT HUGHES

Pat Hughes is the radio voice of the Chicago Cubs.

He's made some of the greatest calls in the history of sports broadcasting. One is the Ozzie Smith home run in 1985. That's the single greatest radio call of a home run that I've ever heard, and I've studied that. I can tell you all the great ones, and that's, in my opinion, the single greatest one. That's, to me, even better than **Bobby Thompson's** homer call by Russ Hodges. It was just perfect—perfect at that moment.

The homer call he made of **Kirk Gibson's** in 1988 was certainly in the top ten that I've ever heard.

Jack was really a funny guy. He joined Ron Santo and me in the booth last June. He was going to appear at the Museum of Broadcasting. It was a "Special Night with Jack Buck" at the Chicago Museum of Broadcast Communications. As Jack sat down, I promoted his appearance that night. I said, "Come on out and see Jack Buck at the museum tonight. The admission is free." After I was done, he said, "Admission is free? That tells you what my value's all about!" He made fun of it, and he really was very self-deprecating and humorous. I thought it was cute the way he was kind of poking fun at himself. He joined us, and then we were calling the game, and there was some friendly back and forth taunting that Cubs and Cardinals

In an Old-Timers' game at Shea Stadium in 1967, Bobby Thompson hit a home run into the left-field bull pen off Ralph Branca...Branca is New York Mets Manager Bobby's Valentine's father-in-law.

Kirk Gibson is the only MVP who never played in the All-Star Game.

fans always do, and we were doing it to each other. He pointed out that he thought the Cubs-Cardinals rivalry was the best in all of sports. Of course, he's seen hundreds of Cubs-Cardinals games.

I'll remember just little things that he said to me and of course memories that I have as a kid. My parents were both from Missouri so on summer vacations we would travel from my home in San Jose, California back to Columbia, Missouri. Of course, that's Cardinal country all the way. I would hear Jack Buck and Harry Caray do the radio for the Cardinals. I think that was my first introduction to Jack, and I was struck by what a great voice he had and how nice he sounded on the air. He just seemed like a genuinely nice person. I found it very appealing at that age, as a kid, when I was ten or twelve. I found that appealing right up until the day he died. I just think he was a very easy person to listen to and an easy person to be around. If you want the definition of "cool," so many people in our society try to "be cool" and to "think cool" or "act cool." To me, Jack Buck was cool because he always made you feel comfortable to be around him. To me, that is the definition of "cool." That was Jack.

That was a terrible, terrible time for the Cardinals. To lose Jack Buck and then to lose Darryl Kile. What a shock for a young ball player like Darryl Kile to die. It happened here in our city. The **Cubs** and Cardinals were ready to play a 2:20 p.m. game in the afternoon and now it was 2:15 p.m. and no pitchers were warming up in the bullpen. The shock of Jack's passing was still very much in the air and on our minds and in our hearts. Now we got the word about Darryl Kile and it all was just overwhelming. I felt sorry for everybody—Darryl's wife and his kids and Cardinal fans everywhere who had lost Jack and then three-four days later they lost Darryl Kile—it was terrible. I'm still sorry they had to go through that.

> The Cubs had never played a home game on Friday or Saturday nights until the "Darryl Kile" make-up game on Saturday night, August 31, 2002.

WHAT'S SHAKIN'…BESIDES CANDLESTICK PARK?

JOHN ROONEY

Since 1989, John Rooney has been the radio voice of the Chicago White Sox. Before that, Rooney spent 20 years broadcasting University of Missouri basketball, two seasons broadcasting Oklahoma 89ers baseball, and two seasons with the Louisville Redbirds, then the Class AAA affiliate of the St. Louis Cardinals.

When I was a kid, my dad was a big Cardinals fan. We lived just outside of Kansas City, Missouri, in the little town of Richmond, Missouri. I was born in Cameron, and most of my parents' family were from the Cameron-St. Joe area. KFEQ radio carried the Cardinals.

Great storytelling is what it takes. You have to pick up stories, and you have to be able to relay those to the audience. Jack always had a way of finding the funny side of the story, and a way to communicate that. When I went to work for KMOX in 1980, Jack told me, "This is the one thing that you'll have to remember your whole career, and if you make it, you'll understand this: you're talking to people who have very little education, you're talking to people who are some of the most educated people in the world, and you're talking to everybody in between. So, make it as simple as possible. That way, everybody can understand what you're trying to say." That's one of the greatest pieces of advice I ever got.

If he wanted to give you a verbal advantage lesson, he could do it. Oh, he could do it! But, he was able to take things and break them down to the simplest terms, while he looked for the light side. We all love to laugh and be entertained, and that's what this is. This is entertainment, and it takes us away from our day-to-day worries.

The first time I met Jack was when he walked into the press box at the University of Missouri. I was just starting to do some Missouri things. He looked around and said, "All right, who's playing today?" He had his bag loaded with information, so he knew who was playing. He sometimes liked to give you the impression that he could just walk in, sit down and do a game. He never did that, though. He talked to everybody he could talk to, and sometimes he might not have had the time to sit down and do the charts and the boards the way he would like, but he gave every minute that he possibly could to whatever game he was doing. That held true whether he was doing the Raiders against the Jets on Monday Night Football, or whether it was **Missouri** and **Oklahoma** in college football, or whether he was doing a basketball game. Jack gave his best to everything that he did.

During the "Earthquake World Series" of 1989 between the Oakland A's and the San Francisco Giants, I was doing pre- and post-game on the radio, and Jack was working with Johnny Bench. We were two or three minutes from air when the earthquake hit. I had already recorded the pre-game show. We used to lay that down so we could have everything timed out where Jack and Johnny could have four or five minutes to set the scene and get ready for the play-by-play. The pre-game show that day had been put to bed probably twenty minutes before the earthquake hit.

When the earthquake hit, Jack was standing next to the table in the booth, next to where he was doing his play-by-play broadcast. All of a sudden, things started shaking. I thought fans were stomping their feet for something on the field. Buck said, "It's an earthquake! See that big guy down there? I'm jumping on him!" Jack was getting on top of the counter, ready to jump over. The earthquake lasted 20-25 seconds. Then, everything stopped.

The first coach's show on TV was hosted by Bud Wilkinson at the University of Oklahoma in 1952.

In the 1983 Holiday Bowl, Brigham Young University quarterback Steve Young caught the winning touchdown pass in a 21-17 victory over Missouri.

Jack ran out of the booth because he knew Carole was arriving at the park about that same time. So, his next concern was his family. People could get trampled on the escalators and who knows what else. I didn't know what was going on outside of the ballpark until I got out the transistor radio and started listening to KCBS. That's when I found out about the fires down in San Jose, problems on the Bay Bridge and the collapse of Interstate 880. No, we weren't going to be playing baseball that night.

The pre-game show actually started on time, on tape in New York. We had a phone—because we needed an extra line—that was on the police trunk. So, the phone line stayed up between San Francisco and New York. We finally got it through the studio person's head that we were having a problem in San Francisco, and they needed to cut off the pre-game show so we could go live over the telephone line. The person in the studio told me, "We can't do that." I said, "That's my studio; I do shows from there, so patch us in. I take in interviews all the time." It took through the first commercial break to do that.

Jack, Johnny and I were on live, passing the phone around, talking about what happened. We told the listeners how we were experiencing an earthquake. Of course, Jack finds humor in everything. He said, "I tell you what, Johnny Bench, the way you ran out of the booth, if you ran like that when you played, you never would have hit into a double play. And I got to tell you, John Rooney, when this happened, I thought my socks were on too tight." He was able to cut through everything, and make it a little lighter to get through a tough moment.

We were on the air for about forty-five minutes, becoming newsmen. During that time is when the newsman in Jack Buck showed up. Milo Hamilton, Jack Buck, Jack Brickhouse, and other people of that era, could talk to presidents one moment, go to a local city council meeting the next moment and then cover a fire down the street. Later, they could walk into the ballpark to broadcast the pre-game show before doing the baseball game. Those people were very special.

Jack Buck (circled left) made his TV debut at WBNS, Columbus, Ohio in 1952. Also circled are WBNS staffers Jonathan Winters and Woody Hayes.

Jack Buck and Harry Caray – 1954. Note call letters KXOK.

Jack Buck and wife Alyce with their Buckeroos in 1966.

When Robert Hyland switched the format of KMOX from music to news/talk/sports in 1960 he donated the station's entire music library to a veterans hospital to ensure he would not change his decision. Here Jack Buck is perusing the titles before they are all carted away.

Marlon Perkins (rear) watches Jack Buck's "Wild Kingdom."

Mercantile Library – UMSL

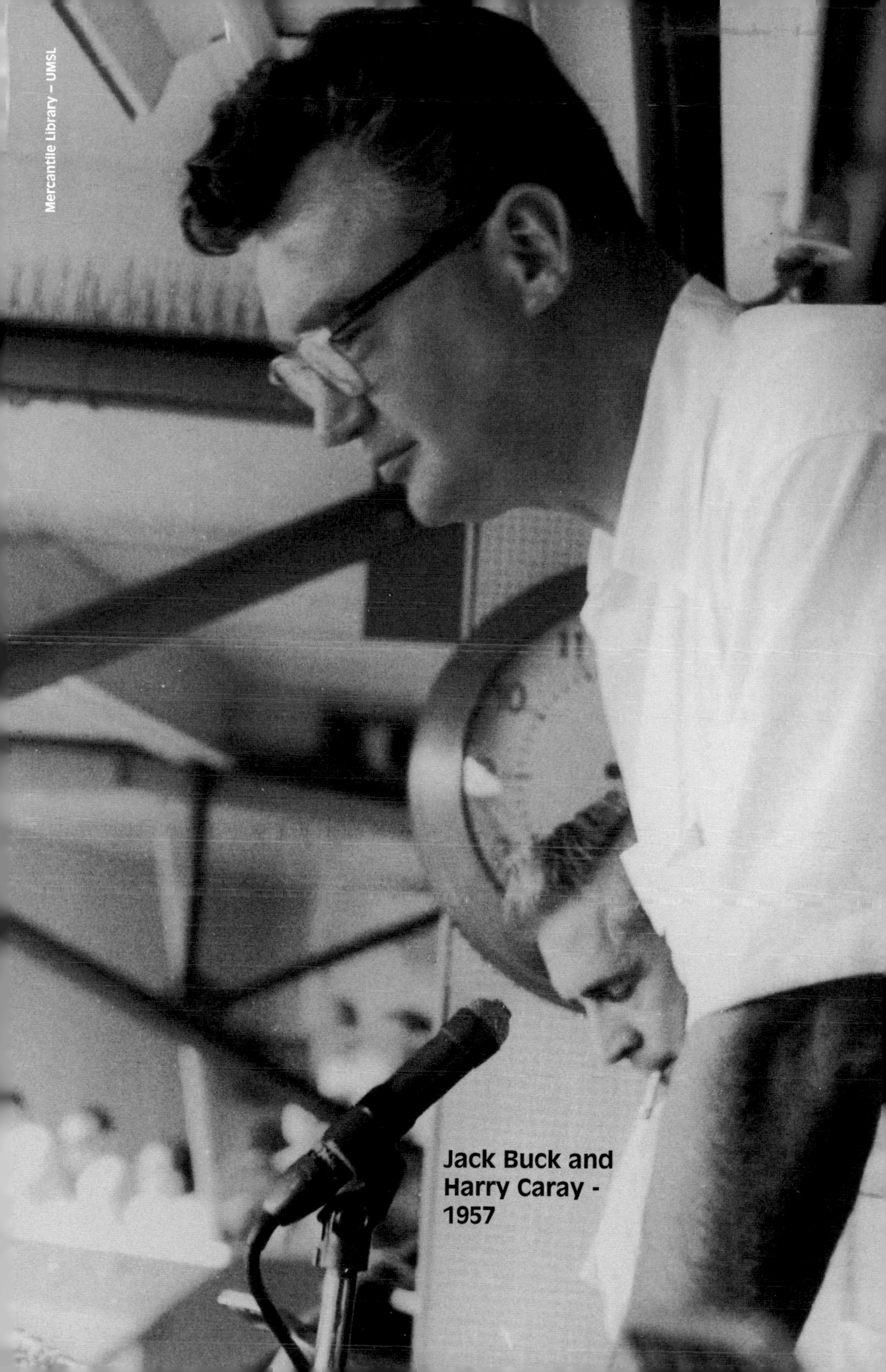

Jack Buck and Harry Caray - 1957

KMOX

Jack Buck interviews Eleanor Roosevelt for his "At Your Service" program.

THIS WRITER IS FROM CHICAGO...NOT THAT THERE'S ANYTHING WRONG WITH THAT

GEORGE CASTLE

George Castle is a Chicago Cubs beat writer for a northern Indiana paper. He co-authored the book I Remember Harry Caray *and wrote* The I-55 Series *chronicling the Cubs-Cardinals rivalry. Castle is the host and creator of Diamond Gems, a syndicated radio show featuring rare audio clips and memories from baseball's past.*

Jack Buck is the last of a dying breed of sportscasters who are able to do everything, not just every sport, but also to do news shows, interview shows, talk shows, literally do anything that the radio station wanted. Toastmaster was his specialty—jokes and all that. From my experience he seemed to be the second most versatile guy in the Midwest in modern times after **Jack Brickhouse**. Jack Brickhouse did everything, but Jack Buck seems a pretty competitive second place.

Joe Buck told me some years ago when I asked him why his father worked so much in the old days doing all sorts of shows, punishing schedule, and he said, "He had to. They didn't pay him all that much." Jack, of course, had a large family. By the time he remarried, he ended up with eight kids. There was a lot of overhead in his house. I've heard stories where he would have to do a Cardinal game at night, and come in to do the morning show the next day. He did it. I know on several occasions he tried to leave the Cardinal broadcast booth for network assignments, but St. Louis was his calling, and he ended up where he should have been.

I met Jack in Wrigley Field when he was a Cardinals announcer. I was a lowly, weekly newspaper guy, and Jack was already a superstar announcer. I will tell you he had a hidden Chicago past. He was the

> For many seasons, Jack Brickhouse was the TV announcer for <u>both</u> the Cubs and the White Sox. The teams would televise home games only.

Bears' TV announcer on CBS telecasts of Bears road games in the mid 1960s. I actually have an audio tape of him teaming with Van Patrick to open the Bears-Lions Thanksgiving telecast in 1964 in Detroit, which is very interesting. He also was one of the celebrity announcers filling in for Harry Caray when Harry was sidelined with a stroke at the beginning of the 1987 season. Jack had the humorous displeasure of having to call a game-winning Andre Dawson grand slam at Busch Stadium against his own team. He was at the mike at Busch Stadium, and he was filling in for Harry, and Dawson came up with the bases loaded. **Whitey Herzog** told Todd Worrell, "Whatever you do, don't walk him." Todd obeyed it to the letter. He gave up a game-winning grand slam. Buck was laughing that all-knowing laugh as Dawson circled the bases. He had a couple of those interesting Chicago broadcast connections.

It seemed like football was always trying to distract him from baseball. His early work with the American Football League on ABC included a Roone Arledge experiment where the announcer would walk out onto the field and actually bring a mike into the overtime coin flip in the AFL championship game in 1962—some famous kinescope shows Jack out there in his overcoat. Then of course he did Sunday work for the NFL on CBS-TV with the Bears and other teams. He was on the "Ice Bowl," telecast in 1967. He did other games, and then he found that real niche as the network football announcer.

Whitey Herzog is the only person to be Manager of the Year and Executive of the Year in the same season.

WRIGLEY FIELD: HOME OF THE SEVENTH INNING RETCH

JOE RIOS

Joe Rios has the enviable job of coordinating singers for the Cubs' famous seventh-inning "Take Me Out to the Ball Game" tradition. On June 5, 2001, Jack Buck gave a rendition that both Cub and Cardinal fans loved. See the appendix of this book for a roster of all the Wrigley Field "singers."

Every aspect of Wrigley Field has its purpose and in 1998, the singing sort of became a new thing of Wrigley Field. Fans really like this new tradition. You'll hear them say things like "Yeah, I went to the game where Sammy hit his thirty-fifth home run, and by the way Ozzie Smith was singing. It was really cool." They won't remember necessarily whether we won or lost or who pitched, but they remember that Joe Mantegna, a Chicago native, sang on the day of the twenty-strikeout game and that was pretty cool.

We wanted Jack Buck to sing "Take Me Out to the Ballgame" because, he's a legendary broadcaster. He came out and he had the red blazer on. I gave him a hat. I was trying to explain to him exactly what was going on. He said, "Joe, don't worry about it." I've got a good routine down. I know what's going on." It was just amazing that I got the opportunity to sit with him for five or ten minutes and just talk with him. I wasn't around for all his great calls, but his mind was absolutely perfect, in good working order—it was just this disease that he had that was just so—you'd think he'd be down, but he was very happy. When he went out and did that, it blew us all away. It was the greatest thing. We had no idea that the *SportsCenter* would be picking it up that night and they showed it for a couple of days. I saw that he had two hats and just thought I would let him do what he wanted to do. He's Jack Buck. I wasn't about to tell him no. We love it when Bob Uecker sings. He always says, "Root, root, root for the Brewers." Harry Kalas says "the Cubbies," but he's got an agenda behind that because every time he sings, and he says "Cubbies," the Phillies win. He gets a lot of guff from the clubhouse guys, but when he sang, if you noticed, the Phillies players all stood up and kind of just folded their arms and looked up at him to see if he'd say "Phillies" or "Cubbies," and he said "Cubbies" again and, lo and behold, the Phillies win.

We always give the guest conductor a Cubs cap that has a little engraving on the side that says the year, and 7th inning stretch. It's up to them if they want to wear it or throw it out. We get eighty-one caps made each year. You can't know sizes of who is going to sing so we can't get fitted caps. I think the cap Jack wore was a fitted cap though. Jack brought the Cardinal cap with him.

We don't have a big Jumbotron so not everybody could see what Jack was wearing. We put the name up and everybody knew it was the legendary Jack Buck when he started singing. He starts off by saying something like "This is the greatest rivalry in sports—the Cubs and the Cards." Then he started singing wearing a Cubs cap. Halfway through the song he takes off the hat and puts on the Cardinal hat. At the point where you're supposed to say, "root, root, root for the Cubs," he said "… for the Cardinals." That place went wild. We loved it. He has that old-time baseball voice that was just perfect. And then he sat and talked to our broadcasters for a while.

The next day Joe Buck said, "I want to thank you for what you did for my father. He had an absolutely great time. I really appreciate what you did." That was the moment where I said, "Wow, this was really good because if Joe liked it then most of the Cardinal fans would have liked it." It was awesome.

Unfortunately we didn't have the opportunity to have him do a repeat performance. Stan Musial has done it here in1998 with his harmonica, and he also did it in 2002. We always ask whoever's retiring that year to do it, and we've asked McGwire. We asked Cal Ripken and Tony Gwynn. Maybe after a couple of years, after they're out of the limelight, they'll come back. I was pretty impressed that Carlton Fisk did it even though he played on the south side for the White Sox. It's hard to say who has been the best we had. Vin Scully did it and he was wonderful. Our organist feels he's the very best of all time including professional singers.

I don't know how thrilled Mike Ditka is about doing it. He doesn't like to be considered a bad singer. This year he was gonna throw a "Millie Vanilli." He brought in a ringer—the lounge singer at his restaurant who sings Frank Sinatra-style—he wanted him to come out and hide behind the broadcast booth and Mike Ditka would lip sync it without his voice coming through. I said, "You know what—I can't have you do that. People really want to hear you." It would have been super funny, but we finally convinced him to do a duet with his guy so he did that. He did kind of keep it down and let the other guy sing out...We've had a couple of athletes that were just horrible, absolutely horrible, Nancy Kerrigan comes to mind, she was just horrible, and another ice skater, Nicole Bobeck also was absolutely horrible...Looking at some of the baseball players, to tell you the truth a lot of the baseball players sang pretty well—Andre Dawson, **Andy Pafko**, Bill Buckner sang well. Billy Williams did great. Bruce Sutter did great. **Ernie Banks** always has a great time with it. We had Jody Davis came on, and he didn't sing that well. Ozzie Smith sang very well, Paul Molitor.

For the most part, the baseball players all sang very well. We had the coolest one the other day, Vance Law and his father, Vernon Law. For the first time we had the guest conductor for "Take Me Out to the Ball Game" also sing the National Anthem. It was just incredible. They have the greatest voices. Vance is head baseball coach at BYU and Vernon has just retired. It's just amazing that we have these two guys, former big league players, who sang both songs. Only Wayne Messmer has sung both songs here for us...Susan Hawk was a character on *Survivor*, and she was absolutely horrible...We had some hockey players who were pretty bad. Chris Chelios has gotten much

In the very first set of Topps baseball cards, the first card (#1) was Andy Pafko.

Ernie Banks and O. J. Simpson are cousins. Their grandfathers were twin brothers.

better as the years go by. He's sung it four or five times. Brian Urlacher, the Bears linebacker, he's just absolutely horrible. We had Dan Hampton, who just went into the Hall of Fame, do it.

Tony Orlando is a big friend of the St. Louis Cardinals and he's really into baseball. He knows Joe Torre really well, I think he grew up with him. As soon as he found out that Jack had passed away, he took the red eye from Vegas to St. Louis and went to the funeral. He was talking with Joe and Mark McGwire and some of the older players, and he said the weirdest thing. The topic of conversation at the time he was there was Jack singing "Take Me Out to the Ball Game" at Wrigley Field, and how cool it was, and what a great job he did. I guess it was fresh on their minds. They had played it at Busch Stadium. I think there was talk about the Cardinals playing that for the rest of the season during their seventh inning stretch. That was kind of interesting they would actually be talking about this. It must have affected everybody in a great way, and he must have enjoyed doing that. It worked out great for the Cardinal family and our family and everybody involved.

Famous Calls

On Ozzie Smith's home run against Los Angeles in National League playoffs, Oct. 14, 1985:

"Smith corks one into right down the line. It may go! Go crazy, folks! Go crazy! It's a home run and the Cardinals have won the game by the score of 3-2 on a home run by the Wizard!"

HOW DO YOU KEEP BEARS OUT OF YOUR BACK YARD? INSTALL GOAL POSTS.
STEVE ROUSEY

Steve Rousey of Champaign, Illinois is a Chicago Bears season ticket holder and a Chicago White Sox fan. His last check to the devil must have bounced.

I'm a **Bears'** season ticket holder; have been for a number of years. I was going to a Bears game, a Monday night game, in Chicago. Jack and Hank Stram were doing the Monday Night radio broadcast. I'm wandering around the downstairs, walking around down there, and it's about twenty minutes till eight. The ball game starts at eight. I see this guy coming toward me, and of course he's unmistakable. He had on this really loud, plaid jacket and that silver gray hair of his. I'd never met him, and I'm somewhat intimidated. But I just couldn't help myself. As we passed by, I said, "Mr. Buck, I just want you to know that I'm a big fan of yours. I want to thank you for all the years of enjoyment that you've brought me, as a young child and as an adult, listening to you." He stopped, "Well, that's very kind—always nice to hear that. When we do radio work, we don't have interaction with our audience so it's always nice to know that people appreciate the job we do." I'm ready to walk on. He asks, "What's your name?" I told him. "Where do you live?" I told him, "Champaign, Illinois." "What do you do?" "I'm a retired police officer." By this time, I'm looking at my watch and thinking that this guy's got to be upstairs doing a national broadcast in fifteen minutes. "Well, thank you for your time. It was very nice meeting you. You've got a game to do." "They'll wait." I thought, "My god, how many people of his stature would ever stop and talk to a person?" Usually it would be, "Yeah, thanks." And go on. He acted like he didn't have a care in the world. It was really moving. I've told that story over the

> The Bears' season ticket holders live in 46 different states...the Bears have the same colors as the University of Illinois because their founder, George Halas, was once a star player for the Illini.

years to many people. Long before he died, I would tell people about Jack Buck. Then after he died, I told that story to a couple of people. They go, "Yeah, we keep hearing that." Not knowing Jack Buck personally, I had no idea what he was like in his personal life, but now I hear other stories and that's basically how he treated everybody. I've got to tell you—that was about seventeen years ago, and that has stayed with me. That really was a strange thing. It impacted me. I'm not a celebrity person. I really wouldn't care for an autograph or anything like that. I've never looked for autographs. I just was happy to tell him thank you for all those years of enjoyment he'd given me.

I've been to a lot of Cardinal games in my life. My first Cardinal game was about 1955 in Sportsman's Park. Other than seeing him up in the broadcast booth at an occasional Cardinal game, I'd never been close to the man. I never saw him. It was just one of those chance encounters. I was just wandering around checking out the inner sanctum of the old Soldier Field here, and here he comes walking along.

The five minutes that he spent with me made a lasting impression in my life that a person of his stature would take the time. I've met people like that. In my work, I could give you a hundred stories of people of celebrity status who wouldn't give you the time of day. People like Whitney Houston, who came to town to give a concert one time. I was going to take her from the hotel to the assembly hall and then back to the airport. This person was so darn rude. When you see celebrities like that, you stereotype them. You think they're all like that. Then you have somebody of Jack Buck's stature. I grew up in central Illinois, and of course you're either a Cardinal fan or a Cub fan. My first ball game was a Cardinal game. I liked to listen to him on the radio like millions of other kids did—on the transistor radio when he and Harry Caray were broadcasting, long before Harry ever left to go to **Oakland**. Then later when Harry went to the White Sox, I became a big White Sox fan, and I'm a White Sox fan today. I'm not really a Cardinal fan, but I loved Jack Buck.

> The Oakland A's colors are green and gold because their late owner, Charles O. Finley, grew up in LaPorte, IN and loved Notre Dame...when he bought the Kansas City A's, he changed their uniforms to those colors.

Chapter 4

Buck Fever!

Steve Lane

Mark Beck

Darryl Meyer

Barb Gass

Tom Mullaney

Rick Schwarz

Dustin McKinnis

Redbird Fandemonium

I HAD NEVER MET JACK BUCK PERSONALLY, BUT I KNEW HIM MY WHOLE LIFE
STEVE LANE

Steve Lane grew up in Tiptonville, Tennessee listening to almost every Cardinal game with his dad. Lane now lives in Lewisville, Texas.

When I met Jack Buck, I told him about how my father, who had passed away at age 54, and I had listened to him and Mike Shannon at night on the radio as they broadcast the Cardinal games. I told him he made us feel as if we were there at the game when we listened to him. I had always wanted to meet him. I thought how I would love to just sit and talk to this man for five minutes if nothing else.

I had the opportunity to meet him back in 1996. I went up to a Cardinal game. I went down to the Hall of Fame—it was there in the stadium. Al Hrabosky and Bob Carpenter were there at the time doing a talk show. I walked by them and waved, and Al waved back. I stood there for a minute and thought, "He might be able to help me meet Jack Buck." He got off the air and I went up to him and introduced myself and had my picture made with him, and I told him that I'd always wanted to meet Jack Buck. He told me, "This is how you can do it." I went up there to the press level and talked to the security guard. Al Hrabosky was up there at the same time, and he told the security guard, "Take care of this man. He wants to meet Jack." He told me to stand right there and that Jack would be coming out of an elevator there in about five minutes. Sure enough he did. He got off the elevator, and he came right up to me. I was just shaking in my shoes. I shook his hand. I took my picture with him. He stood and talked to me for about five or ten minutes. I told him about how he made me feel growing up as a Cardinal fan, and how my father just loved listening to him. He was just a very professional man all the way. I wasn't surprised at how nice he was to me. I just had a feeling that this man was going to be nice when I would get to meet him. There was no doubt in my mind. Just listening to him and the way he treated people, talking to them, and everything on the radio. You just knew that this man was real. I wish my dad could have been there to meet him—and I think he was, in a way.

I like to have my picture made with sports celebrities and whoever, and I've got four 5 x 7s, and in the center of this, I've got an 8 x 10 of Jack and me. The other pictures are of me with Bob Lilly, Chad Hennings, Troy Aikman, and Rafael Palmiero.

I make it a point now every year when I go down to a game to go up to the press level; I've met Mike Shannon and had a chance to meet Ozzie Smith up there one night.

On June 19, I got up at six-thirty in the morning. My alarm is set for a sports radio show here in town, and they announced that morning that he had passed away. I couldn't believe it. I knew he had been sick. Then a friend of mine called me, and we talked about it a little bit. It was kind of like a family member of yours has died. It was just sad. It really was.

It was just the way Jack called the game. He had the type of flair for just sending chills up your spine when he was making a certain call. Even to this day, when you hear that call, like when Ozzie Smith hit that home run in 1985. Even to this day when I hear it, I just get chills.

> *"A lot of wonderful and exciting things have happened in my life. There isn't too much I would have done differently. I have no regrets. I've tried to live life to the fullest."*
> Jack Buck

JACK BUCK WAS AN ITCH THAT DIDN'T GO AWAY WITH ONE SCRATCH

MARK G. BECK

St. Louis dentist Mark Beck has something most Cardinal fans would love to have: Jack Buck's voice on his home answering machine.

My mom was going to **Pittsburgh** to visit my sister who was pregnant. She was in the airport and ran into Jack Buck there. He was going to Pittsburgh, too. It turns out it was his last football game for CBS Radio. She was telling Jack about being kinda upset about my sister's pregnancy and stuff. My mom had to go up to the airlines desk for some reason or another. Jack followed her up, and while she was talking to the gal, Jack asked, "Is there any room in first class?" He was told yes there was room, so he pulled out a voucher and said, "Put Mrs. Beck in first class." I thought that was real neat.

She also told him about our having his voice on our answering machine at home. We bought this recording deal at a silent charity auction for two hundred dollars, and Jack made a recording for us. Somebody from the Cardinals called and told us to write out something we would want Jack to say. We only really wanted him to say, "Thanks for your time this time. Till next time, so long." He pretty much ad-libbed the rest of it. He starts out and says, "Hi. This is Jack Beck coming to you from the Bucks. No. This is Jack Buck coming to you from the Becks. I can't get to the phone right now 'cause I'm doing the dishes here at the Becks. But if you'll leave your number, they'll call you back. Thanks for your time this time. Till next time,

There was never a no-hitter at Pittsburgh's Forbes Field…but it was the site of Babe Ruth's last home run…as a Boston Brave in 1935.

so long." In the background you can hear the crowd noise and some guy selling peanuts or something.

My friends just love it. I couldn't tell you the number of times we'd pick up the phone and they'd say, "Hey, I got a guy here who wants to hear this on the recording." So we'd hang up and let it play so they could hear it. We got a lot of calls like that. Some would leave a message and say, "Hey, that's a great recording." People really got a kick out of it. We hope we're not being sacrilegious or something by still having it on, but people still want to hear his voice.

Three years later, I was able to go up into the booth and watch a couple of games from the KMOX booth. I started to tell them the story, and he remembered it, word-for-word practically. At the time a lot of people thought, "Well, Jack's slowing down. He's not as quick as he used to be." But he sure remembered something as trivial as that.

My memories of Jack are just what a first-class individual he was. And how he was able to paint the pictures of the game where it was more fun to listen to him than even to go to a game.

You'd hear all these different little stories about little kindnesses he would do for people and how he would tip everybody—twenty or a hundred bucks or whatever. Maybe it was Red Schoendienst who said, "He's the greatest Cardinal." I'd have to agree with Red that he was. He'd seen all the players. I don't think there are many people like that who are kind and outgoing—just a great guy. I've heard announcers say bad things about people and put other announcers down, but I don't think I ever heard Jack say anything but a kind word about people.

Now when you listen to games, you never hear the score. When Jack Buck was doing it, and Mike Shannon's the same way, you'd hear the score every couple of minutes. You knew what the score was. Most announcers don't realize that people tune in at any time during the game.

I don't think there's ever going to be another announcer like Jack Buck. Not even his son, Joe—I mean, Joe's a good announcer, but I don't think he paints the picture like Jack did. I don't believe he's as great a person as Jack. I don't know that anybody could be.

SORRY, BUT I CAN'T HEAR YOU UP HERE ON CLOUD NINE

DARRYL MEYER

Darryl Meyer had two dreams fulfilled in twenty-four hours: a healthy baby and meeting Jack Buck, his childhood idol.

Joe Buck's second daughter is one day younger than my son. My wife and I went to the hospital to have our third child—our second son. I had gone downstairs to smoke a cigarette and was riding back up in the elevator when I looked over—the guy standing next to me was Joe Buck. He was looking like he didn't want to be seen or recognized. Kind of under my breath, I said, "You're Joe Buck aren't you?" He said, "Sure am." I told him how I thought he did an awesome job coming up by himself and not begging off his dad to get him the job and told him how much respect I had for him and his father. I thought they both were class acts. When we got off the elevator, he went his way and I went mine. I was there in the room with my wife. Maybe half an hour later, a nurse came over and said that Joe wanted me to come out and wanted me to meet his dad. I went out and he introduced me to his dad. We were all three standing at the glass and pointing out our babies to each other, Jack's granddaughter. It was really neat. Jack stood there and had his arm around me. We talked for quite a while and looked at each other's kids. It was the first time I'd ever gotten to meet either one of them. He was my childhood idol. That was the last time I ever saw him.

My son had been born the day before so I was already on cloud nine because he was healthy and everything. Then I got to stand with a guy I could remember as a little kid having an AM radio stuffed under my pillow listening to the ball games when I was supposed to be asleep. It was like a dream coming true—standing there with one of the biggest names in the business and one of my huge idols as a kid, somebody I totally respected all my life. He had his arm around me while we were showing off our babies to one another. It was just really cool.

When I heard the news that Jack Buck died, it immediately brought tears to my eyes. I knew he had been sick for quite a while. My father is dying of prostate cancer right now. I was sitting right here in my dining room eating breakfast. It was one of those moments you never forget.

I heard it said just the other day: "Jack Buck was the guy that everybody wanted to be." He was the guy that everybody looked at and said, "That's the way I should live my life. I should help other people. I should do this or that." Jack Buck never knew a stranger. He was a lot like my grandfather. My grandfather isn't famous, but he's a self-made man himself. Both he and Jack could talk to anybody on their level and never be talking down to them. They could talk to a banker or a bum at that person's level and never act like they were talking down to them. They were always there for somebody.

We've been blessed with **Hall of Fame** announcers. We've got Bob Costas, Harry Caray, Dan Dierdorf—the list goes on and on. St. Louis has just been absolutely blessed with these guys. Jack Buck and Dan Kelly are probably the two best ever in my book. Joe Buck made it on his own. He didn't rely on daddy to get it. The name opened some doors, but daddy didn't push him through. Joe earned all that on his own. He's now one of the top ones out there.

> Only two players have won two MVP awards and are not in the Hall of Fame: Roger Maris and Dale Murphy...Roger Maris was Roger Maras until 1955. He didn't like for fans to call him "Mar-ass."

JACK BUCK ONCE SAID—JOKINGLY— THAT HE WISHED HE HAD ALZHEIMER'S SO HE WOULD FORGET HE HAD PARKINSON'S
BARB GASS

Back in 1997 my dad and I went to a ball game, and we had tickets to the green seats, behind home plate. On our way down to our seats, we saw Jack Buck. He was by the elevators, and my dad, Donald St. Eve, was all excited. I liked him, but my dad was *really* excited. I go, "Oh, there's Jack Buck. Let's see if we can get an autograph," since we have big fancy tickets for those green seats." He did autograph our tickets, and I had taken my camera along that day, knowing that we had these really good tickets, and thought I might get some good pictures. I asked Jack Buck if he would mind posing for a picture with my dad, and he said, "Sure, no problem." He stood there and he put his arm around my dad. My dad had a ball cap on, and Jack was like, "Oh, take that hat off so you can get a good picture." He was just very nice and didn't act put out at all. I took his picture and it turned out really, really good. I had it blown up and made one for myself and one for my dad.

That was five years ago. Right now my dad is an Alzheimer's patient in a nursing home, and we have that picture in his room. The workers there always make comments about the picture and ask him about it. He doesn't remember much, but he can still remember that day as a source of conversation for him when people come in the room.

That was the only time we met him. Of course, I'd seen him around downtown **St. Louis**, but I never had talked to him personally. We were just in a situation, and we were the only ones around. We went up to get his autograph, and he was just very gracious. I've gotten

> All six games of the 1944 World Series were played at Sportsman's Park in St. Louis. The rival managers— Luke Sewell of the Browns and Billy Southworth of the Cardinals—shared a one-bedroom apartment.

other people's autographs before, and they'll autograph stuff, but they don't really make conversation with you. It was just that he was so nice about taking a picture with my dad. My dad's my dad! To my dad that was like my daughter getting an autograph from Mickey Mouse. That was the most exciting thing that happened to him in a long time.

On June 19, I opened the paper in the morning and read about his death. I was really sad about it. I was driving to work and was listening to KMOX, and I was crying all the way to work listening to everybody else's stories—and just for my dad, and because it brought back memories of my dad when he was not sick. He used to go to the ball games all the time. Just remembering how we got that picture and knowing that it's sitting there in his room at the nursing home.

We've never had season tickets, but I've been to hundreds of games. My dad took me to my first game when I was ten years old. When I grew up, I found it fitting that on special days—I mean who else would appreciate going and sitting in the green seats behind home plate. That's why I would take my dad. My parents were at the 1964 World Series, and we were at all the World Series games in the eighties.

Jack Buck and Don St. Eve, July 4, 1997

EIGHTY-ONE PERCENT OF THE PEOPLE IN KANSAS CITY WHO HAVE SEEN AT LEAST TWO "POLICE ACADEMY" MOVIES AGREE THAT DON DENKINGER WAS WRONG!

TOM MULLANEY

Tom Mullaney has a picture of Jack Buck hanging on the wall above his desk in Conway, Arkansas. This is the story of how the Cardinals fan got that picture.

I grew up in St. Louis. I lived out in the county out past Eureka. We would go to games, but more times than not I sat and listened to them. I always remember Jack Buck coming across the radio. For me, he was always the voice of the Cardinals. He was the person who made me fall in love with the team. He brought me into the stadium when I couldn't be there. He always made me feel like I was in the seat right next to him because he described the game and what was going on so well that you felt part of it.

Then when I left St. Louis and went to college, I moved to Kansas City. Luckily, KMOX has such a strong signal that I was able to pick it up in Kansas City and could listen to Cardinal games and not have to watch the lowly Royals. I appreciated being able to do that. I travel a lot, and it amazes me how I am able to pick up KMOX in all these different states. I get into places where there's not much radio reception. About the time I know the Cardinal game is supposed to start, I go turn on the AM dial and hit "search" and just wait until it hits KMOX and I can pick up the signal whether it was going south to New Orleans or out into Nebraska or up north into Iowa or wherever it might have been. You could always pick up a KMOX signal. It made the long drives feel a lot shorter being able to sit there and wrap yourself in Jack calling a Cardinal game.

I did meet Jack. I met him two years ago at Winter Warm-up there in St. Louis and had a photo taken with him. Then the following year, I'd had it developed, and I brought it with me to see him again, and he didn't sign many autographs during the weekend, but I remember that day he had gone over and was talking to the gentleman who does all the statues—did his and Ozzie's. He was standing there, and the guy who represents Stan Musial was standing there with him. I waited until he finished doing what he was doing and just asked him if he would mind signing it. He looked at me, "Were you here last year?" I said, "Yeah, I was here last year." He said, "Well, I've got to go do something. Follow me outside."

I followed him outside, and there were a bunch of people around trying to get him to sign stuff, and escorts were kinda pushing people away saying, "No, he can't sign. He can't sign." He looked back at me, and he pointed to me, and his hands were shaking because of his condition. He said, "I'll sign that guy's picture." I handed it to him, and he signed it for me, and we shook hands. It was really nice for me because it was great to meet him initially and have my picture taken with him, but to have him take the time to sign it for me in the advanced stage of Parkinson's that he had. It was so hard for him to do it because his hands shook so bad and he had to continually reposition the pen. To sign his first name took a lot of work, and then he had to kind of stop and do the second one. Then he pulled off, and he wrote "Hall of Fame" on it and his year. Then he pulled back and kinda like he started to hand it back to me, but then he pulled it back again and wrote "Go Crazy." He put in parentheses "pffft." It was a nice thing for him to do. He didn't have to do it. He was obviously busy, and it was obviously hard on him. It was a great thing. That's the one thing that I'll remember him for just because he did something so nice and personal for me.

THE DO'S AND DON'TS OF WORKING WITH JACK BUCK—DO!

RICK SCHWARTZ

Rick Schwartz of Crown Point, Indiana recalls memories of Jack Buck from his days as a young man at KMOX.

W ally Moon was a Rookie of the Year for the Cardinals in 1954, the same year that Buck came to the Cardinals. That's a little bit before my time, too, since I was born in 1953. After Moon retired, he went down to Arkansas and became a coach at a small college called John Brown University. Quite a number of years later, I wound up graduating from John Brown University in the class of 1980. In the class of 1979, we had a young man named Jim Winn who was a pitcher, an excellent pitcher—just superb. He went on to pitch with the Pittsburgh Pirates. In the summer of 1983, the Pirates called him up to the big leagues. Jack Buck and Mike Shannon were broadcasting the afternoon game out of Three Rivers Stadium in Pittsburgh. I was working in the Community Affairs Department for KMOX TV, in St. Louis.

I was listening to Buck and Shannon broadcast the game and this kid came on in relief. I knew who he was since I'd been in college with him. Jack mentioned the fact that it was his first game, and he was giving a little bio on the kid, and he expressed amazement. "It says here that he won some baseball awards for John Brown University, but it also says here that John Brown University doesn't have a baseball team. I don't understand how he could be a baseball pitcher for a college that doesn't have a baseball team." Well, I knew what happened. Between the time this kid had graduated and the time he went up to the Pirates, John Brown University, for various reasons, had dropped their entire baseball program. They were one of the best small college baseball teams in the nation, and then they just dropped it cold and so Buck was right, and the kid won the NAIA World

Series and MVP and all kinds of awards. But John Brown did not have a baseball team. I reached over to the phone and called the sports department on the radio side and said, "I can help Jack. I know what happened." I told his producer, "I went to John Brown. John Brown had a team and they dropped it in 1981 so they no longer have a team." I mentioned to the producer, "Oh, by the way, John Brown is where Wally Moon went after he retired. He was JBU's baseball coach for a number of years." He said, "Okay, I'll pass that on to Jack." Ten minutes later on the air, I heard Jack say, "Oh, now I remember why John Brown doesn't have a baseball team." And he said word-for-word what I'd said, but it was from his own memory. He told the radio audience, "You guys remember Wally Moon. I remember Wally going down to John Brown to become a coach after he retired from baseball." And he gave my whole story about the kid, about Wally Moon and everything, but suddenly it was from Jack Buck's memory. I sat here thinking, "Oh, Jack you dirty dog."

Back in 1984, my wife and kids got to meet Jack, but I never did. He was wearing a garish sports coat—my wife will never forget that. When she heard the news that he had passed away, the first words out of her mouth were, "Man, he wore the ugliest sports coat." He was color-blind so he just had no fashion sense at all. I was one year old when Jack Buck came to the Cardinals. I grew up within sight of the Arch—our house was maybe two miles away. If the ground had been flat, we probably could have seen Busch Stadium. So there was never a time in my life when Jack Buck wasn't there. So missing Jack is missing a part of my life. My wife isn't from St. Louis so it's not the same to her. It's not the same to my kids. To them, he's just a name—somebody to mourn briefly in passing. But to me, he's been part of my life since I was a year old.

Jack was Cardinal baseball to most of the people. Every year there are new players. Every year there are new heroes or new goats, depending on how the year goes. Jack was the anchor who was the constant for every year. He was Cardinal baseball.

THE BOY WONDER HAD THE BOYS WONDERING

DUSTIN McKINNIS

Dustin McKinnis, a 2002 graduate of Central High School in Cape Girardeau, spent time with Jack Buck in the broadcast booth. He has undergone more than 100 operations to repair problems related to his tracheal tube.

I met Mr. Buck in the summer of 1995 when a friend who works at Busch Stadium introduced us. After talking for a while, he invited my family and I to the broadcast booth to watch the game between the Cardinals and Reds.

Mr. Buck soon took me under his wing. He invited me to the microphone to interview me on the air. He wanted to talk to me about the 89 operations I had up to that point. He told me I was a true fighter. Before the interview was over, Mr. Buck said he wanted me to try play-by-play. I was honored to share the microphone with a man I respected and looked up to for so many years. I called the final out in the third inning. It was a great thrill. We kept in close contact following that season.

The following season, when I was visiting Mr. Buck in the booth, he said he wanted me to do some more play-by-play. This time he told me, "I want you to yell 'that's a winner!'" When I heard him say that my mouth dropped. I actually couldn't believe Mr. Buck wanted me to use his signature line.

There were two outs, and he turned the microphone over to me. Cincinnati ended up getting two hits. I vividly remember what Mr. Buck turned to me and said, "Kid, I'm going to blow you out of that chair if you don't get this next guy out." A ground ball was hit to second and thrown to first for the victory and I yelled his famous line. I remember Mr. Buck having tears building in his eyes and a big smile on his face. It not only meant a lot to me, but to him as well.

Chapter 5

Sweet Home St. Louis

Mike Roarty

Vince Bommarito

J. Kim Tucci

Bing Devine

Red Schoendienst

John King

Bea Higgins

John Carney

Greg Marecek

I Love Those Dear Hearts and Gentle People

WHAT'S BEER GOT TO DO WITH IT? AT THE '98 ALL-STAR GAME, A GUY FROM MILWAUKEE NAMED BUD IS MADE COMMISSIONER AT COORS FIELD

MIKE ROARTY

Mike Roarty is a legend in the American brewing industry. A Michigan native and a graduate of the University of Detroit (Alumnus of the Year in 1994), he became the major domo of the incredible rise in market share for Anheuser-Busch products during his reign as head of marketing. The proud Irishman, now retired from the beer business, could fill several books with stories from his career. He was one of Jack Buck's closest friends, if not his best friend.

Jack Buck left the Cardinals for one year in his early years. There were three announcers at that time, and since Jack was the youngest, they let him go. That was remedied the following year when he was rehired.

He went to CBS to take part in a television program they called *Grandstand*. It wasn't Jack's format at all. He's a freewheeling, incredibly sharp intellect who had the greatest sense of humor and the quickest response time I've ever seen in any individual. That's what made him such a great emcee. He was so quick. He sized up a situation and he would deliver a line that was just hilarious most of the time. He was one of those natural people.

That year they put him in *Grandstand*, a tightly scripted program. Well, he wasn't a script guy. The thing didn't work. It didn't work for CBS, and it didn't work for Jack Buck. He was very uncomfortable. Jack could have been successful if they had left him alone. Instead of that, they tried to do the scripting. First of all you're dealing with a medium that he was totally familiar with—sports. And you're putting words in his mouth that he was not familiar with, and he would worry about that.

What I did was I kept his job open. We hired a couple of interim announcers. I kept my eye on his career as it was moving along over at CBS. When the thing finally got bailed out, he came back, and so he had that one-year experience. He didn't move to New York, he commuted. It was a sad situation and it was a sorry circumstance for Jack. It bothered him because he didn't like to fail at anything. He was always successful at everything. Buck was replaced on *Grandstand* by Lee Leonard. Lee co-hosted the very first ESPN show when they came on the air in 1979.

Jack appreciated language, and how you used it was important to him. That's why Shannon used to drive him crazy—Mike's own unique way of expressing himself. Jack helped Mike Shannon a lot. Jack would get mad at him sometimes because he hated the see the language butchered, and of course you never knew what was going to come out of Mike's mouth. The two of them were a good team.

Jack Buck and I used to sing together. He was a very good singer, but he wouldn't always sing. For a guy who was in the public eye and who did so much, so many things, in a very public way, he was bashful. He didn't want to sing because he would get embarrassed. Yet, he was terrific. He had a very nice voice and a good delivery. One of the unique things about Jack, he remembered all the verses, all the songs. Where the rest of us would mumble, he would get up and sing. We had a lot of parties at his house, and Jimmy Williams, a piano player, would always be there. Jimmy would start playing a couple of what they call "my songs." And Jack would say to Williams "Take a break." Jack would then sing like you wouldn't believe.

I didn't play golf much with Jack because my game was so bad, but I did play when we would go to Ireland. When I'd come out with my clubs, he would grimace, and he'd be looking for Frank Cashen, the general manager of the Mets, and he'd say, "Frank, you play with him." Frank was a good friend and a great Irishman, and that was an important market for us—New York. So he, being a part of it, was quite natural, because we wanted to get a good mixture of sports people, celebrities from the Hollywood set, and from television.

I like to think I helped save the Irish Derby. What happened was Denny Long was the president of our company back in 1985, and he had a group of soccer people and a mixture of wholesalers and the like over in Ireland. This was really in pursuit of soccer. My wife and I were invited to the Irish Derby, and the Chief Steward was our host. It finally came down to the Chief Steward propositioning us about taking on the sponsorship of the Irish Derby. Remember the Irish Sweepstakes? Well, the Sweepstakes had run out thanks to the lotteries in the U.S. We became attached to horse racing that way. I went over to Denny and said, "You've got to listen to Lord Hemphill and the Chief Steward." Denny couldn't understand Lord Hemphill any more than I could. He was a great old guy, foxy old guy, but he gave us all the reasons why they needed corporate sponsorship and of course we didn't have beer in the country but we thought about it. We needed to attach our normal parameters for consideration of anything like that. It looked good, so we took it on.

After the first year, Jack would say to me, "When are we going back?" He loved horses and Ireland was very special to him. His mother was Irish, her maiden name was Fox and they came from Dingle County Kerry. We got him down to Kerry and he saw where his roots were.

We've got pictures hanging up all over the place of the different Irish events, The Irish Derby. The fun we had in Ireland was just incredible. For the last ten years, I've been president of the Irish Council. We recently had a luncheon in Dublin, Ireland, honoring Sandra Day O'Connor.

Our guests at the Budweiser Irish Derby ranged from Hollywood stars—Stefanie Powers, John Forsythe, Donald O'Connor, Maureen O'Hara, Paul Newman, Robert Loggia, Richard Gere, Lloyd Bridges, Sheila McRae, and other prominent stars. From the music world— Tony Bennett, Colm Wilkinson, Betty Buckley, Tommy Makem, Phil Coulter, Lou Rawls, and many others. Norm Crosby was a frequent visitor to the delight of our other guests who enjoyed his monologues on our daily experiences. P. X. Kelly, former Commandant of the Marine Corps, joined us. The baseball world was represented by Gene Autry, who owned the Angels; Jim Dowdle, who was CEO of the Chicago Cubs; Frank Cashen, who was General Manager of the New York Mets—all were our guests at the Derby. Every morning Jack would race the others for the *Herald* which reported baseball scores.

Jack and Carole fit into our group perfectly, she formerly of the Broadway stage and he of the sports world stage. The Irish loved them, and Jack went out of his way to relate his Irish roots with that great sense of humor. A large number of Irish people expressed their condolences to Carole and the family when they learned of his passing.

We also went to places like the Caribbean, the Riviera, Paris, and Normandy, where Jack wrote a beautiful poem about the thoughts of one of the dead reflecting on the many visitors to that sad and lonely place. Of course, he would cry quietly as he silently moved around the tombstones.

We were pals—as was Stan Musial, Red Schoendienst, Art Pepin of Tampa, FL, Don Hamel, Allan Borucke, Chuck Bauer, Donald O'Connor, Charlie Spoonhour, Joe Arndt, Jerry Clinton, David Pratt, Norm Crosby, and a long list of others.

Every Christmas morning for the last umpteen years, Jack and Carole would host a radio broadcast event from their house from nine to noon. It became a tradition to the point where everybody in St. Louis would listen to that. Carole would add some friends from the church she goes to and various performers that they knew, and then they would sprinkle in local people who would come over and sing or participate in some way. It was always a wonderful day, with a kind of a family attitude. He had eight kids. Julie and Joe, with Carole, and then six from his previous marriage. Those kids were talented. They would come over and sing and were just terrific, and of course, all the grandchildren, of which there were many. It was a very happy event every Christmas morning.

During last year's pennant race, a disputed call caused a lot of rancor toward an umpire. Jack went on the air to encourage the fans to treat the man with respect and appreciation for doing his job. A sense of foreboding hung in the air when the umpire entered the playing field. The fans gave him an ovation which brought tears to Jack's eyes.

His sentimental side was easily evoked. His soft heart made him a champion for the afflicted and downtrodden. He attended over 200 charity events a year. Jack couldn't say "No"! He loved his fellow man and tried to help in every way he could.

He laughed often, cried frequently due to his sensitivity for others, and his joy in his life and the people in it. He enjoyed the trust and respect of the entire community and all of the sports world. He left this world a greater place. Jack was an inspiration to all of us.

There were hundreds of stories, a thousand laughs, a few tears and special moments etched in our memories which will last forever.

Dan Dierdorf, Win Elliott and Mike Roarty enjoy another Jack Buck one-liner.

WHY CAN'T SUGAR BE AS SWEET AS JACK BUCK?
VINCE BOMMARITO

Vince Bommarito owns one of the most famous restaurants in America, Tony's. Tony's is almost directly across the street from Busch Stadium.

Jack emceed a couple of special dinners that meant a lot to me and my family. I was at a roaster for Cystic Fibrosis, which was one of his favorite causes, and we had a packed house, and he had people rolling in the aisles. He made everybody laugh except my mother, she couldn't understand everything.

Jack was caring and the generous moments that he shared are treasures. He had an admirable style. When he would come to the restaurant, he always visited with the staff. Among the thousands of celebrities who walked into our place, Jack was the most gracious with the service people of anybody. We had a little busboy who worked for us for about thirty-five years. No sooner had Jack had sat down, he'd say, "Where's John Hall at? He needs to come over and say hello." Of course, he'd come over, and Jack would make the guy feel like a big man. That was really Jack's style with everybody.

He'd have to go to KMOX on business from time to time. KMOX is right around the corner from our restaurant. He'd stop in at a little bar we operate in our lobby after he had taken care of business over there. He'd go to the bar and he'd kibitz with the bartenders, knew them both by name. They considered him as a friend. And he considers them his friends. He would kibitz with the customers at lunchtime. He was just a good guy. What else can you say?

I had a bypass a few years ago, he called me up half a dozen times to see how I was doing. My wife was sick several years ago. He was very concerned. We had planned a trip, but he said, "Well, when Martha gets well, we'll all go on a trip." She got well, and we went on a trip, and it was great. But best of all, he was just a good guy. I've been dealing with people my whole life, and I can't imagine anybody being as gracious as Jack. His talent goes so far beyond his announcing and his poems. He put that poem book out last year, and I bought one for all my family.

He never made a big deal of himself. But he was a big deal. He was the most gracious guy I've ever known.

Steve Schmitt with some of his prized sports memorabilia, including a lithograph of Cardinals Hall of Famers.

THE SPIRIT OF ST. LOUIS

J. KIM TUCCI

J. Kim Tucci is a busy man. He is the president of the Pasta House Co., a chain of 31 restaurants, chairman of the St. Louis Convention & Visitors Bureau, and chairman of the Missouri Film Commission.

The last time I saw Jack Buck we had a meeting for the Baseball Partnership to promote the stadium, and Jack and I were charter members of that committee. We had a meeting down at the Stadium Club, and it was right before he got sick. He asked me if I would relive the story of when we broadcast together in 1960 at Brooklyn College in New York. It was the 1960 NCAA soccer championship.

In his book Jack says that we were playing Howard University. We weren't. We were playing the University of Maryland. He said it was an NCAA playoff game. It wasn't. It was the championship game. He said I was a former player. I wasn't. I was the current trainer, but I was a broadcast major and so KMOX had me go up there to do the play-by-play broadcast with the producer, an engineer from CBS in New York and Jack Buck. This was in 1960. I went outside in an open-air press box, totally exposed, no windows or anything. Jack was coming down the top row where we were broadcasting. I recognized him. Of course he didn't know me. He introduced himself. I said, "I know who you are." And I introduced myself. He said he was up there doing a New York Titans football game, and they had sent him over to do the play-by-play, and I was supposed to do the color, and that he had never done a soccer game before. He didn't know anything that was going on. He talks about it being the first and last soccer game he ever did.

We did the game and Brooklyn College won the game, but he messed up everything. He knows that. But nobody knew about it because it was on radio—you could say anything you wanted. Except that there were two college students sitting in front us. They could see what was going on down on the field like it was on television. Finally right before halftime, one of the kids turned around to him. Jack was on the kid's right shoulder, and said, "Mister, you don't know what the heck you're talking about." Buck had a cigarette in his hand and immediately without hesitation he punched this guy. He punched him with the cigarette in his hand and said, "We're on the air." Boom. The guy ducked, and he punched the guy in the back of his head. The cigarette breaks off and goes into the guy's hair. I was a little nervous, and Jack didn't do anything. Halftime came, and the two guys left and never came back. They would have probably sued him for ten million today.

That was the first time I ever met Jack—he was thirty-six and I was nineteen. I had been to a couple of places with him because I was involved in St. Louis with sports teams. We would go to an annual banquet or something and I would see him, but I had never met him. We've been friends now for forty-two years.

A couple of years ago, it was the seventy-fifth anniversary of KMOX and the highlight of the evening was to present Jack with a piece of crystal to celebrate his fiftieth anniversary with KMOX. Before the presentation, they had a silent auction. He had spoken to me earlier in the evening and had said, "Look I may want you to come up and tell the **soccer** story." He loved that soccer story—kind of a macho thing. Then he said, "No, I don't think it's appropriate. But if I call you up, you'll do it." But he never did. They gave him the award, and he was shaking because of the Parkinson's—one arm's flying up one way and the other arm's flying up the other way. He always had that hesitant speaking style, and he said, "I, first of all, want to thank all of you for not having an oral auction tonight because three months ago, I bid two thousand dollars for two tickets to the Cardinal game and a visit to the broadcast booth chat with Jack Buck." I just thought that was the best one.

> More U. S. kids play soccer today than any organized sport, including youth football. The reason so many kids play soccer is so they don't have to watch it.

A Gallery of
Jack Buck's Partners

Jack Buck greets new partner
Mike Shannon – 1972

Mike Shannon with scout Joe Monahan on the day he signed with the Cardinals after freshman year at Mizzou–1958.

A Mike Shannon family portrait from 1968.

This picture must have been taken the year before KMOX increased its parade and signage budget.

STARR SHANNON BUCK

KMOX RADIO

KMOX

Harry Caray's last Cardinal broadcast, October 2, 1969

Harry Caray shows Jack Buck how the Cubs choke.

Harry Caray may have had too many Budweisers and perhaps he had one Busch too many but he drank Schlitz on the day he was fired in 1969.

Joe and Jack Buck – 1991

My partner Joe Fresta and I were in **Cooperstown** when Jack Buck was inducted. I went up there for that because I thought he was somebody special. I thought it was really special to be there when he got inducted. I was right there on the infield, the inner circle.

Jackie Smith, a friend of mine, got inducted into the NFL Hall of Fame in Canton, Ohio, and I was there for that. I was at the Missouri Athletic Club, where I'm a past president, and there was a VIP reception before they had the dinner where they were going to honor different people. Buck was emceeing the thing, and they were also giving out the Jack Buck award. I'm in the reception and he comes up to me and says, "Hey, you've got to help me out." I said, "What do you mean?" He said, "Dierdorf has just had some root canal or something out in Denver, and he didn't make it back in. He's supposed to present Jackie Smith with this special award for being inducted into the Hall of Fame, but he can't be here so you've got to do it." I'm thinking, "I've got to do it?" I mean it's a big deal! It's like a minute before we're going on, okay? So I said, "Yeah." Well he just took it for granted, "You just give him the award." I thought it was an honor that he had confidence in me that I would be able to do this." I wasn't even on the dais but Jack called me up and luckily I was there at Canton, Ohio when Jackie Smith was inducted. I relived that moment, and you could hear a pin drop. People were choked up, and it was really something special. But for me the honor was that Jack came to me and had the confidence and said, "I want you to do it." That was special. He gave me his blessing—I want you to do it. So I took Dierdorf's place, and I did it.

Jack talked to everybody. He made a point that if he knew something about that person or about their job or what they did, he always included that. It made them feel good. Those people realized that it was something special for them to be with Jack Buck, but he also realized that they realized it. It wasn't a passing thing with him—he always looked people right in the eye when he talked. That's why he's special. I never thought he would get this national recognition like he did. I went to the memorial service, and sat right behind home plate.

> Cooperstown (N.Y.) was named for
> the father of James Fennimore Cooper.

Then that afternoon I had to go to Chicago. When I got up there the next morning, Friday, they had a whole page with his picture in the *Chicago Tribune*—unbelievable.

They have to sell the naming rights to the new stadium, it gets down to dollars and cents. But let's say you would call it Enterprise Rent-A-Car Jack Buck Stadium, Budweiser Jack Buck Stadium, Monsanto Jack Buck Stadium—that's how they could do it. This is a big ticket. You're talking upwards of a hundred million dollars to name this stadium. The dome got over thirty two million twelve years ago so you can imagine what Busch Stadium would get. I think that would be great. I think this thing would have passed and everybody would have been behind it if Jack was healthy and they could have put Jack on the air. If they had him, how are they going to say no to Jack Buck? No one would argue, and that would be it. Some people might think it's not worth as much, but everybody would go crazy for Jack Buck Stadium.

Everybody says the same thing. Jack was the symbol of St. Louis. More so because of his influence and his power with the media. He was on the air, and calling in all the time at KMOX, being there all the time—that presence. He was definitely more of an influence than Stan Musial. He was on the air all the time. Younger people, little kids, everybody knew Jack Buck. They don't know Stan Musial. They know who he is, and they see his statue. But they don't even know what Stan Musial's voice sounds like. Today as I was going downtown, I'm Chairman of the Visitors' Commission, I saw a new billboard. It said, "The Voice of St. Louis, Jack Buck. We'll miss you." It was signed KMOX. That's the thing. When they say KMOX is the Voice of St. Louis—Jack Buck is the Voice of St. Louis.

Jack Carney and all these key people are gone from KMOX, but Jack Buck had always been there. He was the icon. He's the Voice of St. Louis, not just on radio, but on television, in people's hearts, minds, everywhere—he's the Voice of St. Louis.

DEVINE INTERVENTION

BING DEVINE

*Bing Devine, now retired in St. Louis, was General Manager of the St. Louis Cardinals and New York Mets. He served as General Manager of one of the Cardinals' two Triple A clubs, the Rochester (NY) Red Wings from 1949-1955. Devine hired Jack Buck of Columbus, Ohio in late 1952 to broadcast Red Wing games...about the same time Anheuser-Busch bought the Cardinals and their two top farm teams. As a result of that sale, the Red Wings changed beer sponsors from Old Topper Beer to Budweiser. Because Buck did an excellent job on Bud commercials, he was brought to St. Louis in the spring of 1954. Devine was General Manager of the St. Louis **football** Cardinals for over seven years.*

Jack Buck was a good friend and a fine talent. One of the most interesting stories I tell about him is that when he was in Rochester, minor league clubs didn't do their road games live; they did it with a Western Union wire report. I used to sit with Jack Buck in the radio studio when he was recreating a game by wire report. It was kind of amazing, when he got through, you'd say, "Gee, I wish you could make the game I'm seeing every day look that good."

I'll always remember him as a great talent and fine gentleman who looked upon and treated everybody the same. He didn't let their status in life make any difference. He could broadcast a baseball game live or by wire report as good if not better than anybody I ever saw, heard or thought about, and that includes a lot of real good ones and even some great ones. He was always a fun person to be with because he was usually coming up with some kind of observation or

> Former NFL quarterback Jim Finks was General Manager of the Minnesota Vikings and the New Orleans Saints, and also was president of the Chicago Cubs.

remark that was designed to make you feel better. He was a "feel good" person.

Jack was always a great master of ceremonies, and a great speaker at a banquet. He always had some new stories and you never knew where he got them. He just came up with them. He didn't make notes about them. Somehow or other when he heard ones that he liked or that he thought would be good, they just kinda became embedded in his memory. He had a great memory.

Jack Buck was a great liaison between the baseball team and with the public at all levels because he could relate to the CEO of a corporation and a fellow who was walking the streets trying to find a job. There wasn't anyone he saw or talked to that he looked upon any differently. I don't think you could have a better representative than that. He came to St. Louis from Rochester when the Cardinals were looking for another announcer, another voice, to go with Harry Caray. Dick Meyer was my liaison with Mr. Busch and the Cardinals owned the Rochester club. Dick Meyer called me and said they were getting ready to add a different announcer into the broadcast booth, didn't we have an announcer up there we'd like to recommend? I said, "Yes, we recommend Jack Buck." He had come to me from Columbus, Ohio, which was another Cardinal club. It so happened that the year the general manager of the Columbus club called me in Rochester and said, "You need a play-by-play announcer." I said, "Well, we just lost ours. We had a young man from Rochester proper. We're looking for one." He said, "Well, let me send you Jack Buck. You can listen to him. He broadcasts our games, and we like him. We can't get a sponsor for next year so we're not gonna have a broadcast." That's how we got Jack Buck in Rochester, and that's how he eventually made the move to St. Louis. The rest is history.

GERMANTOWN'S GIFT TO CARDINAL FANS
RED SCHOENDIENST

Red played, managed and/or coached in nine World Series. He played in ten All-Star games. He managed two All-Star games. He was inducted into the Baseball Hall of Fame in 1989. He was Stan Musial's roommate and helped to lead the "glory years" for the Cardinals during the 40's and 50's. Red is currently special assistant to the General Manager of the Cardinals.

I guess the first time I met Jack would have been when he came here to St. Louis to broadcast. It was pretty hard—a new man coming in to call the games. I didn't pay that much attention to him, but after some time here, he was so good at everything he did. It was great that he was here.

Jack always had stories of some kind. The things I remember so much about him would be his broadcasting, his interviewing, his emceeing at banquets and things. And his kindness—he's always been so kind. He was always ready to help somebody no matter where he was or what he was doing. Jack was just a great guy.

When Jack was emceeing at a banquet, you'd know you were going to have some laughs. It was more or less like going someplace to be entertained by a movie star—that's the way it was to me. He could come up with something all the time.

I loved to go out with him on the road. We went out quite often. We played golf together. We went out to eat so many times to all the good restaurants, and took in all the shows.

One day about six years ago we did go to one of the shows in New York. We left the hotel, caught a cab and he dropped us off. We went out to eat close to the theater and then walked to the show. After the show was over, we got into the line waiting for a cab, and it was the same cab driver that had brought us over earlier. Jack said something like, "Did your shoes go out of style while you were waiting for us?"

Stan Musial, Jack and I were all good friends. We'd go out to lunch quite a bit here in St. Louis when Jack was able to get around. We played golf. We'd go out and play nine holes of golf occasionally in the morning. Then we would have lunch and then go to the ballpark. Jack was not a good golfer. He liked to play, but then he got Parkinson's so it was a little tough.

Once I remarked to him, "Jack, you never use any bad words or four-letter words to get a laugh." He said to me, "Well, if I had to do that, I wouldn't be doing what I'm doing.

There's no question Jack helped Joe out. Joe would probably tell you this—Joe would be in the broadcasting booth as a real young man before he ever thought of broadcasting. He got a pretty good idea from Jack and learned his mannerisms of Jack and how he conducted himself in everything. To watch Jack broadcast, to watch him interview somebody, it always was great. He never, that I can remember, ever asked for anybody to call him if he'd like to be interviewed. Jack would just walk up to the young man wherever he was and say, "Could I have a few minutes of your time? I'd like to interview you." That's the way he was. If they said no, it was perfectly okay with Jack. But, I never did hear anybody say no to Jack. After Jack was in the business for some years, they looked forward to coming to town because they knew he was an honest broadcaster and would give you a hundred percent on the ballgame he was doing. He was a Cardinal fan, there's no question about that. But he announced the game so wonderfully and gave everybody credit when they did something well.

When you talk about the Cardinals, there are a lot of great Cardinal players. Stan Musial is THE big boy, the Cardinal player. But Jack Buck has done so much for the St. Louis Cardinals. He's done so much for the city of St. Louis. I don't know how you can recognize the things he has done. You'd have to say he is "the Cardinal" to me, the "Red Bird." In his broadcasting, he sold the Cardinals to everyone who was listening. The Cardinals had a big following, and they'll miss Jack. No matter who Jack broadcast with, he could make that person a better broadcaster.

EVERYONE WANTS TO GO TO HEAVEN, BUT NO ONE WANTS TO DIE

JOHN KING

John King grew up on a farm near St. Clair, Missouri, graduated from CBC High School, St. Benedict's in Atchison, Kansas and St. Louis University Law School. He is a leading attorney in St. Louis and was a friend of Jack Buck.

I'm a Catholic and go to the Catholic Church but I'm a born-again fundamentalist Christian. Carole, his wife, is a strong Christian. I said to her one night, "Has Jack ever come around?" She said, "No, why don't you talk to him?" One time we were sitting there inside the press box, after getting something to eat or drink, and I said, "Have you accepted Jesus Christ as your personal savior yet?" He said, "You've been talking to Carole again, haven't you?" I said, "Yeah." Let me tell you what he said to me. This just so impressed me. It floored me. He said, "You know, John, I've done a lot of bad things in my life. Now that I'm reaching my older years, I kinda feel hypocritical to start believing in God at this point. I believe in God, but doing those things that I think will help me get into heaven...." I said, "Hey, Jack. It's a question of heaven or hell. I think I'd pick heaven before I'd pick hell." He said, "Well, that's a good point." To hear him say that he thought it would hypocritical was just one of the most humbling things I ever heard in my life.

There was a function for Larry Wilson, St. Louis Cardinal football player. They had it down in one of the old theaters on Grand Avenue. I went to the thing. As a surprise to Larry, Jack Buck flew in Larry's mom and dad and paid for their airfare and everything. I tell you—that impressed me so much. It just made a big hit with me because it was just such a great thing to do. Consequently that led me to do it, and I have done it on at least four occasions.

IF THE PHONE DOESN'T RING, IT'S HARRY AND JACK

BEA HIGGINS

Bea Higgins was Harry Caray's St. Louis secretary for twenty-five years. When Jack Buck's part-time secretary, Millie, left to marry football coach Glenn "Bo" Schembechler, she began doing some work for Jack. She is now retired and still lives in St. Louis.

Harry Caray and I first met Jack Buck when he came on board in 1954. I answered all the mail that came for Harry and Jack and the other announcers. I thought Jack was a great guy—very likeable. We had a good relationship with Jack. After Harry left town, I gave up working for them, but I would run into Jack now and then. I saw him about ten years ago. He said to me, "Bea, we're both playing the back nine." I said, "Okay, Jack." He was failing several years back. He was a heck of a nice guy.

Jack's sense of humor was what struck me most. I used to go to the ballpark and bring my one son in particular. We'd always sit in the Sportsman's Bar and used to sit in the booth right next to them. Every time I would bring my son, Jack would say over the air, "Bea brought her father again." My son got the biggest kick out of that. One other thing was when I used to book them on some engagements. I had them one time at our Catholic church for our husband and wife tournament—father and mother meeting. I said, "Jack, you're in the Catholic church. Monsignor is going to be there. Don't say anything blue." "Okay, he says." I introduced him, and then he gets up. He looks me straight in the eye and starts telling a joke. He did it for orneriness with a twinkle in his eye. The only thing was that the Monsignor topped him. He mentioned to me one time before Harry died, "Do you think Harry will ever retire?" I said, "No. You're not going to either, are you?" He said, "No."

THE "CARN DAWG" KNOWS THE ANSWERS TO A LOTTA QUESTIONS THE LISTENERS NEVER ASK

JOHN CARNEY

John Carney first knew Jack through his father, the legendary Jack Carney, during the years they worked together on KMOX. Now Carney does his own talk-show on the station.

One time we were at the grand opening of the Irish Crystal Company and Jack was doing spots for them and I was doing radio commercials for them on another station. They moved to a new place and were having a big opening so I showed up and Jack emceed the event. There were probably fifty or sixty people inside the store and he's gagging and telling jokes and ribbing on the owner and basically making everybody feel warm and comfortable and special, which he did better than anybody. But, there was an Irish band there too and he told some jokes and gags and he walked away from the podium, went back to the band and whispered to the band, a little private conversation, then the band goes into Danny Boy. Jack comes back to the mike and doesn't sing Danny Boy but proceeds to tell the story about Danny Boy and the father letting his son go off to fight the war and waiting day after day for the son to return and he never does because he dies and the way that Jack narrates this thing everyone is in tears. Two minutes earlier everyone had been laughing.

Shortly after September 11th, KMOX had me do the afternoon drive. I've always kind of thought of myself as the village idiot, and not so much the news information guy. So, I was a little weirded out that they wanted me to do this afternoon information slot, right after one of the biggest events in our nation's history, but then I found out that they wanted me to do it with Jack Buck for three hours. I thought this is even stranger because I don't know anything about sports either, what the heck are we going to do. We just went on the air, and it was amazing, the places that we went together and things that we talked about, it was probably in twenty years of doing this, the best three hours that I ever had.

He died on my shift. I was literally three minutes from going on the air and the hotline rang and it was Joe Buck, and Joe told me that his father had just passed away, literally like five minutes before and I said, "Well, you know, I'll pass it along, I'll tell everybody on the air. I'll handle it reverently, don't worry." Joe and I have a real special relationship, we've known each other most of our lives and we well realize that we are members of the Lucky Sperm Club and he's managed to utilize and harness those talents a lot better than I have but, anyway, we experienced things that are hard to describe to other people as far as similarities. He said, "No, I'll go on the air." I said "Well, if you really want to do that, but only if you're comfortable." He really wanted to and that was maybe part of the continuing healing process that he's been a family spokesman for the last few months of Jack's life.

So, I literally started the show, I dropped the theme and we went right on the air and I don't even know what I said to start the show, I was pretty shocked. I know I had a guest that was in the studio and right before we went on the air I said "I'll call you and we'll reschedule, something's come up." So, Joe and I talked probably fifteen, twenty minutes on the air and then the calls came and we took calls for five solid nights. Three of them without any commercials. But that first night, I stayed on the air for six hours taking phone calls and talking about it. I was lucky in that since because I had a chance to deal with it a lot and talk about it a lot with people, as opposed to a lot of other folks who had to go to their jobs and do something else and pretend to not hurt that they had lost a good friend and deal with that in their own space and time.

The guy made me a better person. He made me want to strive to be a better broadcaster. He forced me to work harder at what I thought I was really good at when it came to being the emcee at events.

I SAW IT ON THE RADIO

GREG MARECEK

Greg Marecek is a towering figure in St. Louis sports circles as the president and CEO of KFNS Sports Radio. He has known the Bucks since 1973 when he was a sports editor for the St. Louis Suburban Journal.

We did a thing called SNI Sports Network, which was just the initials of Suburban Newspapers, Inc. Jack Buck did the original show for me to kick off the company. We called it *The Base Burglar.* We're the guys who dubbed the title Base Burglar for Lou Brock. Lou and Jack did a ten-minute, four-time-a-week radio show that aired pre-game to the St. Louis Cardinals baseball on KMOX and the Cardinal Baseball Radio Network. Frankly, I would never have gotten that done without Jack Buck going to Bob Hyland at KMOX and saying, "I want to help this young guy get this company going. I'm going to do this for him." Jack wouldn't take a dime. He did it for four years and never took a cent. If I sent him a check, he'd send it back. He became a good friend.

My syndication company grew steadily and we were doing regional television. We did the first Big Eight basketball tournament The league came to me to be the television coordinator when they decided to do a tournament. I got Jack Buck to do the play-by-play the first year, and Jack did many more shows. If I had a show that needed a host of his caliber, he would do it. In fact, he was my sponsor to get into the country club that I belong to here today. It's one of the more significant clubs here today and it's funny almost to his last days, I'd walk into the press box, and he'd come to me and say, "Hey kid, what did you shoot today?" He'd say that all the time, and I'm fifty three years old. So, "Hey kid," was pretty good.

One of my favorite Jack Buck stories goes back to that Big Eight Basketball tournament. There it was, the first time the Big Eight has ever had a post-season basketball tournament, and they were trying to lift up the league. You know, in those days, and I'm talking the early eighties, basketball in the Big Eight wasn't as big as it is today. Oklahoma was struggling. Missouri, Kansas and Kansas State really held the league up. The tournament was a big step to see if they could actually sell the tickets. Now, of course, you can't get a ticket for the tournament over in Kansas City. But back then Chuck Nienas, the Commissioner, asked me to put together a television network since I was syndicating things like that, and I said okay.

I started looking around the Big Eight Conference trying to get TV stations in different cities to carry the games of this tournament. They'd say, "No. We'll carry one of our home state teams if they're playing, but we won't carry anything else. After doing that for a couple of weeks, I told Chuck, "You know, the games themselves are not selling this deal. I need some more impact. If you don't mind, I'm going to pick the announcers. I'm going to call and see if Jack Buck will actually do the basketball games, and he said, "Well, you know Jack's not even doing basketball." I said, "That doesn't matter because he can do anything." I called Jack and said, "Jack I really need your help on this one. If you can come and do this tournament, it will really help make the tournament. Do the semi-finals and finals. I think that will help me sell it." He said, "Okay. I'll fly back to Kansas City from spring training and I'll do them. As long as I can get back to St. Petersburg and not miss more than a game or so, it'll be okay." The Cardinals weren't broadcasting all their games from spring training down there anyway. So, oh boy, all of a sudden I've got Jack Buck's name out there with Gary Thompson, the color man, and the game started to clear those local markets a little faster.

It comes game night, we're at Kemper Arena and the teams are on the floor. Kansas is actually playing Kansas State. We're in the truck behind the Arena a couple of hours before the game. They're getting ready for the game, and, of course, Jack's flying back from Florida. I said, "Don't worry about it. He'll be here." About an hour and a half before a game, the engineers like to see if they can practice some of the opens and other things, but Buck's still not there. I said, "Well, he probably got stuck a little." Well now it's an hour before the game, and I'm getting a little nervous myself so I call his home and Carole answers the phone. I said, "Carole, where's Jack?" She said, "Oh well, I guess he's not there yet." I said, "No." She said, "Well what you don't know is we had a snowstorm here in St. Louis and his plane was delayed. But he's coming. His plane is in the air. He's already left, and he's coming." I go back in and they're getting ready, and it's all the way down to ten minutes before the game, and there's no Jack.

Finally I walk out into the Arena. I look up into the crowd, I'm looking around, trying to figure out who in the heck is going to broadcast and I see in the third row Fred White, the voice of the Royals. I know Fred. He's done some other stuff for me so I wave at him, and he comes down. I asked, "Fred what are you doing here?" He said, "I came back from spring training for the weekend to pick up some more clothes, and I'm flying back down to Florida tomorrow. I knew the tournament was here so I'm just gonna be here tonight." I said, "You know what. You're working tonight." He said, "What?" I said, "Yeah. Jack Buck's supposed to do it. He's not here." Fred said, "Oh, fine, I'll come down there."

So he steps in and he puts the headsets on and the PA guys announce that it's time for the National Anthem and I go back to the truck. They're just starting to play the National Anthem when all of a sudden, this big voice bellows, "Hey kid, I'm here. Don't worry about it." I look around, and here comes Jack. He's got his suitcase and a coat in one hand, and he's dragging his little boy, Joe, in the other hand. He literally throws the coat and things into the truck. He hands me Joe and says, "You take care of little Joe, and I'll go do your basketball game." He goes out and the National Anthem is less than half way through. He sees where the broadcast position is and he walks under the basket and across the middle of the basketball floor and he keeps walking all the way to that position and spins around and takes the headset. He knows Fred of course so he takes the headset off Fred's head, puts it on his. Fred's relieved. He stands there as they sing the last piece of the National Anthem and he says on the air, "We'll be right back with the starting lineup." With that they go to a break, and he turns to Gary Thompson, and he says, "I don't know who you are. I'm Jack Buck." He shakes Gary Thompson's hand and says to him, "I hope you know this game well because you need to tell me who's in white and who's in dark."

He did a magnificent basketball game that night and on Monday our phone rang off the hook. All these stations said, "You know what. As long as you have Jack Buck doing the games, we'll carry them again next year." He said many times that was the most embarrassing moment of his professional life. He said, "I'm never late. I'm never unprepared, and I would never disrespect the National Anthem. And I did all three that night." But he was prepared as it turned out. He read stuff and he knew exactly what was going on. As the game started, he had the players up and down the floor with no problem. That relates to the way Jack Buck was. He'd always get upset with young people in the business who'd report late to the game, not be on time, and then he remembered he only did it once himself, and it wasn't his fault. It was the snowstorm.

I can't remember the year, but young Joe was moving along fine with his radio broadcast and sharing in some of the Cardinal games when he was young. I think he was still at Indiana, and was either twenty-one or twenty-two. We were at spring training, and I was sitting in the regular press box at Lang Field. One of the ushers came up and said, "Jack would like to see you in the booth." I didn't think anything about it so I go down there, and Jack's actually in the little room next to the booth. He's got Joe with him and he looks at me and said, "Greg, you do those Missouri games, right?" I said, "Yeah. I'm the rights holder. I do Missouri basketball and football." He said, "I want you to help get my kid in television. Maybe he could do those games or something but I want him in television. I want him to do more than I've done." I said, "I'll do everything I can." I went back and asked the University of Missouri if we could use Joe Buck as the play-by-play voice, and they argued extensively against it. They said, "No, no, he's a young kid. We don't know if he can do basketball. He hasn't done any of that." I said, "Now wait a minute. The kid does baseball. He sounds good. He's coming along. I know he's young, but his dad would love to get him involved. This would be a good way to start him in the deal." Finally I said, "Look, there's an early season tournament. Let me put him on that and then we'll talk after that tournament is over. So we did. We sent him out, and I think it was Puerto Rico or Hawaii. He did the games and he was great. On Monday, they came back and said, "Well, he's fine. We'll use him the rest of the way." This is exactly what I knew would happen. It was just typical because they all had their favorites and wanted someone else to do the games.

We are just very, very fortunate that we have a quality guy and tremendous announcer like Joe Buck as a constant and wonderful reminder of Jack Buck.

One of the last times I saw him was at the stadium at the end of last season. I'll never forget because I had enlarged the version of that picture with all of us on the golf tee at Algonquin Golf Club, and it started to dawn on me frankly that all these guys aren't going to be around all the time, and I'd like to get it personalized. So I took that picture down to the ball park, and Jack was doing the game, and I remember it was one of the last games of the year. I showed it to him and he laughed because he remembered the day it had happened. He said, "Darn, if Musial had made that putt on eighteen, we'd have beaten you." I beat all three of them that day, and we had wagered a dollar apiece just to make it interesting. I've got a picture of Stan missing the putt on eighteen.

> *"It was a pleasure to know Jack Buck. It was always an uplifting experience to be in his company. His positive attitude, even in the face of his illness later in life, was a great example to all of us."*
>
> Stan Musial

Chapter 6

Buckshots

Bob Starr told me this story. A group of area bakers got together for a night at the ballpark. The head of the retail bakers came upstairs to the booth with goodies and a young lady in a nice little outfit with a sash across her that said "Miss Checsecake." Miss Cheesecake, who was 17 or 18 years old, sat down next to Jack Buck and he talked to her on the air for a few minutes while doing play-by-play, and then she was excused.

The head of the retail bakers was standing behind Jack holding a box of cheesecake. Jack—still on the air—looked toward Bob and asked him a question. Bob who was standing some distance from Jack, thought he heard him ask, "Do you like cheesecake, Bob?" Bob replied, "Jack, I haven't had any yet, but it looks good enough to eat!" Jack then choked his way through the line-up and then informs Bob during the break that he hadn't heard the question correctly. Jack had asked him, "How did you like Miss Cheesecake?" When Bob got home his wife met him at the door and said, "tell me I didn't hear what I think I heard on the air tonight in the first inning!"

——CURT SMITH, Author, Rochester, NY

We were at the old Tony's place, a restaurant, before he moved into his new location. There was an upstairs. We were upstairs. Harry Caray had come back to start broadcasting again after having a stroke and was in a pretty serious physical condition to the point where it hampered his speech. But he was coming back, and he was getting better all the time. It was his first trip to St. Louis since he got stricken. So Jack and Carole and Harry and his wife, Dutchie, and Lee and I sat down for dinner at Tony's. As the dinner went on, we were having a great time reminiscing and laughing about things that had happened in the past. Nobody was bothering the two guys for autographs or anything so it was kind of a nice peaceful, friendly dinner. And to hear Jack and Harry going at it about the old days was really fun. So as the time progressed and we got up to leave, somebody in the back of the room said, "Welcome home, Harry." With that, almost as if on cue, the whole restaurant stood up and applauded—gave him a standing ovation. Now Jack, being the sentimentalist that he was, started crying. I got teary-eyed. But Harry is saying, "Tha-a-nk you very much. Tha-a-nk you very much." Down the stairs he goes. I laughed so hard. It didn't faze him one bit. It was one of his great moments.

——MIKE ROARTY, retired Marketing Whiz, Anheuser-Busch

I was at a roast for Harry Caray at Bally's back in late 1988. Jack had good jokes: The Cubs and White Sox should merge so that Chicago would only have one bad team. And Harry should be buried in Chicago so he could still vote. He had the audience rolling in the aisles. He outdid all the comedians and sports personalities on the dais. There were a lot of great, talented people who spoke that night but none came close to Jack Buck.

——RON ENDRES, Las Vegas, Nevada

There was a young lady on a trampoline and she was Japanese. We were in Buffalo, and it was cold up in our booth. So we were off the air, but he was pretending he was still on the air, he said, "Well; there's definitely a Nip in the air," as the camera focused on this "Nipponese" Japanese lady. He had a great sense of humor, and I'm sure he wasn't being anti-Japanese. Going across the front of the stadium it showed this young Japanese lady bouncing up in the air, and he said, "There's a Nip in the air."

I was a Cardinal fan growing up, but never a huge baseball fan. I did love to go see Stan Musial jack 'em out of the park. They had good teams. I guess I had gone off to college by the time the football Cardinals moved there so I didn't watch a lot of pro football. I was a huge Hawk fan—Bob Pettit fan. I'd sneak in the Kiel Auditorium. We'd get in the locker room. I was a little kid who wanted to get in there and meet these guys. I didn't want their autographs. I wanted to talk to them. Probably at that time basketball was my favorite sport.

——ANDY RUSSELL, Mizzou and Pittsburgh Steeler star
and former color analyst with Jack Buck

We went into Las Vegas one time. It was against the law to go from St. Louis out to California without stopping in Las Vegas in the Sixties and Seventies, so we always stopped in Las Vegas. We had some fun there. I told him, "Hey, I'll go rent the rooms." He said, "I feel I gotta go right to the craps table." I said, "Okay, here's a hundred dollars. Better go snake eyes for me and I'll go get the room."

So I come back and I said, "What did you roll the first time?" He said, "Snake eyes." I said, "Oh, man, that's 30-1. Great! That's $3,000." He said, "I couldn't go up there and bet snake eyes. Everybody would look at me like I am crazy." He had not made the bet.

——MIKE SHANNON, Cardinals' broadcaster

For many years we would make an annual trip to eastern Indiana on Christmas morning to spend the holiday with my wife's family. Because I was part of the ministry, we always had a major Christmas Eve service at Grace and I could not leave town until Christmas morning. As a result, we would spend cold Christmas mornings in our car on lonely, long I-70 for the seven hour drive. That was when we discovered Mr. Buck's family—and we were "invited" into their home via KMOX for "Christmas at the Bucks." Through those broadcasts that long morning drive became a warm family experience for us, the time flew by faster, and we became acquainted with the culture and great people of St. Louis who passed through their home and whom we met over the radio.

——**BOB PICKETT**, Grace Church, St. Louis

I can remember when the football Cardinals were still in St. Louis. They had a good running back who was also a good kick returner, Terry Metcalf. Apparently, this guy's agent got to him and told him how kick returning was dangerous and the player should tell the Cardinals that he wasn't going to do it. The Cardinals needed one or two more wins this particular season to make the playoffs. I guess Metcalf selfishly told the head coach that he wasn't going to return kicks.

Jack caught wind of this, and sat down with Metcalf. Jack told him how he needed to be thinking of his teammates and how he should re-think his decision. The next Sunday, Metcalf was out there returning kicks. He said that he had a heart-to-heart with Jack Buck, and he saw the light. That's how much respect players had for Jack. He had a great deal of clout with the players. They had the utmost respect for him.

——**BUDDY BATES**, Cardinals Equipment Manager

I remember the 1966 All Star Game. It was played at our new park, Busch Stadium, in St. Louis. The temperature was 103 degrees, and it registered 130 degrees on the Astroturf. They asked Casey Stengel, "What do you think of the new ballpark?" He said, "It sure holds the heat well."

You can't treat the game like Armageddon. It's every day. You'll wear your audience out. You also treat it with respect. The baseball audience knows more about *its* sport than, say, football's because it includes the ladies. A lot of the ladies have been brought up in the game and it's a simple game if you start with it as a kid. So as a broadcaster you're kind of giving already bright people the inside dope—telling what you know because you're on the scene and they're not.

With football it's mechanical, calling each play, telling where the ball is, the down, the distance. In baseball you tell a story as the game goes along. I enjoy *winning* baseball more than anything and I've had the pleasure of seeing the Cardinals win in '64-67-68, and '82-85-87-96-2000. When you have a bad club and you're out of it in August, baseball can become drudgery because you get spoiled. There's nothing like winning baseball when it engulfs the city and lasts through the winter. A successful baseball team has no parallel in sport. It's just a wonderful thing to observe.

———JACK BUCK's entry in Curt Smith's book, *What Baseball Means to Me*

One night I was driving on Interstate 270 listening to the ballgame and it was in a rain delay. I checked my cell phone messages and one was from Steve Uline of Bud Sports. I called him and he said, "Can you do me a big favor and fill in on the radio and do some play-by-play? Shannon's got his Night at the Races, a CBC fundraiser. He has to leave early, so can you come down as quickly as possible?" I was thrilled. I got to do my first Cardinal game on KMOX with Jack Buck. My mom was doing errands and she turned on the game. She said, "Oh my gosh, that's Dan!" She ran home and threw in a tape and I'm glad I have a tape of that game. It was a dream come true doing the game with Jack.

———DAN McLAUGHLIN, Cardinals Broadcaster, Fox Sports Net

One day Jack came up to me in the hallway, and he could see that I probably looked a little overstressed and overworked. Jack knew one of the people with whom I was working, and he made one of his comments that brought everything down to its lowest level. He said, "You know, the guy you're working with doesn't have ulcers." I looked at him like, "I don't think he does either." Then he added, "He's a carrier." I just started laughing. He could see what I was going through and he summed it up so well. The quick wit of Jack Buck was absolutely incredible.

———MARK GORRIS, Kansas City Royals

The first time I met Jack Buck was actually at a seminar in the early eighties in Palm Springs. Chevrolet used to throw this each year for all the teams and radio stations that it sponsored on radio and TV. They would usually bring out one or two of the big-name announcers to speak to the group. Most of the people there were actually advertising sales people and radio station executives and team broadcasting executives. We had a breakfast meeting the first day. I'll never forget, the first thing he said, at seven-thirty in the morning, he welcomed everybody and said thanks for being here and then he said, "I'm glad to be speaking to you at breakfast. I've always thought that breakfast is the most important meal of the day. If I'm not home in time for breakfast, I get in a lot of trouble." It broke the entire room up. Here are all these people who are haplessly hung-over, not ready to get their day going, and he has them falling out of their chair in the first line. As always, the delivery was fantastic. His sense of timing, the pause, waiting for the punch line, was just perfect. The entire day just went great after that.

——ERIC NADEL, Texas Rangers Announcer

Jack and I started chatting and we found out we were in the Army together and we had even both been in the same unit. My unit was in England in November of 1943. At the time, I didn't know Jack because he was a replacement. He joined the Ninth Division in March of 1945. I was a medic in the rifle company and found out that Jack and I were in the same company, but I didn't know him then. I was nineteen and he was twenty. When the American forces captured the bridge in Remagen, Jack was wounded there. We found out through talking that night that I was the one who bandaged him the morning he was hit. I was the only medic in the platoon. I had treated many different people so I really didn't know him at the time but we figured out it was me who treated Jack for the shrapnel wounds of his arm and leg. After that we became friends and I even went to his house to see his wife, Carole.

——FRANK BORGHI, St. Louis

In 1999, I went with a photographer to St. Louis to do a story on Mark McGwire. We were on the field before the game. Jack Buck had just done a dugout interview with a player and was sitting there by himself. I grew up in St. Louis and was a huge Cardinal fan, like everybody else there. I've never really been in awe of professional athletes because I've been around them so much. But I really was in awe with him.

I walked up to him, and I was a little nervous, and I introduced myself to him. I told him who I was and what I did and where I was from. He was the kindest person I'd ever met. He was really interested in what I was doing, and he carried the conversation. We probably had a nice ten or fifteen-minute talk. It was the coolest experience of my life. I've met several athletes, Pete Rose and a lot of different baseball persons, but he was by far the coolest person. It was the neatest thing that's ever happened to me. That has just stuck with me for all this time.

——BRUCE VONDERHAAR, Sports Director, KODE-TV, Joplin, MO

I didn't realize how big Jack was across the country. When he died, he had a whole page here in the San Diego paper. He was known because of his Game of the Week in football, and all his work in broadcasting, particularly the great call on Gibson's home run that still rings in memory. To St. Louis, Jack was huge. Only Stan Musial is there with him. For a guy who wasn't a player, he was huge. And all over the country, for that matter, it wasn't just that town, everybody knew him. He was legendary. He was there with Harry Caray. Harry tended to bury people, but Jack outlasted everybody. Jack Buck was absolutely Mr. St. Louis.

——JERRY COLEMAN, Padre Compadre

I remember talking to Jack about Joe when Joe was broadcasting the Louisville games. Jack was just so proud of the work Joe was doing and how he had gone to the minor leagues to gain experience. Of course he worked alongside his dad. I just remember how proud Jack was. Every time the Cardinals and the Expos played, a series didn't go by that Jack wouldn't talk about how Joe was doing in Louisville. I remember him saying, "He is really good." He said it jokingly, but I think he really meant it. He said, "You know, he's going to be better than I am. He's going to come up here and stay here a long, long time and really do well because he's a terrific young broadcaster." He was a very proud, beaming father who would talk in glowing terms of the work that his son was turning in at the minor league level.

——DAVE VAN HORNE, Florida Marlins, Play-By-Play Man

In all the changes that KMOX was going through the last few years there, and most of the people that were KMOX people, the original KMOX people from the Hyland days, had gone, and it was down to probably only five of us left in the radio station. I had this ostentatious studio and Jack felt very comfortable when he would come in to record his commercials to sit down in that studio and kind of talk about the old days a little bit. He felt comfortable there. He would often say, "You know, boy. You know when I finally go, there are gonna be Cardinal fans saying, 'Did you hear Jack Buck died in the press box calling the Cardinal game?' And the other fan would say, 'Oh, no really, that's too bad. Did the Cards win?'" He used to tell those stories. He had so many stories and he was such a jokester. The man always had a joke on his sleeve.

———**DENNIS KLAUTZER**, Former Imaging Director, KMOX

I was doing an article on Mike Shannon and Jack Buck told me a story about Mike's first year as a broadcaster with the Cardinals. Jack said they were down in spring training and ready to do the first broadcast. Jack says to Mike, "You got the umpires?", meaning did he have their names. Mike says no, so Jack told him to get them, meaning their names. Shannon misunderstood and left the booth, and in a few minutes Jack looks up to see what all the commotion is about. Mike had gone down to the field and dragged the umpires up to the press box.

———**JOE CASTELLANO**, former sportswriter, *St. Louis Globe-Democrat*

The first year I ever followed the Cardinals was 1954. That was the first year he did Cardinal games. I was eight years old, listening to those games on the radio, with a broadcast crew that included Harry Caray, Jack Buck and Joe Garagiola. Without question, three of the all-time greats in the industry. You think about it in later years—to have those people in the same booth together, we didn't know what we had when we were kids listening to that. We just were, "Well, this is our broadcast team for the Cardinals." Then you look at how nationally known all three of them became in later years and you think, "My gosh, that was really the crew that we listened to every night." In those days, Harry was so excitable, and Joe had played baseball, and of course everybody knew about him as a player, not a notable one, but a guy who was known anyway. So Jack was kind of the guy who settled you back down after the excitement of the other two. Then after Harry and Joe left the scene in the seventies, really for the last thirty years, Jack was the true treasure on the broadcast. Because he was the guy that added perspective in his early years. Shannon was learning the trade, and I know Jack helped him a lot, and they were very close friends, but Jack was the anchor of that thing after Harry left. Just listening to him on the air because he made you remember.

——MARK STILLWELL, Sports Information Director, SW Missouri State

St. Louis is blessed with a large number of terrific guys in sports there, but Jack's the guy. Musial was a great player. You admired Stan with that stance and the harmonica and his numbers and his contribution to the game. But in my neighborhood, the broadcasting neighborhood, Jack was THE guy. Jack was THE guy for a couple of reasons. One, he bided his time. He waited his turn till Harry left. Once Harry left, then while he certainly wasn't born there, he was always considered to be the native son. He was St. Louis. That's one of the great things about being a baseball broadcaster, and maybe twenty, twenty-five years from now, I can feel that to some degree because it's all so new to me here in New York, and I grew up here. There he was identified with the town. He was identified as the town. Jack Buck was St. Louis. The voice, the humor, and again I keep coming back to the graciousness. He was Midwestern and all that connotes a positive sense. And yes, he's the only guy who can look good in a godforsaken red jacket.

——CHARLEY STEINER, Formerly of ESPN, now NY Yankees Broadcaster

Sometimes he would talk to me in Italian. Or he would whisper, or sing a little song in Italian, and I just loved that. His Italian was not too bad—he knew a few words. He was so pleasant and sometimes people would ask him for his autograph, and it was no problem. At times I would notice that he would go through the dining room and stop at tables. With his voice, "How you doing?" He really loved people, that man, he really did. And they love him, boy they really love him. Everybody knew when he was in the restaurant.

When he was here, I never saw anyone pick up the check, just him.

——DOMINIC GALATI, Owner of Dominic's On the Hill Restaurants

Jack Buck was an amazingly nice man. My fondest memory is of the time I wanted to do an interview with him. I had called him a week or two weeks in advance and told him I was going to be back east, and could I stop in St. Louis and do an interview. He said, "Sure, I'll meet you in the lobby at five o'clock." It wasn't like, "Call our PR people, and I'll set you up with a credential, and how much time are you going to need or what are you going to write?"

It was just as simple as that. I was a little worried walking through the lobby. There wasn't e-mail back then. I hadn't called him to confirm and I was a little concerned. I thought, "Well, they'll track him down. He said he'd be in the lobby so I'll just go in the lobby and wait for a while and see if he does show up." I was about five minutes early, and he was sitting there waiting. He just took me under his wing and introduced me to everybody. I spent from five o'clock till the end of the game with him.

He introduced me to everybody: elevator operators, reception girl, everybody in the press box, and of course everybody knew him. He just made sure that I met everybody. It was just amazing how courteous he was. I didn't ask to sit with him during the game. He said, "We've got you all set with a headset." He was great!

———LARRY STEWART, Assistant Sports Editor, *The Los Angeles Times*

I went to the University of Missouri, and I don't know if I met Jack when I was a student or not. I got out in 1968, and think I may have met him at some function then. I just remember meeting him at the ballpark one night when I was ready to cover my first game.

Sometime shortly after that, he suggested to me that I go down to the umpire's room and make my acquaintances with them. There's all kinds of signs on those doors—"Don't enter at the risk of bodily harm, or whatever." He said, "You're gonna need to know them if a play comes up where they have to be asked about it. If they know who you are, they'll be much more likely to explain the situation to you," and he was exactly right. I found the umpires to be quite pleasant fellows anyway. That's one of the first pieces of career advice he gave me. Up until that time, he didn't particularly know me from anybody. I had been doing it a few years, but he didn't have to tell me that. We'd always been friendly, but I didn't know that he cared that much.

———RICK HUMMEL, *St. Louis Post-Dispatch*

Jack was such a nice guy. He was one of the greatest that ever got behind a microphone and as a young broadcaster, I really looked up to him. He was always so accessible and so helpful. He would help young broadcasters, not just in how to go about your business, but the way you carry yourself and your relationship with players. He was a great mentor. My first year was '65 with the Astros and I remember seeing Jack early in the season and he was really open and would help me in whatever way he could. I saw him at the end of the season, after I had been enjoying the big league life. I had gained fifteen pounds. Jack said, "Kid if you stay around this game a few more years, you're going to weigh three hundred pounds." I took that to heart.

Jack would always go down on the field before the game and talk to the players. Every broadcaster has a relationship with the hometown team, his own team, but Jack had such a great relationship with players and managers and coaches from the other teams and that was immediately noticeable.

————HARRY KALAS, Phillies' broadcaster, Hall of Fame inductee, 2002

In the summer of 1984, I was debuting a show called The Sports Machine. The show was going to be on in St. Louis. Jack Buck and Mike Shannon started talking about the show and me like there's no tomorrow. I was just flabbergasted. I couldn't believe that I was hearing them talk about this show. I played against Mike Shannon. He was a big quarterback at CBC. He was a great basketball player at Epiphany. I played against him, and man, he kicked my butt seven days a week. Here these guys were saying all these nice things, and I was just blown away.

So I wrote them a thank-you note and then I ran into them the next spring in a hotel called the Don Cesar in St. Petersburg. Jack Buck walks up to me and he said, "You've got it. You're good." I just thought, "You're the guy who is the epitome of what I want to be, and you're encouraging me." Most guys don't do that. Unlike some other announcers, Jack would say, "Don't forget. You owe your career to me, man." Then he would pick up the tab. There's a restaurant down there in St. Petersburg where he would always pick up the tab. He was always over there in this Italian place on St. Pete's East Side. Then he'd come over to the Don Cesar and he'd walk through the lobby, and my tab would always be picked up. We'd be in the

Italian Restaurant, and he'd say, "Don't forget. You're picking up my tab tonight. You owe your career to me." I go to pay my own bill, and it would already be paid. It was just his friendship.

———GEORGE MICHAEL, The Sports Machine

One outstanding thing about Jack that I didn't realize until about a month after we started was that he had been an official for football, basketball and baseball before he went into broadcasting. So he was very up to date on the rules. We were doing a big game in Minnesota, and the officials got crossed up on what transpired during the preceding play. By the time they had it figured it out, Jack had explained everything to the national audience. That's how astute he was with those rules.

Before every game he went down and talked to the officials. Normally that's private property, but they heard he was a former official, as a result they were eager to talk to him.

———HANK STRAM, Buck's CBS radio partner

I cherish the memory of Jack singing during the seventh-inning stretch here in Chicago last year. That was remarkable. If you wanted to catch a caricature, a snapshot, or an image of what Jack Buck was like, get that tape and watch it. I've watched it a couple of times, and it brings tears to my eyes. I think I'm in the background looking at Joe Buck, who was doing the game on the Cardinals radio side, and he's looking at me kind of funny. I mouthed to him, "That is awesome." It really was. It was a wonderful moment for someone who grew up a Cardinal fan, who grew up in St. Louis, to see Jack Buck saluting my grandfather, with whom, at times, he had a very difficult relationship, but in their later years they had so much respect and love for each other that he was willing to be a part of that day. It's beyond great.

He came out in this God-awful crimson jacket and said to the Wrigley Field crowd, "How do you like my jacket?" Of course, everybody starts booing, and he just laughed. Then he started singing. He came to "...root, root, root for the,' everybody screamed "Cubbies!" and Jack said, "No, the Cardinals." Then he threw his Cubs hat out. He knew how to play it up, get people riled up, excited and have fun. It really was fantastic. It was just an incredibly emotional, fun time. Obviously, Jack's health over the last several years was not good, but he never seemingly let it get him down.

———CHIP CARAY, Chicago Cubs Broadcaster

I don't think that I really, at that moment, had any idea of the depth of my connection with him. Listening to Cardinal baseball with my father and my grandfather on the radio in northern Arkansas is one of the earliest memories of my life. I lived in a less complicated time, born in 1952. At my grandfather's house there was no television. That is what you did. You listened to the radio. You listened to the Cardinals at night. That is how you got through summer nights. In a way, it's been a part of my life for nearly fifty years. I don't know anyone outside my family who fits that criteria as closely. I listened to him for many, many years and you had the sense of who and what he is. Then you find out the person is the real deal, plus so much more. It really is a loss.

——JOHN MARTIN, Providence, Rhode Island

Jack always joked about his wife Carole, who is such a sweet lady. I was doing a baseball game in St. Louis for CBS. I flew in on Friday morning, and called Jack's home to say "Hi." Jack said, "Gregory, young man, how are you doing?" I told him I was fine and that I was in town. He said, "You'll come out to the house tonight. You'll sit around the pool. You'll have a bite to eat and a little something to drink." I told him, "Jack, I really can't because we have production meetings tonight." He said, "Very well. I'll see you at the ballpark tomorrow." I told him okay, and to please say hello to his bride for me.

I walked up to him behind the batting cage at the ballpark the next day, and after we exchanged hellos I asked him, "Where's your wife?" He said, "Not going to be here. We had a little tiff." "Serious?" I asked him. He said, "Even now, she's divvying up the furniture." You knew it was all B.S., but he was so funny.

——GREG GUMBEL, NBC Sports

I met him in Las Vegas one time when I was there for a convention. I was walking through the gaming room in Caesars Palace. Jack Buck, Dan Kelly and Mike Shannon were sitting at a blackjack table, and there was a seat open there. Jack invited me to sit down. I sat down next to Jack. One of my salesmen came walking by, and he was a real Cardinal fan, a real sports fan, and I said, "Hey, Johnny, you see who I'm sitting next to?" And he just went bananas. He asked Jack for an autograph, and Jack pulled a check out of his pocket, and wrote "void" on it, and handed him the check with a little note saying, "To my friend, John Horton." I just thought that was amazing.

——HANK GALEOTTI, Lake St. Louis, Missouri

Jack Buck was one of my favorite people. The thing about Jack was that baseball—the game on the field—mattered to him. His passion was broadcasting what happened between the white lines.

No one was better at describing the action. He made a routine groundout exciting.

Today's new breed of announcers try to be funny and negative, forgetting about the game unfolding on the field. Many of them don't understand baseball. That wasn't Jack Buck.

Years ago the Cardinals and Phillies were playing a grueling three-game weekend exhibition series during spring training in the Dominican Republic. The game was thirty minutes from the first pitch when Jack approached me. He was having phone problems and was unable to get on the air. My newspaper had a phone installed so I told him to start his broadcast on it. He never forgot. Just last October at the playoffs, the last time I saw him, he approached me and joked, "If I get in a jam, can I borrow your phone?"

"Any time, Jack."

——HAL BODLEY, Sports Columnist, *USA Today*

The thing I remember about Jack Buck was after the Miracle Mets were in the 1969 World Series, I was living in Memphis working for a glass company in the off-season. Ron Swoboda came down to speak at some sports banquet they were having. Jack Buck was there. I met Swoboda at the Peabody Hotel, and we were sitting there. Jack Buck comes walking by and says, "Hi Ron, how you doing? Hi Jim." It just shocked me that he remembered who I was—I hadn't played in the big leagues since 1965. I was impressed because I was just a one-year deal there, and he was in town for this banquet. The fact that he knew who I was amazed me. He just had that kind of a memory.

——JIM BETHKE, Mets Pitcher, 1965, his only Big-League season

There was a situation a couple years ago when Jack was really starting to be affected by Parkinson's disease. Four or five of us were standing around the batting cage at Busch Stadium one day before a game. Jack came sauntering out of the dugout—Jack didn't walk, he sauntered—and in that distinctive voice of his he said, "Hey boys, what's shaking…other than me?" He completely disarmed us.

He had a sense of humor about what he was going through. He used to make jokes about his pacemaker. A couple months ago when he was really having a tough time getting out of the hospital, he told Joe, "I feel like I've donated my body to Washington University. I wish they'd give it back." He had a good sense of humor and a good outlook about that stuff.

——**BOB CARPENTER**, St. Louis Announcer, Cardinals

I have said this about other people, but not too many people. I have been with CBS during my entire career, 30 years, and I've been directing for 25 of those years. There have been very few people who come down the pike who have that quality that a Walter Cronkite had, which is called the trust factor. Networks used to have a rating that was based on a trust, likeability, connection to the camera, and coming into people's living rooms. I would venture to guess that Jack Buck would have scored very, very high in those ratings because he was somebody who, when he talked to you, was all about trust. If he said something, you knew it was true. There was no embellishing. There was no painting something that wasn't there. You knew it was true. That, to me, is probably the single thing that made Jack Buck. More than how great his descriptions were, and how he would paint the picture, you knew it was true if Jack Buck said it.

——**BOB FISHMAN**, CBS Sports Director

One of the things that sticks out with me was that he and Harry Caray both, after the 1955 season, went out and bought new cars. Jack bought a Pontiac, and Harry Caray bought a Ford. For the whole year, that was brought up about one out of every four broadcasts that Jack could afford a Pontiac and all Harry could buy was a Ford. That made Jack kind of an intuitive character with the people in town. He thought enough about his staying in the job and everything to buy a Pontiac. They considered Harry the man about town, the guy who would push his money out wherever he could, and Jack, a guy who already had a family started, he already had quite a few kids then, and it was a trademark through those years that he was able to buy a better car than Harry. Everybody got a kick out of that back in the fifties.

——**JOHN RING**, Illinois radio personality

Two Americans were caught in Mexico attempting to smuggle drugs, one was a Cub fan and the other a Cardinal fan. They were brought before the captain of the firing squad who informed them that he would grant each one a last wish providing that it was reasonable. The ugly Cub fan said he could die in peace if he could hear Harry Caray sing "Take Me Out To the Ballgame" one more time. The captain said "This is your lucky day. We have cable in the palace, our head of security is a moron as well as a Cubs fan and he tapes every game." The captain turns to the Cardinal fan and asks if he has a reasonable last wish. The big, good looking Cardinal fan replies, "I sure do, señor!" The captain says, "Well, what is it?" And the Cardinal fan says, "Shoot me first."

——JACK BUCK, at a Harry Caray Roast at Bally's in Las Vegas, November 19, 1988

Jack Buck was fair. There are broadcasters who argue with the players half the time over comments they make. Jack wasn't that way. Whether you were playing good or bad, he was fair. He had a terrific, dry sense of humor.

As an example of his humor, I could see him winking to his broadcast partner and pointing to a statistic that a guy hasn't stolen a base all year as he says on the air, "He might be running on this pitch." He was that way.

I also remember how much Jack worked. He was a workaholic. Going back to our younger days, he did Cardinal baseball, which was one hundred sixty two games, plus spring training. Then he jumped into his football schedule. I was with him one day when he got his St. Louis Billikens basketball schedule. That was in July, and he was planning his winter schedule. In baseball, he had his network duties on top of the Cardinals. He was the sports director at KMOX. It seemed like Jack Buck was on the air all the time. I remember it so well that it struck me forty years ago that I didn't know when he took time to eat or sleep. That's a full load, and it doesn't include his preparation time.

——RAY SADECKI, Cardinals' Pitcher 1960-1966, 1975

The big memory for me was being able to meet Jack Buck in person. He was just the type of guy you would imagine, if anybody had the ability to be stuck-up because he was such a great talent, and an overwhelming personality, it would have been Jack Buck. He was the furthest thing from that. It was like hanging on a back fence and lighting up a smoke and having a Budweiser and talking with your next-door neighbor. That's the kind of man he was. I will never forget that demeanor. I will never forget the way he would come across on radio in very much a conversational manner, very much a friendly manner. He would bring you the story of the ball game, and you could almost smell the aroma of the ballpark. You could hear the sounds, and you could visualize it in your mind's eye so nicely because of the way he would call a game.

——RAY SMITH, Illinois Native, Pennsylvania Radio Networks

I remember once at Wrigley, it was one of those red-hot days in the summer. Our booths at Wrigley Field are not air-conditioned. It's one of the oldest ballparks, and as a result, it's somewhat antiquated in many ways. You can really roast as a broadcaster with your headsets on and one of those ninety-five degree days. Jack Buck took a break in about the seventh inning, and he's in the air-conditioned press-room. I don't get a break—I do every inning of every game for the Cubs. Jack would always look over and smile at me and say, "How you doing, kid?" I came in about the eighth inning, and I'm just sweating like crazy. I had to get some ice water. There's Jack sitting there, and he looked at me and smiled, and he said, "Pat, they don't pay us for nothing." I'll never forget that. He's absolutely right. It's a fun job and a good job and a well-paying job, but some days you really, really have to work hard and you really suffer. That was one of those days.

——PAT HUGHES, Chicago Cubs Broadcaster

I joined the Cardinals May 1, 1973 and worked with Jack and knew him and was friends with him ever since. I've worked with him in lots of different ways. One of the last things we did was selling a print to benefit the Backstoppers. With the help of David Pratt, one of the Cardinals' owners, matching what we raised through selling the print, Jack raised $1,000,000 for Backstoppers. The night before he went into the hospital he went to the annual dinner at the Missouri Athletic Club to announce the sale of another print, this time to raise money for the Herbert Hoover Boys and Girls Club. That was the only reason he went to the dinner.

Julie, Carole, Joe and Jack Buck – 1985

Wrigley Field, June, 2001

Where have you gone Ted Williams?
Joe DiMaggio and Jack Buck want to know.

You heard what they saw

Jack and son
Joe working
together, 1991.

Jay Randolph left, and Jack at Variety Club Telethon.

When good shots happen to bad golfers; Jack Buck, Stan Musial, Greg Marecek and Whitey Herzog

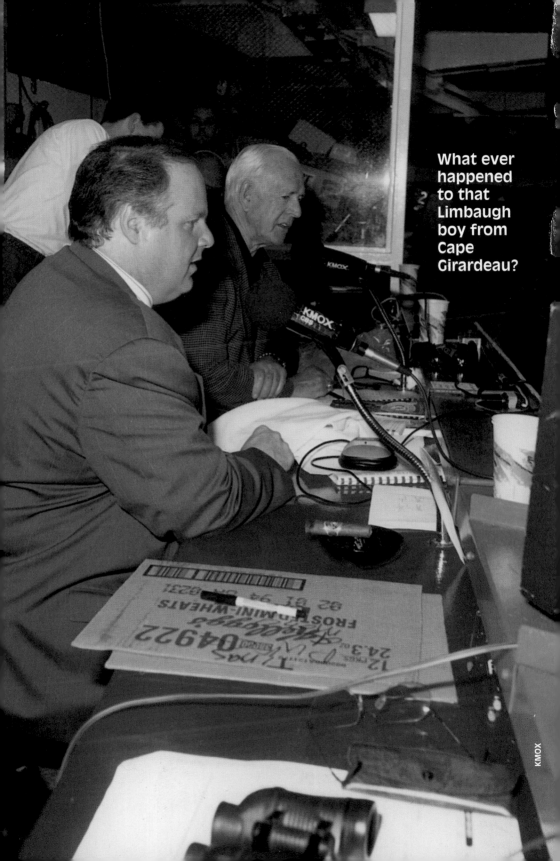

What ever happened to that Limbaugh boy from Cape Girardeau?

KMOX

I attended most of the dinners when Jack spoke. I would steal a couple of his better jokes because I make a lot of speeches and I would always credit him. We'd be standing around in the office and I'd ask him to tell them such and such a story, and he'd say, "You tell them." That happened to me on more than one occasion. You'd think I'd learn my lesson. How much pressure can there be to tell the master's joke with the master sitting there critiquing it.

——MARTY HENDIN, Cardinals vice president of community relations

I remember Jack at Holy Cross Camp, that was a parity camp. It's gone now. He was just a guy in the neighborhood. There was word that Jack Donnelly could have gotten Jack Buck to be baptized in the Catholic Church, now I'm not too sure if that's true or not. The priest that supposedly baptized Jack Buck was Father McGraw, a neighborhood priest here at Holy Cross Church.

Jack Buck did come back to Holyoke, several years ago. We had a superintendent of schools, Moriarity, who wanted to get in touch with a noted baseball person. Someone recommended Jack Donnelly to do that. Jack Donnelly at that time worked for the parks and was out raking the ball diamond. The superintendent couldn't believe a guy just working in the park would be able to get in touch with Jack Buck. Somebody asked him if he could get hold of Jack Buck, and he said, "Yeah." Well they said Jack Buck would come to speak if Jack Donnelly would also speak. Well, Donnelly was no college man whatsoever, but he gave a speech you couldn't believe. It was right on the button. He was the one who introduced Buck and the whole thing. It went over very well.

——GEORGE HOGAN, Childhood friend, Holyoke, Mass.

I was a student when I met him. I was a beer vendor at Busch Stadium when I was in college. I had wanted to get into broadcasting my entire life. I was going to the University of Missouri and had to make a decision to enter journalism school my junior year.

My family was pressuring me to go to law school or something different because journalism was a lot of work and low pay and tough to get into, etc. I was kind of having second thoughts as I was working at Busch Stadium about changing some things around and making a career change. I had a chance meeting with Jack Buck outside of Busch Stadium at which time I told him about my situation.

He didn't know me, but was very direct and very influential, having a conversation with me about pursuing your dream and how to go about doing it the right way. All the while, I'm sitting there wearing my red, blue and yellow clown Sports Service beer vendor suit, which I was sort of embarrassed about. It was just kind of a turning point really in my life in terms of pursuing something or not pursuing something based on a chance meeting with somebody that I grew up listening to my entire life.

———TIM WOODBURN, Sports Radio, Lexington, Kentucky

One day Jack asked me if we had a little 8x10 rug in the basement. I told him that we did and I asked him why? He said, "Well Shirley, who is up in the booth, near the end of the season when it's getting cooler, has to sit there with her feet on the ground, and I don't want her feet to get that cold." So he took that rug down there, and he put it under her feet.

———CAROLE BUCK, Jack's wife

I live on the "Hill" in South St. Louis. I know the people that live in the house that you once lived in. I know some people that met you and they told me that you were the nicest guy that you could ever meet. I got you a gift certificate to Missouri Bakery. Missouri Bakery is the best bakery on the Hill. I hope you enjoy some of their pastries.

———JOSEPH TORRETTA, sixth grader at St. Ambrose Catholic School,
in a letter written to Jack Buck in April 2002

Chapter 7

Cardinal Virtues, Cardinal Sins

Bill DeWitt, Jr.

Mike Shannon

Buddy Blattner

Milo Hamilton

Bob Carpenter

Sally Rains

Ron Jacober

Pete Vonachen

Harry Weber

Jim Jackson

Paula Homan

BIG BIRD

BILL DEWITT

As principal owner of the Cardinals, William O. DeWitt, Jr. serves as Chairman and CEO. DeWitt grew up in St. Louis, the son of former St. Louis Browns owner, William O. DeWitt, Sr., graduated from Yale and was a partner with President George W. Bush in owning the Texas Rangers. As a nine-year-old batboy for the Browns, he was part of baseball lore when he loaned his uniform to a midget.

I was a kid around the ballpark in St. Louis. My father and my uncle had owned the Browns and sold to Bill Veeck around 1950. The Eddie Gaedel deal happened in 1951. I was nine years old and my father came to me and said, "You've got the only uniform that will fit a smaller player, we need to borrow it for something that's going to happen between games of a double header. This smaller player is going to come in and pinch-hit." So I said, "Fine, take the uniform." It was the only one of that size that was an official uniform. Back in those days, those kinds of uniforms were not for sale.

I'd been told a couple of days before. They said, "don't tell anybody, but a midget is going to be playing and we're going to put 1/8 in the score-card. A couple of days ahead of a time nobody will really know what was happening and then that day it will read 1/8-Eddie Gaedel." It was a double-header and between games of the double-header Gaedel popped out of a cake wearing my uniform and pinch-hit in the second game. It was quite a thing. Gaedel was 26 years old and died ten years later.

I got my uniform back and left the 1/8 on there. It's on loan to the Baseball Hall of Fame in Cooperstown. They are doing a tour of *Baseball Is America* and it will be one of the things on tour along with other baseball memorabilia so it's turned out to be a good attraction. I'm happy to have them use it up there.

I was sitting in the box next to the dug-out with my family and watched Gaedel bat. Everyone in the stadium had a feeling of bewilderment, amusement, not sure what was going on. It was a bit of a mixed reaction.

Before I really knew Jack Buck, my father was a good friend of his; they were both in the St. Louis baseball scene. My father had grown up working for both the Cardinals and the Browns and then owned the Browns in the late 1940s so I knew Jack somewhat when he first started broadcasting. He was obviously a great announcer even back then, and then he and Harry Caray were such a great team.

Jack had great subtlety, he had great humor and Harry was more of a play-by-play, more inflection in his voice. They were a great team, both great announcers. As time went on I didn't see Jack for a number of years and then when we bought the Cardinals in 1996, I remember Jack coming up to me at a press conference and he said, "I remember you being around your dad as a kid. If you are as good a baseball man as your father was, the Cardinals are in good hands." That made me feel good, he spoke highly of both my parents.

He was so good on personal things. He did a poem I thought was particularly good about Spring Training. It's terrific. The gist of it is when your team's out of the race and it's near the end of the year you realize that Spring Training is around the corner. It's just a really great poem. I thought it was so baseball oriented having been around the game. I asked him if I could get a copy of it. He said, "Oh, sure," and he got me a copy of it and signed it. He wrote me this really nice personal note on it saying what a great job he thought I was doing with the Cardinals. It really meant a lot to me that he did it.

George W. Bush and I were in the oil business together. He was a great baseball fan and he said one day, "Let's buy a team" so I worked with him in putting together that ownership group in the late 1980s and I stayed with the Rangers until maybe 1994 when I tried to buy the Baltimore Orioles. I ended up being a smaller partner there for a year or two and then the Cardinal thing came along and I was able to get involved.

We've been doing a statue program at the stadium of the great Hall of Famers. We did George Sisler, the great Browns player and then we wanted to do a Negro League player. The one who fit the bill there was Cool Papa Bell. We did that earlier in 2002 and his daughter, Connie was there. Cool Papa Bell had died about 10 years earlier. Connie told the story that when Cool Papa was elected to the Hall of Fame, Jack Buck said to her, "I want your father to have a big party for his election into the Hall of Fame" and she said, "Well that would be wonderful." He said, "I'll arrange to do it and I want to host it." She said that, kind of unbeknownst to anybody, Jack had invited their family and friends. Cool Papa wasn't in the position financially to afford that kind of a party. Jack threw the party and picked up the tab. The party was held at a club where Jack was a member. Cool Papa was alive when he was inducted to the Hall of Fame and Jack had wanted him to have a big party. Connie got tears in her eyes when she told that story.

After September 11th, we were the first game played and it was on television. At that time Jack was not well but he got up and did that poem and it was just really moving.

Jack Buck was there for all the great moments in the last 50 years of Cardinal baseball. You think of all the great things that have happened. All the signature events. Jack Buck was there describing them. When you remember when Musial hit five home runs in double-header you think of Jack Buck describing it. He was quite a guy.

WHO DIED AND MADE BILLIE JEAN KING?
MIKE SHANNON

Mike Shannon first knew Jack Buck as a young boy growing up in St. Louis, then as a player on the Cardinals and for more than 25 years, his broadcast partner on KMOX Radio.

Jack knew everybody. We walked in one day and Al Davis was just standing there. He introduced me to Al Davis, the promoter king. We were in New York doing a game and there was the other king, Larry King, and Don King. There's no telling who you'd run into when you were with Jack.

I went into the broadcast booth in 1972. Jack really took care of me. He was my teacher and my mentor. All I did was learn and observe. He was very kind to bring me along the way he did. It was a wonderful relationship. We had such a good time. We liked a lot of the same things. He enjoyed going to the race track, playing golf, he enjoyed the games. We got along splendidly.

I don't even know if I would have taken this job if it weren't for Jack. I knew when I walked into the booth that I had a friend there. I had a person who would take care of me. I had confidence that if I went to Jack and I said, "Hey, can we do this thing?" He'd say, "Don't worry. I'll take care of it."

Jack and I were with each other almost daily during the season. After the season, we never saw one another. If we ran across one another at a banquet, that would be the only time. That also helped the relationship. You know, Jack, even though he slowed down at the end, he would be at the ballpark every day when he was working at home. Of course, he came on the road a number of times also.

I sat next to Jack hours and hours, day in and day out. I could just see his mind spinning all the time. He had an unbelievable sense of knowing how what he was going to say would sound to the people that were sitting in Arkansas or Tennessee or anywhere. I don't think I've ever run across a person that knew how what he was going to say would sound in the ear of another person better than Jack Buck. He was unbelievable when it came to that.

He used to always say in a kidding manner that "Mike knows even where the Unknown Soldier is buried." And I used to say, "That's right, Jack." And then, lo and behold, when they did come out with all the DNA, it ended up that the Unknown Soldier was a gentleman from St. Louis. And of course, after that Jack said, "I'll never say anything again." That was one thing.

One night we had a banquet. One of the football coaches—I won't mention his name—had way too much to drink. Once Jack started the Master of Ceremony duties, all the servers and the busboys left. At one end of the head table, one of the football coaches was there. He enjoys drinking Budweiser. There must have been some other people who helped him. There must have been three or four cases of empty bottles on the table. Someone got up to get a standing ovation, I think Woody Hayes, and what he did, he jumped over those three cases of Budweiser bottles and they went flying everywhere. Jack always had a sly comment. He said, "Coach, I think the right side is clear now."

Jack was very involved in fundraising for Cystic Fibrosis and still has the longest running golf tournament in St. Louis to benefit Cystic Fibrosis.

One time he brought a young man up to the booth who was gravely ill with a disease and he sat behind us. A foul ball came up, hit the wire and hit the table in front of us; it went up and hit the counter behind us, then it went up and hit the ceiling, then it went over to hit the wall, came back and hit the counter. There was an empty hot dog box sitting on the counter and that ball rolled right into that hot dog box and right in front of that young man. And the smile that was on his face was enough…well, it was just a wonderful, wonderful moment. Jack Buck lived for moments like that.

I never will forget one time when we were out in Vegas. A friend of Jack's was a great Joe Louis fan. And, of course, a friend of ours out there was Ash Resnick at **Caesars Palace**. Ash employed Joe Louis at the casino there, and they were good friends. Anyway, this guy wanted to meet **Joe Louis**, so Jack says, "Well quick, come on. I know where he is. He's over there at the craps table." So they went over there. Joe was rolling the dice. Slowly but surely, this guy inched up behind Joe Louis. He was just mystified with Joe Louis; his boyhood idol and hero. Joe kept running the dice and there was a big crowd around the table. Finally, the guy got right up next to him. Joe Louis sevened out and he turned around and Jack's friend was right there. Joe said, "Are you messing with my money?" I thought this guy had to go back to the room and change his shorts. Jack said, "Well, did you get close enough to him?"

As sophisticated as Jack was, and he was as sophisticated as any gentleman you would ever want to run across, when he got on the golf course, he was dangerous. Jack had the one great quote—he was out playing golf and said to his caddy, "Young man, you might be the worst caddy in the history of golf." The caddy answered, "Mr. Buck, that would be too much of a coincidence."

He was a character out there. We'd go out and I'd say, "Jack, what are you going to shoot today?" He'd respond, "I'm probably going to shoot a hundred." So we'd be playing and he'd be upset. And I'd say, "Well, what are you mad about?"

We used to have so much fun together. We used to go play golf in the morning, we'd go to the racetrack in the afternoon, then we'd go to the ballpark at night. So we had just an unbelievable time.

Jack raised so many millions and millions of dollars for so many charities and people that you couldn't count them all. He was on stage. It was like a Broadway play. It was orchestrated. Jack was the conductor. He took care of everything.

> The Caesars of Caesars Palace has no apostrophe and the Dr in Dr Pepper has no period. Both confound editors around the country…Joe Louis died almost destitute and his funeral was paid for by Max Schmeling.

DIZZY DEAN DRESSED TO THE THREES
BUDDY BLATTNER

Buddy Blattner is a legendary baseball and bas-ketball radio announcer. Among other teams, Blattner has broadcast for the St. Louis Browns, St. Louis Cardinals, California Angels and Kansas City Royals. He also was the voice of the St. Louis Hawks of the NBA. During the 2001 summer, the Lake Ozark, Mo., resident won the singles tennis championship at the Summer National Senior Games—The Senior Olympics in Baton Rouge, La.

Although we were in the same business, our paths didn't cross that many times; we didn't share a booth together, or do any particular event together because when he took over with the Cardinals, I was under contract with Gene Autry and the Angels in California. After that long stint, I then went to Kansas City for the first seven years of the Royals. I've now been at the Lake of the Ozarks for twenty-five years.

Jack had been brought in from AAA ball in 1954 to work with Harry Caray. Harry could be tough to work with. Joe Garagiola was going to work with Harry, while the advertising agency wanted me on that team. There were just too many broadcasters, so that was when Jack was let go after the 1959 season. Garagiola wasn't meshing with Caray, so they put Garagiola and myself on television doing those games. I believe Stretch Miller was doing radio with Caray. After the 1960 season, Stretch was gone, and they brought back Buck. It was a good move. Joe was ready to move on to New York, and I was ready to move to a long-term contract with the Angels.

The second time around, Jack and Harry got along much better, pri-marily, I think, because of Buck. He was not pushy, and he kind of let things flow. He wasn't given much work; he did his two or three innings. They enjoyed his work. When Harry was moved out, Jack took over. Jack Buck was the best.

MILO HAMILTON IS A TOUGH ACT TO FOLLOW...MAINLY BECAUSE HE TAKES THE MICROPHONE WITH HIM.

MILO HAMILTON

A legendary member of baseball's fraternity of radio broadcasters, Milo Hamilton has seemingly seen it all. The man who worked for the St. Louis Browns (1953) and the St. Louis Cardinals (1954) was behind the microphone for Roger Maris' 61st home run and Hank Aaron's 715th home run.Hamilton has been with the Houston Astros since 1985.

I first met Jack in 1954 when he came to St. Louis. I had been there the year before with the Browns, and then the Browns went to Baltimore and became the Orioles. The Cardinals hired Jack, and I to work with Harry Caray in 1954, but Jack and I never worked together. During the first half of the season, I was on the road. Then at the All-Star break we switched roles.

The next year, the Cardinals wanted to go back to their player analyst, so they put Joe Garagiola in the booth. I went to Chicago to do the Cubs, so Jack and I obviously crossed paths then. We did not lose touch when I left.

We had something in common because we broke into the big leagues at the same time, so we were interested in following each other's careers. We also were in a situation in those days when the second guy on a broadcasting staff didn't get much airtime. Of course, if you were on the air with Caray, you got about as little as there was. In fact, I didn't start getting a lot of airtime until the early 1960s. Buck

The public address announcer for the Astros (Colt '45s) in 1962 was Dan Rather. John Forsythe, the actor and friend of Jack Buck, was the P.A. announcer for the Brooklyn Dodgers in 1937 and 1938.

wasn't getting a lot of airtime in the 1950s, either, so we could commiserate about that.

As our careers went on, our kidding was based around how long we were going to keep broadcasting. When we'd see each other in spring training each year, we'd go through the regular questions of asking about each other's family, then he'd ask me what I did all winter. "Well, I did football and basketball," is how I usually replied. He'd say, "Why do you keep doing all that? Why do you want to work all the time?" I said, "Jack, I'll make a deal with you. As soon as you stop doing Monday Night Football, I'll stop doing basketball." Of course, we both knew we weren't going to quit, because we liked it too much. You don't do this for fifty years, as we both did, unless you enjoy it.

Believe it or not, I was never able to interview Jack on one of our baseball pre-game shows, because all the time I was interviewing the manager. My sidekick would be doing a player or the other manager. But, Buck interviewed me every time our teams played each other. When Jack passed away, I was on KMOX that morning and again at the evening drive. The host said that when the Cardinals and the Astros played, either in Houston or at Busch Stadium, they always knew Jack was going to have me on the pre-game show. If a guy who wasn't even on the sports staff remembered it, I must have been on there a lot, and I was!

Jack always had me on because our days went back to 1953 and 1954. He always started the interview by saying, "Let's see, Milo, we've been doing this how many years?" He'd always open the interview the same way, and then he'd start asking me about our ball club. I must've had a bushel basket full of the gift certificates from him for doing those interviews over the years.

The secret is to not put yourself above the game, and don't talk down to the audience. To me, baseball fans are the most knowledgeable. At the same time, we can't take for granted that everybody listening is knowledgeable. So, you walk a line to educate and witness the fact that people will tell us that they learned the game of baseball by taking their radios to the game. Jack fit into that mold in every way.

Jack could disarm you because he'd say something about you. I don't think he transposed his wit too much into the broadcasts. It's the old story of not shoving something on the audience if it doesn't fit. That wit is what helped him do a great job of emceeing dinners.

The last time I saw him, it was more than just "how are you doing." He also brought me a copy of his poetry book, autographed. Then we ate together before the game in the press lounge, and talked about the poems. We had a nice visit on the air and a nice visit in the press lounge.

The last time I talked to him was the first week of January, after his first surgery. He said, "I'll see you in spring training because I'm going to be there to do the games." At that time, I didn't realize how serious things were. After three months, we all expected any day to get the call, because nobody could take all of what he went through— the surgeries, the diabetes, the Parkinson's…the deck was stacked. He battled it.

As somebody said, "He's better off now than the way he had to spend his last two or three years."

We had a lot of things in common. We both grew up in the Great Depression era of the 1930s. We both were in the Second World War. We both broke into broadcasting in the 1940s, and our careers were kind of entwined big-league wise. So, when you have that many things in common, you have a friendship and a mutual respect. In this business, you have acquaintances and some friends, but you don't have a lot of great friends. I can say without any fear of contradiction, that Jack and I were great friends. He always referred to me on the air as an "old friend." That was special between Jack Buck and me.

BUSCH STADIUM—THE LAND OF AHS
BOB CARPENTER

Bob Carpenter, a 1971 graduate of St. Louis McBride High School, had his broadcasting dreams come true on April 3, 1984, when he called his first Cardinals' game for the Sportstime Cable Network...with Jack Buck as his analyst. Since that time, Carpenter has called Cardinal games for several St. Louis television outlets and KMOX radio. Today he is one of the main play-by-play announcers for ESPN, calling Major League baseball, college football and college basketball.

Jack was pretty much the guy that I looked up to when I was a young broadcaster, and I liked to pattern myself after him. I was a St. Louis kid. My sister got a job with the Cardinals in 1967, when I was fourteen years old. So, I was around the ballpark a lot in my teen years. After listening to Jack on the radio for a number of years, I then got to observe him firsthand...that was cool to get to know him on that basis.

Remembering one-liners and jokes is how Jack kept his mind sharp. There was no indication at all, to any of us, that his mind had slowed down. He was quick-witted, sharp and funny. The problem he was having on the air was the congestive problem he was having that he sometimes struggled to talk. The functions of the mind were right there, though.

But, you talk about a guy who led a full life. He pretty much squeezed every ounce of fun and laughter out of his time that he possibly could. Everybody's going to miss him.

Sometimes he would just walk up to you, tell a joke and walk away. He could get away with all sorts of jokes like nobody else could. He was Irish and he loved telling jokes. A lot of times, a conversation with Jack would consist of you saying, "Hi, how are you doing?", he'd tell a one-liner, then walk away and tell it to someone else. Or, he probably had a different one ready for each person. He was quite funny right to the end.

I picked up some things from him over the years. The Cardinals and the **Montreal Expos** share a complex in Jupiter, Florida. So, each team had an office adjacent to the main stadium. The Cardinal offices and clubhouse are beyond the right-field fence in a two-story building. There's a balcony where people can go out, sit under umbrellas and watch the game.

Last year during spring training, Jack and I ended up out there talking for about twenty minutes. We were swapping stories. He was telling me about a basketball game that he had to do in Kansas one time. He had all kinds of weather problems trying to get there. He said he literally sat down to do the game as the official threw the ball up in the air. He said, "I rushed into the building and I sat down. I wasn't as prepared as I normally would be. The referee threw the ball up, 10 guys jumped up in the air after it, and they never came down." That was Jack's way of saying that the game was a total fire drill for him because he just walked in and did it. I'm sure he did a good job. It was interesting to me to sit out there and have a real conversation with him. We watched the game for a while. Pretty soon he said, "Well, I'm outta here." He had enough sun and fresh air on the hot day, so off he went.

That's how Jack was. Sometimes he was kind of like an apparition that would pop into your life for thirty seconds, and then disappear again.

When he was down on the field before a game, all the players, coaches and managers from the opposing teams knew him, so he'd talk to everybody. He just kind of sauntered from one station to another, and after he got the interviews that he needed for his pre-game show, he'd disappear into the dugout and off he'd go. Jack definitely marched to the beat of his own drummer, but he never

With the Expos in 1993, Moises Alou hit six consecutive home runs over a span of four games.

hesitated to slow down and pay attention to other people. That was one of the charming, generous things about his personality.

I remember the first day I worked with him. That was on April 3, 1984. It was my first day doing big-league baseball, and I was in Dodger Stadium doing the **Cardinals** and Dodgers with Mike Shannon. Jack would come over and work with me on TV for the middle three innings. Here I was, a young play-by-play guy and I was Jack Buck's analyst. I'm thinking how in the world am I going to add anything to this show. But, Jack was gracious and it all worked out.

One night, after we had been on the air for a couple of weeks, he said to me during a commercial, "OK, kid, I want to hear you do play-by-play. This next inning is yours, and I'm going to sit back and listen to you." Great…all of a sudden, Jack Buck is my analyst. As I mentioned before, he was gracious about it, and it went quite well.

He had a way of disarming what could be an otherwise tense situation with his humor. At the same time, as a young announcer, I really got the feeling that he was checking me out. He wanted to see if I was worthy of the opportunity I had been given to be in there. He told me to take my media guide and notes, and put them away, then just watch the game and do it. That's advice I've tried to think about for a lot of years. Jack was one of those guys who didn't believe in having a lot of prepared notes. He figured you should just do the game, and if you were good enough, that'd be enough. That's a simple philosophy, but Jack was not a guy who was going to sit around for a couple days before a series, researching the other team. His research was on the field, from talking to guys and interviewing them. That's where Jack Buck did his homework.

As a network broadcaster, I've tried to strike a balance between doing a certain amount of research and just doing the game. If I'm doing a baseball game for ESPN, they send me enough research to kill several trees. This stuff is unbelievable. Jack has taught me to strike a balance between the two. I have to do certain things to satisfy the network people, but at the same time, I want to be true to the game and

The last forfeited game in the major leagues was August 10, 1995 in Los Angeles. The Cardinals won 2-1.

not overwhelm people with a whole bunch of extraneous info that doesn't have that much to do with what's happening on the field.

When you're doing 180 games in a season, counting spring training, you have to be lighthearted and have fun. I've been in a booth with a couple of the same guys for a whole season, and it's like being with your family everyday. If you don't have a sense of humor about some of the bad things that are going to happen, it's going to be a long season. There are teams out there that have broadcasters who work together everyday, who don't like each other. That's kind of a mind-boggling thing to me. I'm sure Jack wasn't best of buddies with everybody he worked with, but he always kept it light. That's how you get through a long season, especially if you have a team that's not going to the World Series. Jack's philosophy along those lines was very solid.

Jack was a great help with Mike Shannon early in his career, too. Mike came aboard with no broadcasting experience, but over the years, he has developed into a very polished broadcaster.

Famous Calls

On Mark McGwire's 61st home run, tying Roger Maris for the single-season record, Sept. 7, 1998:

"Look at there, look at there! Mark McGwire Flight No. 61 to Planet Maris! Pardon me for a moment while I stand and applaud!"

WHEN IT'S RAINS, IT'S SCORES

SALLY TIPPETT RAINS

Sally Tippett Rains was a producer in the sports office at KMOX, who worked with Jack Buck and Mike Shannon in re-creating baseball games during the strike in 1981.

As it became apparent there would be a major league baseball players strike in 1981, Jack Buck and Bob Costas talked with Robert Hyland about how KMOX would fill the air time. As is still the case today, the baseball games were very valuable to KMOX; their highest listenership was always during the baseball season and the station could not afford to let its ratings drop.

They came up with a great idea: re-create baseball games and invent fantasy games. They re-created old World Series games with Jack and Mike Shannon broadcasting. They also did fantasy games like "What if Dizzy Dean's Cardinals played Bob Gibson's Cardinals?"

There was no need to re-create the Cardinals World Series games because they already had been done. These games were of other teams. For instance, we did the seventh game of the 1971 World Series between the Baltimore Orioles and the Pittsburgh Pirates.

We went to *The Sporting News* and got the game summaries. Jack wanted it to sound like it was actually happening, so we called the National Weather Service to find out what the weather was the night of October 17,1971 in Baltimore, Maryland. We researched what songs were popular at that time, what was going on in the news, and interesting tidbits about the players.

The regular KMOX baseball credits rolled, and on came Jack Buck saying something like, "Hello everyone and welcome to Memorial Stadium in Baltimore, Maryland. I'm Jack Buck and along with my partner Mike Shannon we'll be bringing you the play-by-play of game seven of the World Series between the Orioles and the Pirates.

It's a warm night here at the ballpark and we'll be right back after this with the starting line-ups."

Clarence Nieder, a producer/engineer was just a whiz at sound effects. He had all sorts of sounds to use to make it sound like a live ballgame. There would be music from the time playing in the background as if being played at the ballpark and Clarence had sound effects like the crowd and the crack of the bat.

If you did not know these were re-creations you might think they were doing the games live because they went to so much trouble to make them perfect. Jack and Mike put in so much time and effort on those re-creation games, and the public really liked them.

Jack of course had done re-creations of games before, when he was a minor-league broadcaster. Those announcers didn't travel to the away games. They sat in the studio and took reports off the ticker, detailing each pitch during each at-bat, and "re-created" the games. The one thing Jack said he learned about those broadcasts was to never talk about the weather—in case the ticker broke, you could create an imaginary rain delay.

It was just a brilliant idea. Back in 1981, I was a twenty-three-year-old kid. Who knew that years later Rob, my husband, and I would be friends with the Buck family and it would be Rob who Carole and Jack would ask to co-write his autobiography. Jack and Mike were just a delight to work with on those re-creations. They were very nice to both Steve Overby, a KMOX sports assistant, and I. We were just little peons, but they really put a lot of trust in us as we did much of the research and gave them the information. I don't know if that type of thing would be done today, there was so much work involved, but they planned ahead and we worked long hours and they turned out great.

KMOX—THE SPORTS GIANT OF THE MIDWEST

RON JACOBER

Ron Jacober has "done it all" in his long broad-cast career and for the last 16 years he has been Director of Sports Operations at KMOX Radio in St. Louis.

Most of my contact with Jack was work-related in a sense. I would see him here at the office. I would see him at the ballpark. There wasn't a great deal of social contact with him because we both had our own lives. I've known Jack for twenty-five years because I was on television here in St. Louis for fifteen years prior to coming here to KMOX. I did Cardinal baseball on television and always did a pre-game show before those telecasts on the NBC affiliate when they had the rights. I did work with Jack some doing Cardinal baseball, not a tremendous number of games, but I'd do ten games a year probably. I wasn't the principal guy but I would replace Jay Randolph when he had a conflict.

For the last ten years, Jack really did not have much of a daily input into programming here at KMOX. It was pretty much mine. I remember calling him seven or eight years ago about something and said, "What do you think we should do?" He said, "Do whatever you want to do." I would see him frequently if he would come in here before he'd go to the ballpark when he was healthier. I talked to him on the phone frequently about a variety of things. He'd come in and regale us with stories and jokes in the office here.

I produced a two-hour special last year and aired it about four times. It was called "Jack Buck, the First Fifty Years." I wrote, produced, and hosted it. It was really kind of a trip through his broadcasting career here at KMOX with a lot of highlights and a lot of his poetry and a lot of his humor.

I recall the first time I worked with Jack. It was the first Cardinal telecast I ever did and we were at **Wrigley Field** in Chicago. I was petrified. I don't think I was petrified so much at doing the game—I was petrified at working with Jack because of his status. But the thing that amazed me was how easy it was. He made you feel so comfortable and so relaxed. I remember he said to me fairly early in the game, "You're here to do some play-by-play aren't you kid?" I said, "Yes sir." He said, "Well, do it." So he let me do a lot more play- by-play than normal, probably because he knew that's what I wanted to do.

After that when I had guys I knew were going to work with him for the first time, and they probably felt the same way I had, "My God, I'm gonna work with Buck. What should I do?" Or, "How should I approach him?" I would tell them that, "He will make you feel more comfortable than anybody. He is easy to work with. You'll pretty soon realize you can be very relaxed."

Ironically I was asked to stand by for his last scheduled appearance at the Missouri Athletic Club. It was in December, and they have a big sports banquet every year. I got a call and was told, "Jack is not sure that he can make the evening. Would you be willing to stand by as the emcee?" I said, "I'd love to, but I can't." We had a managers' retreat out of town. That was his last public appearance because he began that evening and did not finish and drove himself to the hospital for lung cancer surgery, so I didn't get to see him then.

The thing that I remember so warmly about Jack was his sense of humor. The man was a master of ceremonies beyond compare. No one could come close. I've done a lot of that and have often thought how inadequate I am compared to him. He could have been a stand-up comedian. He was so funny. He'd come prepared and he would rarely eat at these dinners—I'd see him writing all the time and

> More NFL games have been played at Wrigley Field than at any other stadium in the country. Mile High Stadium in Denver was in second place until demolished in 2001.

looking at the crowd and checking out the room—who was there or wasn't there. He'd come prepared with material, but he developed a great deal of it after he got there. He did baseball writers' dinners for many years. He did the Missouri Athletic Club dinner for many years. For most people, even though these were essentially award dinners, the highlight of the evening was Jack's stand-up routine, usually in the beginning. He'd have people laughing in the aisles. He was funny. No question, that will certainly be one of my lasting memories of Jack—his ability to make people laugh. He could do it. He could get away with things at dinners that nobody else could either. He could zing people that nobody else could zing and get away with it.

Now, his play-by-play skill was just phenomenal. He was so good. He was very good at football, he's in the Football Hall of Fame. He even did hockey. Most people don't know that he did a lot of the Blues' games the very first year of their existence. He called their first goal ever. His great love, I'm sure, was baseball.

There was a great headline in the paper when he died: "The Voice of St. Louis and The Soul of the City." I thought that just put it so well. He really was the soul of the city. He was pretty outspoken when it came to his feelings about this country. He was a patriot. I said, "If you could look at his heart, there's probably an American flag on it." He would cry. I used to kid him that he'd cry when the sun comes up. I think the National Anthem made him cry a lot. Men and women in uniform were very special to him.

The thing that I guess I was most impressed with him as a person was the way he treated common people—bellhops, busboys, cleaning people. He would know their first names. A lot of people that I know looked down upon those people. He came from poverty so he understood where they were. He'd be sitting in here at a talk show and the cleaning people would come to empty the trash can, and he would get to know their name and their family. That so impressed me.

We have a lot of young producers here, kids in college, or kids right out of college, who never had much money. He'd come in sometimes and say hello to them and shake hands with them and they'd find a fifty or a hundred in their hand. He did that a lot. He was very, very generous especially with people that he knew needed it. Stories are legendary about him. We heard so much on the air when he passed— stories we'd never heard of from people we'd never heard of—about things of kindness that he did, not necessarily money.

There was a story about a young guy who was slightly retarded who worked at the ballpark. I guess he was going to lose his job because he had lost his ride, or he didn't have a car or whatever. Jack would go pick him up, bring him to the park, and take him home afterwards. There was stuff that we heard that just made me want to cry. I knew he was a very generous guy, and I saw the evidence of that a lot. I've seen a bowl of soup cost him three hundred bucks after games— because you could never pick up a check. You could never pay a check. I don't know how he worked it out. I guess he'd tell the maitre'd, "I don't want that guy paying." Somehow he worked it out. He'd always pick up the check.

I was in the booth when **Mark McGwire** hit number sixty-two to break Roger Maris's record. Mike Shannon made the call. I was just sitting over in the corner because there was no other place in the darn ballpark to sit. Between the next half inning, Jack looked at Mike, and said, "Mike, I'm glad you got to call it." Obviously it was one of the most historic calls in baseball history—breaking that long-standing home run record. They both had tears in their eyes.

Mark McGwire's brother, Dan McGwire, once a starting quarterback for the Iowa Hawkeyes and a former #1 pick of the Seahawks, is the tallest NFL QB ever at 6' 8". Former NBA star and Toronto Blue Jay, Danny Ainge, is the tallest major league second baseman ever.

WILL IT PLAY IN PEORIA? THEY DID!
PETE VONACHEN

Pete Vonachen is the King of Baseball in Peoria, Illinois. He owns the Cardinals' Class A Midwest League affiliate. The legendary Vonachen was a very close friend of Harry Caray and through Harry became a big buddy of Jack Buck.

I knew Jack Buck very well. He worked with Harry Caray from 1954 to about 1969 when Harry left. I spent a lot of time with Harry. Jack and Harry got along very well. They were really, really good friends, and Jack really respected Harry. Their styles were different but they meshed together. Because Harry had so much respect for Jack and vice versa, they just got along famously. I don't know of any time when there was any disagreement on the air.

Jack used to come to Peoria, but not lately because he wasn't feeling good. He used to come on those Cardinal Caravans all the time—he loved the caravans. Jack was a real people person. He realized that a lot of these players wouldn't go on the Caravan—that was beneath them. That's why these press Caravans aren't as successful as they used to be. That's why the Cubs have dropped theirs because they can't get any players to go. I remember the last time Jack was here, he and Al Hrabosky were like kids in a candy store. They were having a great time. I think one of the last bastion of stars to come was Whitey Herzog. Whitey loved to come on the caravans, too, but the players—I think they paid them two thousand bucks or so, and with the salaries they're making, they're not going to ride around on a bus in the middle of winter for four days. I remember back in the 1960s when the Cardinal Caravan would come here, and they'd have Harry Caray, Jack Buck, Lou Brock, Red Schoendienst, Joe Cunningham, Dal Maxvill; one year they had Stan Musial. All the big guns came then on the caravan, but then you get this new breed of players that you've got now, and they won't sign an autograph let alone ride around on a bus in the middle of winter. It's different.

When Jack would come to Peoria, I'd tell the guys, "Don't eat." They'd usually have a chicken dinner or something like that, but we have Jim's Steak House which is probably one of the best steakhouses in the country anywhere and we'd all go there. We'd have dinner and then we'd start making the rounds. We'd hit the good Budweiser saloons, and we'd just have a ball. These guys didn't say, "Well, I don't want to go in these places. I might have to sign an autograph." That wasn't the attitude at all. They'd say, "Hey, where are the good places? Let's go. Let's have some fun." It's altogether different today.

Whenever I went down to St. Louis, I would always see Jack. I knew Mike Shannon from coming on the Caravans. He used to like to hunt and I could line him up with duck hunting up here. Bob Harland, now chairman of the Green Bay Packers, was running the Caravan in those days. The first time he came up I was involved on the original board of the Children's Hospital of Illinois and so I set it up for them to get here early so they could go to the Children's Hospital. Jack Buck and Mike Shannon were unbelievable, the way they whistled through those kids and the way they got the other players involved with them. He is just a great, great PR guy for baseball.

> "I thought Jack was a genius. I really meant that. The man had so many talents. I don't think a lot of people have a full understanding of how gifted he was, not just as a broadcaster."
>
> Tony LaRussa

JACK BUCK WAS A BUST!
HARRY WEBER

Harry Weber was raised in south St. Louis, left for a number of years and returned to Bowling Green, Missouri. There he became a full-time sculptor, with the Cardinals as his biggest client. He has recently finished a statue of Jackie Stiles, Southwest Missouri State's record-setting Lady Bear hoopster.

In 1996, I went to the Cardinal management and showed them a little statue of Ozzie Smith. They said they didn't want to do a statue of him right away, but they wanted to do statues of all the Hall of Fame Cardinals with retired numbers, which was a great job. It has been a lot of fun. There are four, and Ozzie now makes five, living Hall of Famers, and we've done all five of them. The five are Ozzie Smith, Stan Musial, Red Schoendienst, Bob Gibson and Lou Brock. The statues are right outside on the north side of Busch Stadium. I also did Dizzy Dean, **Rogers Hornsby**. Cool Pappa Bell, and the late Enos Slaughter.

I first went to the Cardinals because I thought maybe there was a shot at doing a statue of Ozzie, not even a big one, just kind of a small, commemorative one. I was quite surprised and very pleased and thrilled when they said they wanted to do a bunch of them.

I guess the second year we were into it—we'd already finished Gibson and Musial and Schoendienst—these were already finished and up. The Cardinal owners knew at that time that Jack Buck was ailing. He already had pretty advanced signs of Parkinson's and they wanted to do something for him before he retired because he was

> Rogers Hornsby holds the single season batting average record for three different major league teams—the Cardinals, the Cubs, and the Giants.

making noises about possibly retiring within the next couple of years. They wanted to make sure to get something before he did that. The original plan was to put the statue, which was a bust, just outside the broadcast booth—on the wall outside the broadcast booth. Then as everyone sort of contemplated, they said, "Heck no. He's as much a Hall-of-Famer as any of the other guys so let's get a special spot." It is directly outside the main entrance of the administrative offices and the ticket office on the west side of the stadium. They had a ceremony for him that year, and it was one of the most exciting things I've ever done. There were just wall-to-wall people and wall-to-wall celebrities.

Before I actually started, I went to see Carole and I met with Jack a couple of times. Jack is—was—I keep saying is because it's hard to realize he's not around. There's so much of him around that it's hard to believe that he's not. He had an amazing ability to be gracious regardless of the situation. He was a very humble character, but he took this with amazing good grace and seemed to like it. The statement he made when we put it up was "If you want to ever find me during the winter, come by, and I'll be cruising around the stadium looking at my statue." He wanted the owners to know that he really did see it as an honor and a tribute.

My stock in trade is action portraits—people actually doing something, moving. I usually look at films and make sketches off the films. In Jack's case it was a special kind of thing because most people don't see Jack Buck, they hear him, and they've got a mental image of what he looks like when he talks. So the challenge was to make a sculpture that looked like Jack Buck sounded and show that friendly confidence that he had, and beyond that, a sense of wit and a sense of finding joy in darn near everything. It was a lot of fun to do. He came up here two or three times to Bowling Green.

When he'd come up here, we'd sit down and have lunch—he survived my chili. We would look at all the pictures that Carole had collected. We didn't pick any particular one. We just picked an age for this statue. We said, "Let's make him about fifty." The challenge was you've got a living adult close to eighty years of age. His career started when he was twenty-five, and where do you pick an age to immortalize him. Everybody sort of agreed that it was the "silver fox" era where his hair was gray and he was just a real slick looking character. Once you're around him, that voice matches the face and the mannerism so well. I'm not very good at words but it was a quiet confidence that he had about every situation that made everybody comfortable immediately. I think his big talent was that he made everybody he met feel better themselves and act better than themselves most of the time. He raised the level of the people he met.

He and Carole came up and punched around with it a little bit. He wanted to make sure that one ear was covered. He said he had the world's biggest ears, and he wanted to make sure that at least one of them was covered. The old-time broadcasters' trick of putting your hand up against your ear so that you can hear the way your voice is broadcasting out was what we did. The statue is a bust and all busts are hollow so it only weighs a couple of hundred pounds. But you put it on the granite column, and you've got some tonnage there. It shows Jack from his chest up. Both his arms are visible, and he's holding a pencil.

We took it down to St. Louis in the back of a truck and installed it like all the others. Jack makes eleven statues that are down there now. When Jack died, I got several calls and interviews about the process of creating the statues.

The day I first went down to the Cardinals to talk about doing a statue for them, I met with Fred Hanser, one of the owners. Bill DeWitt and Fred were the ones who wanted to do this program. The funny thing is if you put up a sculpture, it's like a billboard and people keep asking who did them, and I get calls and I've had fortunately all the work my body can hold for the last seven or eight years, which is delightful.

I was traveling, showing horses, when Jack died. We came back to St. Louis to go to the service down at the ballpark and to the funeral. His death was something everybody had been prepared for, but I don't think anybody really was prepared for it because he meant so much to so many people. It was an odd situation for a celebrity—when a celebrity dies, there's usually a large amount of curiosity, but there's less empathy. But here it was ninety-nine percent empathy.

The way I got into sculpting just happened naturally. I was drawing even before I could talk. There hasn't been a day I've been alive I haven't drawn at least one picture. Sculpting is just an extension of that. I found out it was actually easier for me to work three-dimensionally than it was in two dimensions. It's something I've always done for fun. When I came back from Vietnam, I realized people would actually buy the stuff. I had, what I euphemistically call, a real job that kept the family fed and did sculpting on the side. Over a period fifteen or twenty years, the sculpting became a bigger money producer than the real job and finally about ten or twelve years ago, we shut down the real job completely.

A lot of the work I had been doing was wildlife, equestrian pieces, anything with a lot of movement in it, so I really wanted to get into sports. I knew there was an opportunity there, plus the fact I loved baseball, and had played baseball a little bit in college. I grew up a Browns fan and when they left town, I switched over to the Cardinals. I thought it was a good opportunity so I just took a shot at doing a statue of Ozzie. This was evidently in the back of their minds for a long time to do something to feature the Cardinal legacy and the tradition of the franchise. The owners have done a better job than any bunch of owners of putting the teams' history on a real-life basis. You see Brock and Musial and everybody there all the time. They're taking part and it's great.

JACK BUCK COULD EVEN CRY IN SPANISH
JIM JACKSON

Ask any broadcaster about the producer-engineer, especially a broadcaster who has spent several years with one team, and one will likely hear the value of that person. Even though fans listening at home hear the producer-engineer's name but almost never hear his voice, a good one is as valuable to the broadcast as the announcers. Longtime radio producer-engineer Jim Jackson first met Jack Buck while working an NFL game in St. Louis. Currently, Jackson is in his fifth season as the producer-engineer for the Cardinals Radio Network, four of which he worked closely with Jack.

This is my fifth season with the Cardinals, so I suppose I only worked four seasons with Jack since he never made an appearance in the booth this year. I have to say that the experience was unbelievable; it was terrific. I've been doing sports as an engineer and producer for about twenty years. I've had the opportunity to work with a lot of different people. There is no one who was as good to work with as Jack was. His son Joe, while younger, is right there. But, in my experience, there was nobody like Jack.

Obviously, I stepped into a mature broadcast where Jack and Mike Shannon had been working together for twenty-five years. After we'd gone through the first couple weeks of spring training in that first season of working with these guys, I said to Jack after a game, "I'm still new to you guys, so is there anything that you would like me to do differently? Is there anything that you'd like me to change? What's your comfort level?" He gave me this real quizzical look and said, "Well, like what?" Again, I asked him if there was anything I could do to help them, or make them feel comfortable with me. He said, "You're doing fine, kid, don't worry about a thing." He called everybody "kid."

Upon occasion, in spring training, for example, if perhaps Joe wasn't going to make a game, Jack and I would ride together to wherever the game was. Jack was the best traveling companion that I had ever been around. He'd get in the car, and maybe we had to drive a couple of hours, but he never took a nap when he was in the car. He told jokes, sang songs, recited poetry and had a conversation from the time he got in the car until the time he got out. He didn't do it to the point to where you would want to tell him to give it a break, but he was just a great traveling companion.

It was a real thrill when I first stepped into the booth to work with him. It was even better than I thought it would be. I had been told that he was great to work with, but until I actually sat in there and experienced it, it was incredible. There were days in the last few years when he was battling Parkinson's, which was very difficult for him, but he never complained about it. He would make a joke about it, and you could tell that he was uncomfortable sometimes, but I never saw him in a bad mood.

I held the microphone for him during interviews the last few years for a couple of reasons. Number one was because of the dexterity issue with the Parkinson's. Secondly, we had gone to digital recorders instead of cassette recorders, so that technology was a little foreign to him—like it is to a lot of people.

Doing that got to be fun for me. I'd go along, and he'd interview Tony LaRussa, the opposing manager or a player, and it was fun. Plus, it wouldn't matter if they were an American kid or from one of the Latin American countries, because a lot of times with the Latin players, Jack would break the ice by talking Spanish to them. I can't tell you how good his Spanish was, because I don't know, but apparently, it was passable. He always made his point and seemed to understand what the other person was saying. Sometimes when you go to interview a young player from, say, the Dominican Republic, he may not be comfortable with his English and doesn't necessarily want to do an interview because of that. So, Jack would break the ice by talking Spanish to the player first, and putting his mind at ease about the interview. Invariably, the people that he interviewed would walk away with a smile. It was interesting to see that.

When you sit down and analyze his play-by-play, especially on the Cardinal network, not only did he tell you about the action, but he did it at the same time that he was telling stories. Here's a guy who had been in the game since the early 1950s. He met so many great players, but he also did so many different types of talk shows at KMOX. There are pictures in our booth at Busch Stadium of Jack in a radio studio doing a call-in show, with Dizzy Dean. Next to that photo is one of him doing a call-in show with Jackie Robinson. These are not pictures of when these guys were players; they're from when these guys were beyond the game. He had a wealth of knowledge from doing this for such a long time. Ernie Harwell is another one. These guys have so much experience, that not only can they call an enjoyable baseball game, but in the meantime, they can tell these stories, spin yarns, and talk about the old days of baseball. Jack was a great storyteller. Even if the game was bad, the broadcast was interesting.

There's a place in St. Louis called Carl's, where they make their own root beer. He loved the hamburgers at Carl's. He found out one time that I went to Carl's, so every once in awhile during a game, he'd pull the owner's business card out of his pocket. He'd ask me to call over there and see if they were busy. Carl's is just a tiny place with two little counters, but I'd call over there ask if they were busy. Usually they'd be pretty busy. I'd tell Jack and he'd say, "They ain't seen nothing yet, kid." Then he'd plug Carl's on the air, and about ten minutes later he'd say to me, "Call Carl's and see how busy they are now." He and I always joked that we'd meet over at Carl's one day. We never did get around to eating at Carl's together.

He didn't plug Carl's all the time. In fact, he'd maybe do it twice a year. When some announcers mention a place like that on the air, you figure that they got a free meal there, or there's something else being comped. Jack, I can guarantee you, never got a free hamburger from Carl's. Even though I never went there with him, I can guarantee that he never accepted a free hamburger. If anything, they'd probably try to comp him his two-dollar hamburger and his one-dollar root beer, and he'd leave a 20-dollar bill on the counter.

So many of Jack's significant calls have been played since he passed away. One that got a lot of play was McGwire's 62nd home run. That's

Photo courtesy of Christine Buck

Filming a Busch Bavarian Ad in the late 50's.

In 1979 Busch Bavarian was the top-selling beer in St. Louis
when Anheuser-Busch decided to drop "Bavarian" from the
brand name.

"No, Gussie. It says I'll work for free if I'm the exclusive beer distributor to Harry Caray."

Jack Buck, St. Louis University Basketball Coach John Bennington and Ed Macauley.

Post-Dispatch

Most bowlers are steroid-free. Jack Buck's Bavarian Bowling Team. Roy Sievers is on the left (1959).

KMOX

Dick Groat, Jack Buck, Bob Broeg and Bob Burnes, 1965. Note construction of the Arch and Busch Stadium in the background.

not my favorite. My favorite is number sixty. It starts out with, "Lookie there, lookie there…" That's something that just popped into his head. I like that one better than number 62. My favorite Jack call, and I didn't work with him at the time, was the Ozzie Smith home run.

I do remember during the 1964 World Series celebration, when I was just a kid, they were having a locker room celebration, and of course there was champagne and probably some Anheuser-Busch products being spilled all over the place. I remember seeing a clip on TV from that where he said something like, "Watch out, boys. You can get that stuff on my two hundred dollar suit, but watch out for my five dollar tie."

In the Abbott and Costello routine "Who's on First," the name of the team was the St. Louis Wolves. Only two real major leaguers were mentioned in the full skit: Dizzy Dean and his brother Paul.

YOU CAN'T GET INTO HEAVEN UNLESS YOU'RE A CARDINAL FAN

PAULA HOMAN

Paula Homan is the curator of the Cardinals' Hall of Fame and Museum and was in charge of cataloging all of the items that were left at Jack Buck's statue after his death.

Jack died on a Tuesday and by Wednesday and Thursday the amount of items people had left at his statue was pretty amazing. The following Monday was when we chose to pick everything up. We did that in part because there were chances of rain every single day that week. I just thought it would be a real disservice to leave the gifts out there and then have it get rained on repeatedly. Even after that next weekend, there were a lot of people standing around on the day we were picking things up. They all wanted to know what we were doing with it all. I said that we were collecting it and were going to try to organize it and present the list of information to the family so at some point they could figure out what they would like to do with it.

The list of contributions covered around 40 pages of the things we decided to list. None of the stuff in binders is listed, and none of the signs are listed. We couldn't figure out any way to list a sign. You need to see the signs. Amazing!

So much stuff was left there that it was really overwhelming. It's one thing to just stand and look at the stuff as a piece. It's another thing to actually have to be the person that goes through and touches every item and tries to write a list. I was just consistently amazed at people who composed poetry, little kids would do drawings—you would find some little note scrawled on some scrap of paper torn out of a magazine or something. It was like people would be there and would say to themselves, "Oh, my God. What can I put in here? I need to put something in here." Then you can just imagine them going to the car and scrambling around looking for something in their car that they can write their note on so they can go drop it and have it be in there as part of that memorial. Then there were people who spent a great amount of time and effort and made huge banners. One lady created stuffed pillow-like shapes. I mistakenly thought it was like a rather primitive looking Cardinal, but someone pointed out to me that it was a broken heart. It was half of a broken heart. I was like, "Oh, that's so much better." There were candles. Some guys left beer. There was one thing that was like an open can of Busch beer and it had a bill—a buck—one buck, stuck on the opening. Whatever that meant? "This Bud's for you?" Or something like that. I did notice that at some point there was a six-pack of bottled beer out there. The next day when I was actually collecting, there weren't six any more. Somebody probably thought Jack didn't need that many. People left radios. Somebody had left a little radio they had tuned in to KMOX so the whole time that people are out there and observing and sort of reverently attending this memorial, they were listening to the radio. You could hear this small tinny KMOX in the background.

It was interesting that there was so much variety and it was interesting that there were so many things that were the same. I had one whole box of flags and patriotic things. I had one whole box of batting helmets of all sizes—the ones that actually fit on your head down to the ones they serve ice cream and nacho chips in at the stadium. Most of those had writing on them. Then there would be one box that would be toys—teddy bears and beanie babies and different little stuffed animal things. Then the people who would leave candles. And the people who would leave caps—I can't imagine how many caps we really have.

When we first brought them down, the caps were all piled on one table. It looked like it was piled three-feet high.

How proud his family must feel.

Chapter 8

West of the Arch East of the Pecos

Denny Mathews

Ned Reynolds

Dick Kaegel

Fred White

Jerald Andrews

EVERYTHING'S UP TO DATE IN KANSAS CITY
DENNY MATTHEWS

Denny Matthews, the oldest of four boys, grew up in the Illinois twin cities of Normal and Bloomington. His dad, George (Matty), was a Cardinals fan and listened to Jack Buck and Harry Caray seemingly every night during the summer months. In 1969, at the age of 26, Matthews teamed with Buddy Blattner to form the first radio crew for the expansion Kansas City Royals. Today, 34 seasons later, Matthews continues to be the voice of the Royals. He is one of a handful of major-league broadcasters to have called games in each of five decades.

Jack had a tremendous amount of professionalism. He certainly was versatile—he did a lot of things such as being a disc jockey, did basketball, baseball, football, among pretty much everything else. He was a great emcee with a great sense of humor. He was always very helpful for me. He was easy to get to know, easy to talk to. He never gave off the impression that he was one step above you.

His mannerisms, to me, were funny. I would see him in spring training before every season. It was never, "Hey, Denny, how are you?" or "How was your winter?" The first time we saw each other during spring training he'd walk up to me and say, "This is how many years for you?" That was always the first thing out of his mouth. Then he'd usually ask if I was married yet, and ask how my family was doing in Illinois. I always enjoyed that, because I could tell you what he was going to say.

He was very quick-witted and off the cuff. I remember one night when I was listening to a game when the Cardinals were playing in New York at Shea Stadium, where the planes were roaring out. It's tough to talk above the roar, so when a plane would go over, he would pause for twenty or twenty-five seconds and then continue with the game. This particular night, that went on for five or six innings. Finally, after pausing for a plane he said, "Well, there goes some more lost luggage."

As a listener, particularly a young listener, you're probably picking up some phrases and such through osmosis. I'm sure there's some Harry Caray-type description in the way I call a game. I'm sure there is some Jack Buck descriptive style or phraseology that's there naturally. I know there was a tremendous influence from them. When I was growing up, I was thinking more about playing than broadcasting, so the games were secondary. For me, the broadcasts were just a conduit through which I enjoyed baseball, got the info and followed my team. As I sat there wanting the Cardinals to win, with these guys describing the games, I wasn't thinking that I wanted to do that one day. It was more of my subconscious picking it up. Even if I wanted to, I don't see how that can be avoided.

Buck told me a story one time about when he worked at KMOX-TV. Apparently, there was a guy in the St. Louis area who was in his early sixties, playing full-check hockey. He was ramming people in to the boards and that type of thing. Jack called him wanting to do a feature on the guy. When he talked to the guy, he said, "I do all of that stuff, but that's not much of a story. You should do a story on my dad. My dad is eighty-one years old and he does Tae Kwon Do, bowls and plays golf. He's an incredible athlete. You should do the story on him."

Jack said he got the guy's name and number, and called him. The guy said, "Sure, I do all of that stuff. It's fine if you want to do a feature on me, but you ought to do one on my dad. He is absolutely incomprehensible. This guy gets up every morning and eats breakfast before going out to jog half a mile. He comes back and calls his buddies to play golf or go bowling. He does some aerobic things at the gym. He's a great athlete." Jack said he asked, "How old is he?" The guy replied, "He's coming up on his ninety-ninth birthday. Besides that, he's getting married!" Jack said, "Why would a guy ninety-nine years old want to get married?" The guy replied, "Well, he didn't *want* to get married…" Buck just carried that story on and on and on. I was rolling when he delivered the punch line. That's a pretty typical Jack Buck story.

THERE ARE TWO WAYS TO GET RICH IN LOCAL SPORTS TV: MARRY A RICH GIRL OR WORK HARD FOR 30 YEARS AND THEN MARRY A RICH GIRL
NED REYNOLDS

Ned Reynolds of KY3-TV in Springfield, MO. Has been a towering figure on the Ozarks TV scene for years. He will soon commence his 37th year on air.

Jack Buck has come here to Springfield on a number of occasions. Of course we have interviewed him and he is a member of the Missouri Sports Hall of Fame, too. We've entertained him on several occasions down here in that capacity. He has been nothing but genuinely an outstanding individual.

I first met Jack back in 1969 or 1970. He had accompanied the Cardinals down here with the Cardinal Caravan. I had the opportunity to visit with him then and interview him. He gave me a terrific interview. I was nothing but impressed with him on that occasion, especially with his wit and marvelous sense of humor. He took his profession seriously but was able to combine that with quite a bit of humor. I think that's what made the man very special.

The last time Jack Buck came down here, he was becoming more severely afflicted with the Parkinson's symptoms at the time. He actually made sport of the whole thing. I remember him standing in front of a Springfield audience in May, 2000, with Stan Musial. We had an auction, and there were probably seven, eight hundred people there, and we were auctioning off various items, one of which was a painting. It may have been a Ken Griffey painting, but whatever it was, he held his hand up and bid for it and won it. When he got up later, he said, "Well, actually I wasn't bidding. That was the Parkinson's that you saw. But I'll get Ken Griffey, Jr. to sign this painting, and I'll make five thousand dollars on it." That brought down the house.

He was the consummate professional, a man who had a brilliant sense of articulation. Really in all honesty, he was the best—the best— baseball announcer that these ears have ever heard, and probably ever will. The man was articulate to the point that he flowed so smoothly. While it sounds easy, and he made it sound easy, it is not. It's a very difficult talent to be able to maintain that sense that he was able to on the radio for so many years. He was just brilliant in his profession.

As I left the station in mid-June, word came over on the wire that he was gravely ill. Normally the Associated Press doesn't report on anything like that unless an individual's death is imminent. So I thought, "Uh-oh, this is not good. Looks like it's probably within the next twenty-four to forty-eight hours." But the very next morning, when I came in to do our sports reporter show on the radio was when I found out that he had passed on. It wasn't surprising of course since he'd been in the hospital for five months. Still it's a sense of a loss for a guy who has been part of our whole sports fabric here in the Ozarks—well all over, as far as that's concerned. When someone like that is taken away from you, while it isn't a surprise, it still comes as something of a shock.

After his death, we called in my partner here at the station at four a.m. He did a two, two-and-a-half minute pictorial piece on Jack Buck, which we ran in our morning and our noon newscast. We pretty much covered and encompassed everything that went on there. We did not cover it on our own. We don't have the staff to do that. Since the event was going on, and was covered on television, we just took what happened there in St. Louis. We had a number of people from this area who identified very strongly with the Cardinals and with Jack Buck go up to the ceremonies.

It won't be the same.

RAPP SINGER

DICK KAEGEL

Dick Kaegel has long been known as one of the most respected baseball writers in the Midwest. The St. Louis native was a Cardinals beat writer for the St. Louis Post-Dispatch *during the 1970s and early 1980s, before heading west to the* Kansas City Star, *where he has covered the Royals since the mid-1980s.*

The best story I can remember about Jack was in 1978 when Vern Rapp was the manager. He and Jack didn't exactly get along too well. I think Rapp was reluctant to do interviews, which Jack of course needed from the manager all the time.

We were in Montreal, and I got a call from my wife at the time, she said there was a big hubbub on KMOX. Apparently, Jack had broken a story that he was in the Cardinal clubhouse when Rapp was having a meeting with Ted Simmons. Rapp made the mistake of leaving the door partly open. Several people, including Jack, overheard Rapp call Simmons a "loser." Jack decided to break the story on the evening talk show. Of course, that caused a big commotion in St. Louis because Simmons was a very popular player.

I called Simmons in his room and told him about it. He said, "Oh my gosh! I can't talk to you now, I gotta go talk to Jack."

We were an afternoon paper then, so I had some time before my deadline for the next day. Being the "clever" reporter that I am, I figured Jack would be in the bar downstairs of the Le Centre Hotel. I went downstairs, and sure enough, he was there, so I sat down with him. A few minutes later, Simmons came running down. There we were—Jack, Simmons and me sitting at the table. They were having an agitated conversation about the story. I was a little concerned because a couple tables over was Jack Herman from the *Globe-Democrat*, St. Louis' morning paper at that time. I knew I had a story in front of me, but I was concerned about Jack Herman overhearing us, and getting the story for the next morning.

For whatever reason, he didn't overhear what was happening, his office didn't call him and tell him what was going on at KMOX. I absorbed quite a bit from the conversation between Jack and Ted. I wrote a story about it, it was breaking news, and it caused a big commotion in St. Louis.

The next day we had an afternoon game. I finished my story, and I was walking down Crescent Street, which is where all the restaurants and clubs are in Montreal. I was ready to have a nice night on the town. I walked by a restaurant and who walks out of the door, but Jack Buck. With a toothpick in his mouth, he said, "Well, they did it, didn't they?" I asked him, "What do you mean, Jack? They did what?" He replied, "Oh, they fired Rapp." Needless to say, I had to make a quick U-turn, and my evening plans changed dramatically.

I will always remember that about Jack, because if I hadn't run into him that night on Crescent Street, I might have missed the whole Rapp firing story.

Famous Calls

On Kirk Gibson's home run agains Oakland in the World Series, Oct. 15, 1988:

"Gibson swings, and a fly ball to deep right field. This is gonna be a home run! Unbelievable! A home run for Gibson! And the Dodgers have won the game, 5-4! I don't believe what I just saw!"

THE BIGGEST HOMER ANNOUNCER IN THE BIG LEAGUES
FRED WHITE

Fred White grew up in the small Midwestern town of Homer, Illinois—a town of about 1,000 people, located nearly halfway between Chicago and St. Louis—baseball loyalties in the White household were divided. His dad was a Cardinals fan. His mom and brother were Cubs fans. His sister couldn't care less. Fred's loyalties went south to the Cardinals. (Homer is also the hometown of sports marketing guru Ray Compton, currently with the Indianapolis Colts.) Although he has worked college basketball and football games for CBS, NBC, Raycom and ESPN, White gained notoriety as a longtime radio announcer for the Kansas City Royals. In fact, he spent 25 years behind the microphone with Denny Matthews. White currently is the Royals Director of Broadcast Services and the Royals Director of Alumni.

I still lived in Central Illinois when Jack started with the Cardinals in 1954. I listened to him when I was a young guy growing up. I was a Cardinal fan, and I wasn't sure Harry Caray could be replaced until I heard Jack take it over. When Jack became *the* guy with the Cardinals, and he expanded his horizon, so to speak, there was no doubt that Harry could be replaced and had been replaced.

I think the best broadcasting pair ever was Jack and whoever he was working with. Harry and Jack were good together. Harry was bombastic, and Jack had that dry wit. I remember being at a function with them when they worked together. Harry said something like, "I would go to H--- to do this." Jack replied, "Good, I'll probably be in H--- doing the middle innings."

Jack had a great sense of humor. He could be dry or he could be caustic. He was smart enough to realize Harry's style, play off Harry, and make something out of it for himself.

JACK BUCK WAS JUST A REGULAR GUY WHO SOMETIMES WORE A CAPE

JERALD ANDREWS

Jerald Andrews is the executive director of the Missouri Sports Hall of Fame in Springfield. He was raised near Bolivar, Missouri.

In May, 2000 Jack was named a Missouri Sports Legend, which is the highest level of recognition that the Hall of Fame has designated to be placed upon anyone related to Missouri sports. Then we had him back in 2001, and he and Stan Musial came together. At that time, the Missouri Sports Legend program had advanced far enough that we had bronze busts of both of them commissioned and they were both here to unveil their bronze bust. Both of them spoke that day as well.

I asked Mike Roarty to introduce Jack. Mike said, "I'll do it, but I'm gonna do it with a tape and I'm gonna have Jack introduce himself." He brought this tape and everybody refers to it as the Fathers' Day tape. Jack did not write it; he merely read it. In essence, it's a short epilogue of baseball in America and growing up playing catch with your dad. It ends by saying, "I don't know about you, but I'd give anything if I could play catch with my dad just one more time." It's a wonderful piece. Although Jack did not write it, it represents everything that Jack Buck was.

I grew up on a dairy farm west of Bolivar. If you've read Grisham's book, *A Painted House*, it could just as likely have been written about me as it was about a kid in a cotton farm in Arkansas. I grew up listening to Buck and Caray call Cardinal games. About our biggest form of entertainment was either playing baseball or listening to the Cardinals with my dad.

Chapter 9

So Say You One, So Say You All

A friend invited me to join him at a Cardinals-Braves game in August, 2001 to spend two innings in the broadcast booth with Jack and Mike. On a perfect late summer evening, we sat in field box seats for the first two innings and then were ushered to the elevator where we road to the press box area—riding up with Bob Broeg—and then into the area where writers sit and watched another inning waiting for our turn. Then we were ushered into the KMOX booth. It was just as dusk set and the lights were beginning to glow. As we walked in and stood at the top of the booth behind Jack and Mike, it was as if we had entered "heaven," for all we could see was the field and it was bathed in a golden glow. We spent the next two innings sitting behind the broadcast team, enjoying the experience and tasting Cardinal heaven. Jack graciously welcomed us and shook our hands as did Mike. I will forever treasure that memory.

——BOB PICKETT, Grace Church, St. Louis, MO

On a road trip in Pittsburgh, Bob Starr, who was sleeping in the buff, got up to relieve himself at about 2 a.m., he came out of the bathroom and half asleep opened the door, which happened to be the door to the hallway and went out. The slamming of the door behind him woke him up and he realized he was stark naked in the hotel hall. After a while, a bellboy came and an embarrassed Starr waited while he went to get a master key to let him back in. The next morning Starr told this to his broadcast partner who would also be one of his golfing buddies that day. Jack Buck told the rest of the guys including Mike Shannon, Tom Barton, and Lee Thomas. Jack said, "Excuse me, I've got to run upstairs and get my golf shoes. I'll meet you guys at the cab out in the front." When Bob got back he called his wife and once again she said "Tell me I didn't hear Jack Carney say what he did this morning after talking with Jack Buck!" Buck had gone up and called Jack Carney who broadcast it all over the airwaves.

——ROB RAINS, Author, St. Louis, MO

When Stan was recuperating from an operation, Jack would come by every day and bring him ice cream or he'd bring him pizza from his restaurant, J. Buck's. He'd walk in and say, "Well we're gonna play gin rummy today!" He brought magazines for him to read. He loved Stan and Stan loved him.

——LIL MUSIAL, wife of Hall of Famer Stan Musial.

Jack called me one year on the Fourth of July. I was cooking outside. The team was away. He said, "Are you listening to the game?" I said, "Yeah." He said, "Did you hear what Shannon just said to the Cardinal Nation?" I said, "What?" He said, "He just said that America is the greatest country in the USA." I said, "What are you gonna do?" He said, "I think I'm going to jump off the third deck here."

————MIKE ROARTY, Retired Marketing Whiz, Anheuser-Busch

When I was at KMOX, I worked with Jack Buck. Previously, I was marketing director at the largest bookstore in town, and had worked with him when his book came out. I had a big book-signing for him. That's where I got to know him. Having listened to him all my life, it was awe-inspiring to meet him. It was a privilege. The morning of the book-signing, we had KMOX there doing a live interview show at which Jack was the only guest. We had a live audience there. As he was leaving to go to lunch, one of the guests who had come to be on the show was a gentleman named Russ David. He'd had a big band back in my mother's era. His wife, Patti, was a singer in the band. They had come in to perform on the show that day. The three of them were going to go to lunch.

As they were walking out, I was standing there to say goodbye, and he was going to walk through this narrow walkway between a couple of book shelves. There was a bookseller there stocking the shelf. Her name was Jenny, and I guess she was in her early twenties. She pushed her cart to the side and stood to the side to allow Mr. Buck and the other two to go through. Jack goes up and sticks out his hand and says, "My name's Jack Buck. What's yours?" She said, "My name's Jenny, Mr. Buck." Apparently there's some song with Jenny in the name that was big way back when, and he started singing it to her. He said, "Have you ever heard that song?" She said, "No, Mr. Buck." "Well, your mother probably has." Here comes Russ and Patti David and the three of them are serenading this twenty-something-year-old who's turning all sheets of red. That's just the way he was. He was just so personal and sincere and charming, oozing charm to everyone.

————NANCY HIGGINS, St. Louis Public Relations Executive

We played the police department in an annual exhibition softball game. I'd play third and Marty Marion was playing shortstop, Red Schoendienst was at second, and Stan Musial was playing first base. Jack was the pitcher. We had Joe Cunningham in the outfield. We had a pretty good team.

The police department had a great big policeman who was a heck of a player—he was a heck of an athlete. Evidently, the Cardinals had signed him years ago and then released him. He was still upset because they released him.

He hit the hardest ball I've ever had hit at me in that game. I was playing third so I mean that's the hardest ball I've ever had hit at me. Willie Mays had hit them at me. This guy was hitting balls way back on the rooftops out of this ballpark in South St. Louis.

Anyway, after this guy hit a line drive, I went up to Jack and said, "Hey, pitch this guy outside, will you?" He said, "I'm closer than you are." I said, "OK, I'm backing up though, big boy."

———MIKE SHANNON, Buck's Broadcast Partner

There was a young boy, ten or eleven years old, here in St. Louis who was lighting a barbecue pit by himself with charcoal fluid. I was down there one day last summer, and I told him, "Jack, that thing you did for that O'Leary kid, is just absolutely the greatest thing I've ever heard." He said, "How do you know about that?" I said, "Well, none of your business. My wife is close to him, and I heard about it." He said, "You know, a lot of players went over to the hospital with me so that wasn't such a big deal." To me that was a big deal because Jack was always the one taking the players over there. Then he said to me, "Let me tell you one thing. That kid's a bigger hero and a got more bravery in his little finger than I've got in my whole body." That's just the kind of person he was. He was just unbelievable.

———JOHN KING, St. Louis Attorney

I worked on-site for Jack's last two CBS Radio broadcasts—Super Bowl XXX and the Pro Bowl. Those great moments, and great calls, will outlive me. They will outlive my kids. We don't have play-by-play calls of Ty Cobb, but because of technology, Jack's calls will live on.Anytime I hear any of Jack's calls, I can't help but smile. It's cool to be able tell people that I worked with Jack Buck.

———HOWARD DENEROFF, CBS Sports

We were doing a game in San Francisco, and we were all bolting to take the red-eye flight after the game. One of Jack's friends from the Bay area was at the game with his son, who was eight or nine years old. This guy was going to take us to the airport after the game. The game ran longer than we expected, and catching the flight was going to be on the tight side. As this guy was getting out of the traffic pattern to get away from the stadium, we came up to the last exit before you can get on the freeway. The guy made an illegal left turn. The cop wanted him to go straight and he didn't. The cop pulled him over, and the guy felt terrible. Jack and I were in the back seat with this guy's son. All of a sudden, I looked at Jack and he was reaching into his pocket. He peels out a hundred dollar bill. He hands it to the kid and whispers, "Give this to your dad, but not until you get home." Jack was taking care of the ticket and he didn't want the kid's father to know about it. It was amazing.

———PAT McGRATH, CBS Radio Statistician

There's a retirement home in St. Louis, Mari de Villa, and Jack was telling a story about when he paid a visit there to connect with all the elderly people. He said he gave a little talk about the Cardinals and so forth. Afterward, he saw a lady who was quiet, elderly, and unfortunately in a wheelchair, over in the corner. Just like Jack, he wanted to spend extra time with the person he felt needed it the most, so he walked over to her and said, "Ma'am, it's a pleasure to meet you." She gave him a bewildered look, so he said, "Ma'am, do you know who I am?" She said, "No, but if you go to the front desk they can tell you."

———MARK GORRIS, Kansas City Royals

The magic number is derived by adding one to the number of remaining games and subtracting the number of games ahead in the loss column from the second place team. The magic number decreases by one when the first place team wins or the second place team loses—this is also the recipe for chili.

———JACK BUCK, during a late season game in 1982

My mom lives in a rural area of Illinois, Knoxville, and they have a radio station, WGIL, in Galesburg which is part of the Cardinals network. My mom asked me one day about some show on the radio called Bucket Bat. "I don't understand what that means. What does that mean – bucket bat?" She says, "I'm imagining there's a bucket and there's a bat, but what does that mean? Bucket Bat—is that some kind of game?" I said, "Gee, mom, I don't know." Here's where my museum background comes in.—*I don't listen to KMOX radio very often*—I had to say, "I don't know what Bucket Bat is." It wasn't too much longer after that, I was telling my historian about it, and he said, "Oh, you mean "Buck at Bat." I said, "I'll bet that's it—Buck at Bat." That was Jack's pre-game show.

——PAULA HOMAN, St. Louis

One of my coaches here at the high school, baseball coach Dan Hecht, was at Busch Stadium as a very young boy. He had written a poem about the success of the Cardinals that year. They were in the pennant race. His father took the poem to the press box and gave it to someone up there. Mr. Buck actually read it during the game. He took it up there just kind of on a dare to see if Jack would read it. Actually they didn't even think they'd be able to get to the press box to get it into Mr. Buck's hands.

I'm very much a Cardinal fan. My lasting memory of Jack Buck would be as a young boy growing up just south of St. Louis. During the summer, everyone in our whole neighborhood was Cardinal fans. You could just walk in the neighborhood at night and could hear the radio at any number of houses. I remember walking home from playing ball at night. You would walk through our neighborhood and could yell over to Mr. So and So, "What's the score?" He'd yell the score. Then a couple of blocks down, you could yell at another neighbor, and be updated on the game all the way home.

——KEVIN BOHNERT, A.D. at Jackson (MO) High School

Jack Buck brought the game alive on the radio. You could almost picture the game better with him broadcasting it. His enthusiasm for the game. He was the kind of guy who was a Cardinal fan from the word go, but he was for other teams, too. He never came on like some of these announcers and would be prejudiced and say this or that. He was just an honest, good, truthful broadcaster. He loved the game. He was brought into it, and he started from scratch and worked his way up the ladder. The thing I remember most—I could just listen to him broadcast a game, and I could see what's happening. He made it live.

Jack was a broadcaster's broadcaster. He enjoyed the game, and he passed it on to you and made you feel good listening to it. I liked his line, "Thanks for your time this time till next time."

——DON SEBILLE, a 68-year-old fan in Iowa

In 1987 we were playing against San Francisco in St. Louis. They only had to win one game to win the pennant. Before the series I told Jack, "You know we're down, but by the end of this home stand, we're going to be headed toward the World Series." Jack replied, "Hey, I like that, but we better do something quick!" He said that so loud in front of the other guys. He was one of those guys who could keep everybody upbeat.

I remember catching Jack when he threw out the first pitch before a game. I remember that day like today. Before he threw it he told me, "I don't know if you're going to be able to reach over there, Tony, but just make sure you catch the ball." The ball made it to me and I caught it. When I handed the ball back to him he said, "I knew I could make it."

——TONY PENA, former Cardinal player, current KC Royals manager

Jack was the master. He could pick up something and make it work. I remember his cleverness, and how his mind was always at work. This game was dragging, and nothing was going on that anybody would want to listen to or watch. Up comes the catcher named Hal Naragon. Jack is babbling away about the game, when he says, "Hal Naragon coming to the plate. Do you know what a Naragon is, Carl? That's a no-sided figure." He just pulled that kind of stuff out of the air.

——CARL ERSKINE, Buck's broadcasting partner, early 1960s

My initial relationship with Jack happened in 1960 when the American Football League started. Jack did some work for ABC, and they televised some of our games. He'd come in the locker room and talk to the players. I saw him over the years, when he started doing the Monday night games on radio. When I retired in 1975, I would bump into Jack because I was a business manager for the Raiders. I did some color work on the games and worked with Jack. He worked hard to make me look good, and I really appreciated that.

Over the years, whenever I ran into him, he always called me his "TV mate." I'm a Midwest boy from Wisconsin, and somehow he knew that. He came up and would slap me on the back and wish me well. That was the type of guy he was. He liked to mingle with the athletes. He was friendly with everyone all the time. It wasn't a show. He was genuine. If you talked to any other athletes that knew him, they would tell you the same thing. That's what makes the greatness in the man.

——JIM OTTO, Retired Oakland Raiders Hall-of-Famer

One of my sign guys does all my signs at the Mallards…I didn't ask for him to do this, but he came out and gave me a beautiful sign as a surprise. On the back, it has the two Cardinals, but their heads are bowed. Underneath it is the script "Jack Buck." On the very top of it in the circle is the Darryl Kile #57 circle in remembrance of him. He made up a few of them. I put them up around the Mallards ballpark. I made the trek to St. Louis a week later and put the sign where the Buck and Kile flowers, caps, etc., were piled next to the offices at Busch Stadium. I put it down to the side of Jack Buck's picture. It's very fitting. It's the birds in the back, but the birds have their heads bowed and Jack Buck in black underneath the bat. It really came out cool. I have it in the store, too. So I have it in Busch Stadium, which I'm pretty thankful for, the Madison Mallards ballpark, and here in the store.

——STEVE SCHMITT, Black Earth, Wisconsin, a huge Cardinals fan and the owner of the minor league Madison Mallards and The Shoe Box, the largest shoe store in the Midwest

One day shortly after his book came out, I asked him if I got a book if he would mind signing it for me. He told me to go to Sam's Club, that they were cheaper there and we laughed. The very next day I was in the Cardinals locker room and here came Mr. Buck with one of his books signed to me. The first thing that came to my mind was, he went to Sam's himself? I was amazed first, that he remembered and second, that he took the time to go out of his way to give me the book personally.

——JOHN LACKEY, Cardinals Batting Practice Pitcher

I was working at WOSU, the Ohio State student station, when Woody Hayes was hired as the head football coach. When Ohio State was deciding who to hire in 1951, the *Columbus Dispatch* was endorsing Paul Brown of the Cleveland Browns. I didn't think the newspaper should dictate who the school should hire, so I said on the radio that the university, not the newspaper should make that choice. I didn't know Woody Hayes, but I said on the air that he would be a good candidate. Some of the fans didn't like it that I had taken a stand against the newspaper and found out where I lived and threw garbage on my front porch.

When football season began, I needed to learn more about his coaching style, so I enrolled in a football class he was teaching. Most of the other students were players on the team. I was sitting in the back of the class when Hayes singled me out one day, "Who are you?" he demanded. I told him who I was and explained that I broadcast the games and had enrolled in the class to learn what he was going to try to do. "Try to do?" he screamed at me. After a moment, he added, "Okay, but don't miss a class. If you miss one class, you're out." Years later when I was doing *Grandstand* for NBC-TV I was assigned to cover Woody and the Buckeyes during the Rose Bowl. Our cameraman sneaked into the dressing room ahead of time and was filming Woody while he was talking to his players. Woody stopped talking and barked at the cameraman, "What are you doing?" the cameraman said, "I'm with Jack Buck," I walked in about that time and when Woody saw me, he said nicely to the cameraman, "Okay."

———JACK BUCK, in *I Remember Woody Hayes*, by Dale Ratermann

I remember an incident in St. Louis about four years ago. Mark McGwire was called out on strikes by a rookie umpire, and he ended up getting ejected. The place went nuts, and it was like they were going to tear the place down. The next day Jack was doing something before the game, a pre-game ceremony. When he was done, he said, "When the umpires come out here, this is a great baseball city, and let's show the umpires. They had a tough day yesterday. Let's show them what St. Louis is all about." They tell me that forty, forty-five thousand people got up and gave the umpires a standing ovation for walking to home plate to show them that yesterday was yesterday and today is today. Jack had set the whole thing up. That's unheard of. He was that type of a people guy. He was always looking for plusses, he was not looking for minuses.

———BRUCE FROEMMING, Long-time National League Umpire

I knew Jack since the early '60s when I met him at The Boardroom, a bar in Clayton. A lot of the gang used to be there when it was in business and then we had a lot of card games over at my house.

For many years I went to spring training with Jack. It was a lot of fun. We'd go to the dog track once in a while. That's where they had the best food in the area. Jack was never a big eater, but he enjoyed good food. I remember at spring training, Jack had to work four days a week and two games a weekend and was off two or three days.

Whenever he went away to a ball game or football game, I'd pick him up at home. He'd get in my car, and he'd drive me up to the airport, and I drove home. He always wanted to do the driving. I would tell him, "Jack, I've never had a fatal accident."

Jack had more friends than Dierdorf has hair.

———JOE ARNDT, longtime family friend

One story that I recall that gives a good illustration of who Jack was happened in Philadelphia. There was a nice coffee area in the lobby of our hotel, and I was sitting down there one morning. One of the people working there was an older black lady, who was obviously retired and just working there for spending money. I chatted with her a little bit, then went on reading the sports page. Jack walked by on his way to the gift shop. The lady was pouring my coffee at the time, and I told her that there was a guy who was in the Hall of Fame, and he's very famous. I was proud of the fact that I was connected with this guy. She studiously watched him walk by.

A few minutes later, Jack came over, sat next to me and ordered a cup of coffee. He took a drink and asked that waitress, "Is this coffee flavored?" As a matter of fact it was, with hazelnut, which Jack didn't like. She turned to him and said, "You sure is picky for a Hall of Famer." Naturally, Jack slowly turned and looked at me like he was going to get me back. Knowing Jack, he might wait three years, and it might be at the baseball writer's dinner in St. Louis, but he'd spot you out and get you back. He never forgot things like that. Anyway, I left for work and Jack sat there and talked to the coffee shop lady for another hour. You know they had absolutely nothing in common, yet he sat and talked to her just like they were next-door neighbors.

———BUDDY BATES, Cardinals Equipment Manager

I do know that every time —every time—you ran into him, you came away smiling. If it was just him calling you by your nickname or telling you a joke or "how you doing?" and he had a dark, black comedy sort of sense of humor often. He was so funny in later years. I'd say, "Hey Jack, how you doing?" He'd say something like, "I know why you're asking." I'd say, "What do you mean?" He'd say, "You've got the Jack Buck voodoo doll over there." He would just always break you up. He was so funny in that regard.

When an opportunity came along to get in the TV booth in 1997, his way of congratulations was perfect because it wasn't the typical "hey, congratulations." He sidled up to me in the press box of my first game, and he said, "I guess you're proof positive that if you hang around long enough, you'll finally get in here." Just little things like that, little special asides, are what you remember about Jack Buck.

———BOB RAMSAY, former Cardinals TV broadcaster, now with KFNS Radio

In the mid '80s, my girlfriend and I were walking out of the stadium when we saw Jack Buck. I was thrilled as we walked side by side and a simple conversation began. I took a moment to introduce Jack to the naive female who had accompanied me. "This is Jack Buck," Dumbfounded, she replied, "So?" I was embarrassed, until he took the matter into his own hands and quipped, "What's your name young lady?"; "I'm Kris from Waterloo!" Then with a shake of his head, and in such an endearing manner, he replied, "So?"

———MICHAEL ROBERTSON, Cardinals fan

In all the years that I knew him, I never, ever heard him complain. A plane could be late. The food could be bad. Situations would come up. Problems would arise. Yet, he never, never complained. It was always, "Hey, well, we'll get it done. What do you need? The plane's gonna be three hours late, let's play cards." Or "I've got a good book I can read, or whatever." He just loved his work and he loved people, and he just fed off that on a daily basis, lived every day to the fullest and truly I say he had that remarkable quality where he just loved life and loved people and in all those years I never, ever heard the man complain once about anything.

————JAY RANDOLPH, Friend and Fellow Broadcaster

When I was 14, I began my radio career working the Cardinal games at the affiliate in Kennett, MO. Every inning and a half the "local" station break came. Turn down this knob. Turn up this knob and push the button to play the local spot commercial. It was exciting for a 14 year old....Every half-hour I got to open the mike after Jack Buck said: "This is the St. Louis Cardinals Baseball Network...wolf." I never understood what that wolf meant or why the guy said it but he did it every time. Then it went quiet for 10 seconds, crowd noise only, as I crammed as much information into 10 seconds as was humanly possible; "This is KBOA FM in Kennett, Missouri. 85 degrees at 4:30. The forecast calls for partly cloudy skies today with an 80% chance of scattered afternoon showers. Stay tuned after the game for Platter Party!" Those West coast extra-inning games that began at 10 p.m. were a killer for a high-school student who walked one mile home across the cotton fields at 2:30 a.m. I only prayed that Gibson was pitching because he didn't waste time worrying about the hitter. It was a thrill years later to meet Jack Buck in the pressbox. "Hi, Mr. Buck, I work with Christine at KPLR, I'm the weekend sports guy, My name is Jeff." He introduced me to Roger Maris who just happened to be there, but I was more thrilled to meet Jack Buck than Roger.

————JEFFREY PYLANT, former co-worker of Christine Buck

Jack Buck was a regular guy. He wanted to be a regular guy. He didn't want anybody to treat him like Jack Buck, the celebrity. Everybody was just another guy, and he was just another guy.

The one thing that really struck me about Jack Buck was how he would make his way through the players during batting practice. They'd be out on the field stretching. Generally you stay away from the players when they're stretching, but Jack would just kind of weave his way through the players, even the guys on the other team, and he'd be introducing himself, "Hello, I'm Jack Buck,"—like they didn't know who he was. He knew enough Spanish to speak to the Hispanic players in Spanish. He really seemed to enjoy doing that. As much as anybody I've seen in this game, he really liked being around the players and just shooting the breeze them. A lot of announcers, especially as they get older, and no longer have much in common with the players, don't do that anymore. But Jack never stopped doing it. He just really enjoyed being around everybody who had anything to do with the game.

——**ERIC NADEL**, Voice of the Texas Rangers for 23 years

Last time he was down here, spring of 2001, he held up the program for the events of the day, and he said, "Look at this. It says Musial and Buck on here. That kind of annoys me. That's not in alphabetical order." Everybody thought that was funny. Then he turns around and says, "You people think that winning seven batting titles and being in the Baseball Hall of Fame and being a Most Valuable Player and being a Legend is more important than having served thirty years with Mike Shannon. Well, you can go ahead and think that." That absolutely brought down the house.

——**NED REYNOLDS**, Sports Director, KY3-TV, Springfield, Missouri

I remember when the Buffalo Bills were playing the Dallas Cowboys in Super Bowl XXVII in Pasadena, California. The Bills had been to two straight Super Bowls before that one. Jack was convinced that it was time for the Bills to win. I don't know with whom he had placed the bet, but he had placed a bet on the Bills. He would never, ever let it be heard in his voice, but every time Dallas scored, he reached into his pocket, pulled out a 10-dollar bill, crumpled it up and threw it out the window. He literally tossed the money out of the window. That was his way of venting frustration.

——**GREG GUMBEL**, NBC Sports

I saw Jack quite a bit during the World Series in 1968. At that time, Harry Caray and Buck were doing the Cardinals, and George Kell and I were doing the Tigers. For the first time, they decided that they would have two announcers from each team broadcast the World Series. The games started in St. Louis. Pee Wee Reese and I worked on NBC radio when the games were in St. Louis, and then Jack worked with Pee Wee when the games were in Detroit. Curt Gowdy was doing the TV for NBC, and Harry Caray worked with Gowdy when the games were in St. Louis, while George Kell worked with him when the games were in Detroit. Our paths crossed much during that series.

Whenever I would go into St. Louis to do games for CBS, I'd see Jack. A couple years ago I was on the field at Busch Stadium, and I went up to the batting cage. Jack was hanging around and we started some small talk. Master of the one-liners, he suddenly blurts out, "One great thing about you, Ernie, is that you'll never die young!"

———ERNIE HARWELL, Detroit Tigers Broadcaster

I'd met Jack Buck a few times but got to know him through the Pro Football Hall of Fame Selection Committee. Of course, I was certainly familiar with his work because I write a sports column. The committee meets for four or five hours on the Saturday before the Super Bowl to pick the final candidates, and you get to know people there. Of course he was one of those guys you're in awe of only because you've heard him so often over the years. I heard him on national broadcasts. I went to the University of Missouri in the late sixties, and heard him do Cardinal games. He was one of the giants in the business, but never acted like he was one of the giants in the business. He was just another guy who had strong opinions and was a delight to be around.

Jack stayed on that committee primarily because he wanted to get two of his friends in, essentially. One was Jackie Smith, tight end for the Cardinals, who went to the Cowboys at the end of his career. The other was Dan Dierdorf who Jack helped make a successful transition from player to broadcaster. His speeches were impassioned at these meetings. He really made a case for people. There had been some resentment toward Dierdorf as well for being a broadcaster. I guess there were people who didn't like his broadcast work which Jack always insisted never should detract from what he did on the field, although Jack liked his broadcast work, too. But he really overcame all those things, and as soon as both guys got in the Hall of Fame, he resigned his position on the board.

———LEONARD SHAPIRO, *Washington Post* Sports Columnist

I was working with my salesmen in Marion, Illinois. We got into the Holiday Inn about six o'clock and the Cardinal caravan was there. They had my room blocked, and I couldn't get to my room so I just stood there and waited for them. Jack Buck took note of me standing there and I guess maybe I looked a little forlorn or something. He came over after it was over. He said, "Hey, couldn't get to your room, huh?" I said, "No, I couldn't. But that's okay. I enjoyed the program." He said, "Come on. I'll buy you a beer." We sat down for about a half hour and talked. He was one of the nicest, most gentle guys I've ever met. I was a perfect stranger to him, and he made me feel like I'd known him for years. He's just a great guy. When we were sitting down with that beer, I told Jack that I remembered him announcing Chicago Bear football games back in Chicago where I'm from. He said, "You're right." He said he and George Connor used to work together as Bear announcers. It didn't last long, maybe a year or so. He was really open and conversational about everything.

———HANK GALEOTTI, Lake St. Louis, Missouri

There are so many young guys who finish their playing careers and go into broadcasting, and they'll ask me what I think. I tell them to shut up. It's television, so the viewer can see what's happening. New color guys talk too much. I talked to one guy in particular, who told me that he was getting criticized too much. I told him to quit talking about when he played because nobody cares. When somebody chooses to watch a game, those are the two teams they want to watch. They want to know about those two teams. Viewers don't care what a color guy did as a player, or how much homework he did. These are the things you learn from guys like Buck. I hope that some of these young play-by-play guys can learn those lessons and pass them down, because they have to teach it. There's no school for what we do.

The thing about Jack is that he was so relaxed, everybody listening and watching was relaxed. You didn't have to strain to listen to Jack. With some announcers you want to say, "This guy's *on* again?" With Jack, you would say, "This guy is on again." That's a big difference. He was relaxed, so he made the people working with him relaxed and he made all the listeners relaxed. He made people understand that it's only a game.

———PAUL MAGUIRE, Former CBS Football Color Announcer

My dad took me to a Cardinals' game, and I took my transistor with me. We lived closer to Kansas City in Sedalia, Missouri so we would normally go to see the Kansas City A's, but we saw a few Cardinal games, too. Harry was describing a "hot smash" to Kenny Boyer at third base. Well, it was a routine two-hop ground ball. So Harry did not rank very high with me in credibility. Credibility was important, and Jack was right there at the top.

——**BILL BROWN**, Houston Astros TV Announcer

I first met Jack Buck at the opening game in Montreal in 1969 because the Cardinals played Montreal in the first major league baseball game played outside the United States. Montreal was an expansion team, their first year on the field was 1969, and the Cardinals were their first home series.

Montreal had a contending team from 1979 to 1982. Then the Montreal management started to take that team apart and by the mid-eighties, the Expos were really having a tough time. We were in St. Louis for a series against the Cardinals, and I sat and talked with Jack, as I did so many times, and told him that this was tough. This losing was getting to me, and the team wasn't very interesting at the time, and it was really difficult to keep the energy level up day after day while broadcasting a hundred and sixty-two games. While I was talking, Jack just shook his head. He reached into his pocket, and he pulled out a one hundred dollar bill and he gave it to me. He said, "Here, take this to your mike stand. It'll remind you what you're there for."

——**DAVID VAN HORNE**, Florida Marlins Broadcaster

In 1997, my last year in St. Louis, our station happened to break the story that the Cardinals were being sold. We interrupted our broadcast in the morning to make the announcement and say that there was going to be a press conference at 1 o'clock. Of course, all of the other stations thought we were crazy, and they couldn't get any confirmation. Sure enough, about 20 minutes after we made the announcement on our air, the Cardinals sent out a press release saying that there was going to be a press conference for a major announcement from Anheuser-Busch. Then, everybody knew we were on top of the story, and that was obviously a huge story.

I was getting ready to go on the air live, when somebody sneaks up behind me and said in a gravelly voice, "Way to go, kid, you scooped them all." That was Jack. That was about as cool as it was going to get. You know he could've broken that story at any time on KMOX, but he was so closely associated with the team that he would never do that. His statement about us scooping them all was classic Jack.

——**TREY WINGO**, ESPN

I will always remember how personable he was, how genuine he was, how he had the ability to interact with his audience, with his crowd. The first time we had him here in May of 2000, we had a little auction that was taking place. We sell about five pieces of memorabilia at each one of these luncheons that we do. We had a nice portrait of Ken Griffey, Jr., but it was not autographed. It was something I picked up somewhere for a few bucks. Our auctioneer started the bidding, and he started it too high—at about a thousand bucks. All at once he said, how about eleven hundred—no one had bid on it. Well, Jack bids. I'm like, "Oh, no." Here Jack Buck just bid eleven hundred bucks for a picture that I gave less than a hundred for. I'm a little embarrassed about it. One, because I know it's not worth that. Two, because no one is going to bid against Jack. I know he's going to get stuck with it. So after the auction is over, and it's time for Jack to speak, he pops up, and he goes, "You know I do suffer from several ailments. One of those is Parkinson's. Like during that auction, I didn't intend to bid on that piece. My arm got away from me." "But, he said, "don't worry about it. I'll see Griffey in two weeks. He'll sign this thing for me, and I'll sell it for five thousand dollars." He just had the audience in his hands at that point in time. He always had the ability to do that.

——JERALD ANDREWS, Missouri Sports Hall of Fame Director

A friend of mine was down outside of Perryville, Missouri, and he had gone to church. There was a Jesuit missionary there who was talking about how he'd been in Africa, and he was able to listen to the games there over the Armed Forces Radio Network. The guy was originally from St. Louis or somewhere in Missouri. He'd set his alarm at like three a.m. so he could get up and hear the Cardinal-Cub games. Here this guy is living in a hut or something in some part of Africa. His alarm would go off at three a.m., and he'd turn his flashlight on trying to dial in the transistor radio, and he sees this movement in the corner of the hut. It's a snake. So he kills the snake and throws it outside the hut and listens to the game and goes back to sleep. He said the next day a native said to him, "You know, Father, that was a poisonous snake. If you hadn't seen it, you would have been dead in ten minutes." So he said, "I owe my life to Jack Buck."

——MARK G. BECK, St. Louis Dentist

Jack would reach millions of people, but he was on radio in places like Baton Rouge, Louisiana, and Little Rock, Arkansas. People didn't know what Jack looked like. Even people here at the lake. We had a golf tournament here for the hospital and Jack came down from St. Louis. We were standing around talking when a guy came in who obviously didn't know who Jack was. Jack introduced himself and the guy practically fainted. It was almost as if it hit him, "Oh my, that's Jack Buck!"

Jack made sure he talked to everybody at the tournament. He didn't let anybody down. That's just the way Jack was.

——**BUDDY BLATTNER**, Lake of the Ozarks, Missouri

The thing about Jack's passing is that we all knew Jack in the context of the ballpark. A ballpark's a happy place, a fun place. The thing I always remember about Jack was just how happy he was every day at the ballpark. Some guys after they've been around as long as he was get a little jaded, get a little tired of the travel, get a little fed up with the ball players—you hear it all the time. Every time I saw him at a ballpark, he always had a joke. He always had a funny story, an anecdote to make you laugh. It reflected the way he is.

A thing I remember about him was when he said, "Hey, we broadcast baseball, and we've got one of the best deals going. Let's not ever forget that." He was right. You can forget sometimes when you're away from home and your traveling builds up. But—what's the alternative? The alternative is having to go to work for a living. Jack, in my opinion, never lost that perspective.

——**JON MILLER**, ESPN and San Francisco Giants Announcer

I was called in to do radio two years ago because Mike Shannon had his annual night at the races, which is a charity event he has in this town. I came in, and by the time I got there it was my inning to work, which was the third inning. There had been a long rain delay. The Cardinals were playing the Dodgers. The week before we were in Los Angeles so I had a ton of notes on each player on the Dodgers—the history of the Dodgers and all that kind of stuff. I'm in the booth and Jack says, "What are those, kid?" I said, "These are my notes." He said, "Aha." He grabbed my notes and just tore them up and threw them in the trash can. At this point, my job's on the floor and I'm scared, and he said, "That's not the story." Then he pointed out to the field, and he said, "That's the story." His meaning was "describe what you see—that's the game." And he walked out. He taught me one of the great lessons I ever learned—that the game is the story.

——DAN McLAUGHLIN, Cardinals Broadcaster for SportsNet

Jack was emceeing the Italian-American society banquet. He said, "Italians are close to my heart, close to the Buck family's heart. During the war, an Italian woman hid me in her basement for three months. Of course, she was in Cleveland."

He was just a great guy. My mother was listening to the ceremony for the unveiling of the statue. Jack always did the unexpected and I didn't even know he knew my father, who also was a toastmaster and a speaker. He and Jack used to do the same dinner sometimes. So during his little speech that Jack gave, he said, "I want to thank sculptor, Harry Weber, whose father, Carl Weber, was a great friend of mine, and the best toastmaster this city ever had." That's the kind of thing Jack would pull out of his back pocket and do for everybody. He made everybody who knew him just feel so good and so special. He told me once that he had an ambition in life to have everybody like him. He said, "I don't believe this business about you shouldn't care whether people like you or not, I want everybody to like me."

——HARRY WEBER, Sculptor of Jack Buck's Statue at Busch Stadium

Jack was doing a function for Amadee, the great sports cartoonist here, on his ninetieth birthday. Jack was asked to host this. He said, "I've got diabetes. I've got Parkinson's. I've got high blood pressure. I've got cancer. I wish I had Alzheimer's so I'd forget what the heck I've got." At that same function we went down to Springfield, we were sitting there under an open tent. Jack had a couple of funny things to say about Parkinson's. "I was sitting next to Bob Broeg, a sports writer here, and I looked over and he had food all over his bow tie. I said, "Bob, how in the heck does a guy get food on a bow tie?" Bob said, "Sitting next to a guy that's got Parkinson's."

——JACKIE SMITH, NFL Hall-of-Famer

I don't remember specifically the first time I met Jack. I guess you could say I met him when I was five years old because dad always had the games on the radio. Some of my first memories, from when I was four or five years old, are hearing the Cardinals on the radio. I wasn't lying there listening to them, but his and Harry Caray's voices were in our house almost every night.

As I got older, I took my baseball cards and put them in teams, and in order of the starting lineups. Then I had the pitchers, bench players, managers and coaches at the end of the stack of cards. I could keep track of who was in the game and in what order they were batting. I'd lie there, shuffle cards, look at the pictures and listen to the game. Most of the time, that was to the voices of Harry Caray and Jack Buck.

———**DENNY MATTHEWS**, Kansas City Royals' Announcer

Baseball broadcasts are different today because of television. The reason that the Bucks and the Hamiltons and the Ernie Harwells have been around for fifty years is that when something happens on the field, we can relate it to something that happened in the past, and make a story out of it. On television, you can't really do that because they're interrupting you on your headset all the time. It's too bad that the young guys don't get to paint a picture anymore. That's not their fault, that's just the way things have developed in our business. I think we still felt that we wanted to tell the stories; we wanted to bring up things that happened in the past. For instance, if we see a young player, we can compare him to a player in the past so the fans have an idea of what that older player was like. However, if you're on television and you have to talk about the six graphics that they just put on the screen of how this guy hits on a grassy field or how he hits in the moonlight, you don't have time to tell a story. That's part of the charm that Buck had. It turned out to be like you were listening to an old friend, and somebody who was as big of a fan as you talking about the game.

———**MILO HAMILTON**, Houston Astros Announcer, formerly with the Cardinals.

Best HE Buck
Fred

Red Schoendienst, Jack's childhood friend Herb Rosenberg, Stan Musial, Jack Buck

Photo courtesy of Mike Roarty

Cardinal President Mark Lamping, Carole and Jack Buck and Mrs. Chuck Knox singing at the Irish Derby in Ireland. It was a great party but the lady on the right is not wearing the lampshade.

Carole, Joe and Jack Buck — New
Years Eve – Tampa, 1987.

Jack Buck's eight children help celebrate his 75th Birthday

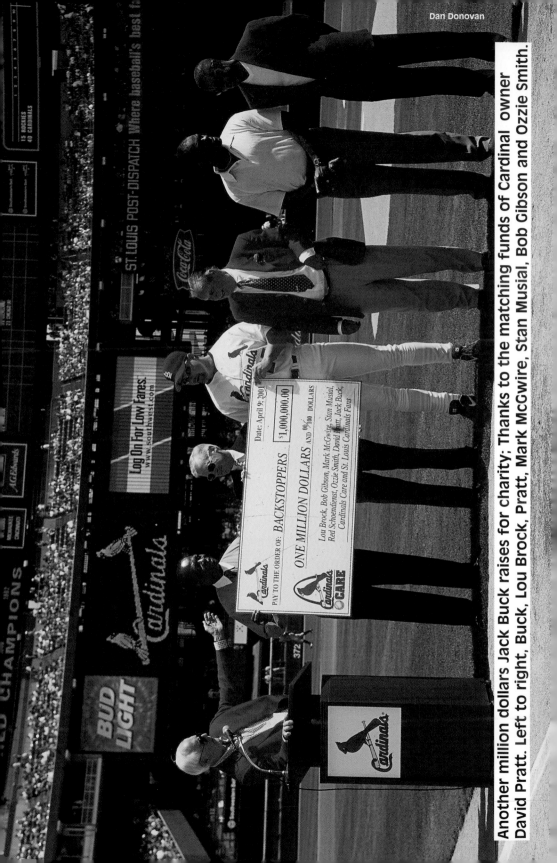

Dan Donovan

Another million dollars Jack Buck raises for charity: Thanks to the matching funds of Cardinal owner David Pratt. Left to right, Buck, Lou Brock, Pratt, Mark McGwire, Stan Musial, Bob Gibson and Ozzie Smith.

Dan Donovan

YOU WILL BE MISSED JACK

MR JACK BUCK
THANKS FOR THE
MEMORIES

thanks
for the

AMBASSADOR

Thanks For Your Time This Time, Till Next Time, So Long......

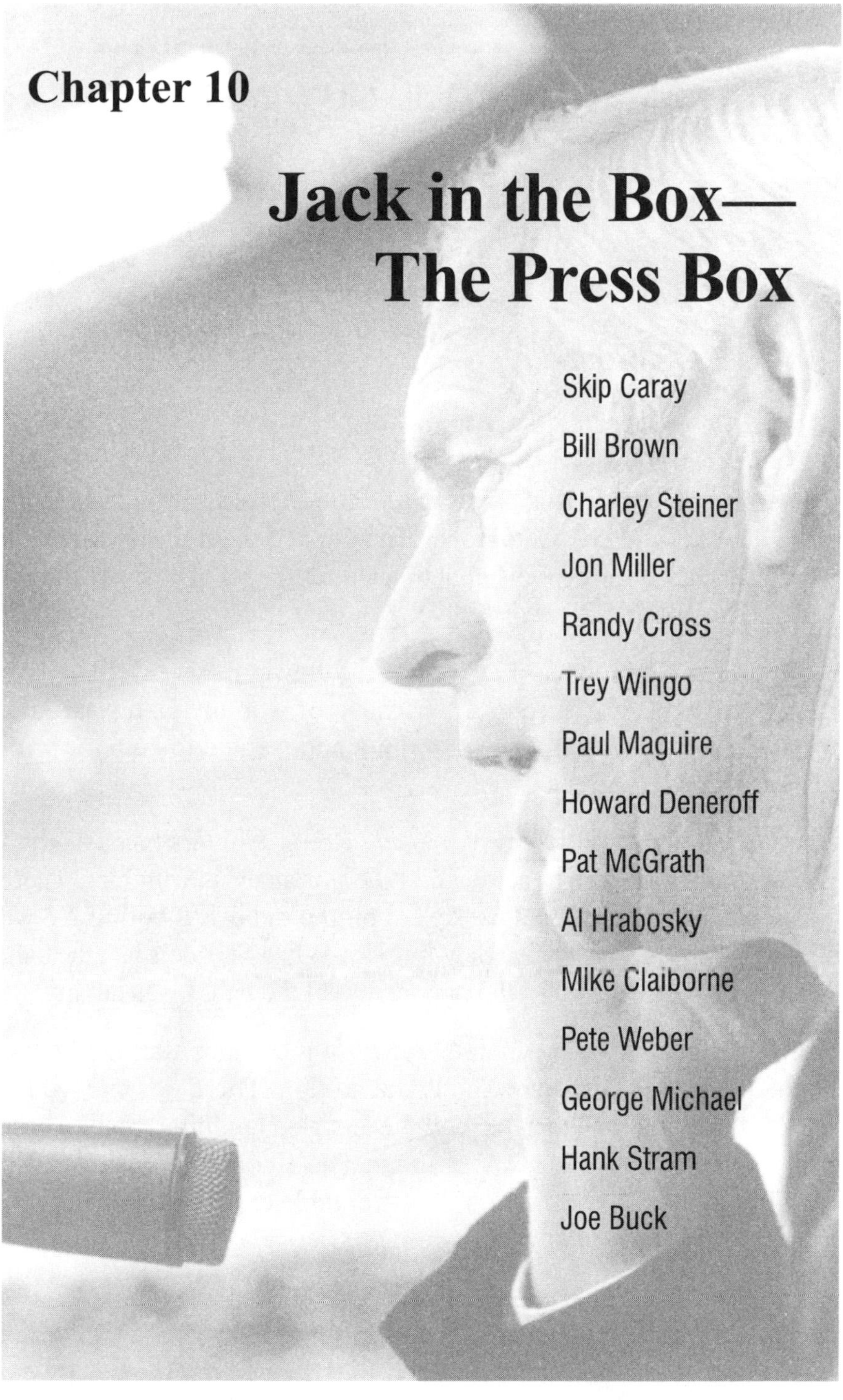

Chapter 10

Jack in the Box— The Press Box

Skip Caray

Bill Brown

Charley Steiner

Jon Miller

Randy Cross

Trey Wingo

Paul Maguire

Howard Deneroff

Pat McGrath

Al Hrabosky

Mike Claiborne

Pete Weber

George Michael

Hank Stram

Joe Buck

A BRAVE MAN, A COOL GUY IN HOTLANTA
SKIP CARAY

The son of Jack Buck's 16-year broadcast partner Harry Caray, Skip Caray worked at KMOX before moving to Atlanta, where he has been the longtime voice of the Atlanta Braves.

I remember when Jack came to join the St. Louis broadcast team with Dad and Joe Garagiola. He adjusted right away, followed Dad's lead and was somewhat of a leader for Joe. I always thought he became an instant success.

It seemed like he took a liking to me right away. There were always people trying to warm up to me because of who my Dad was. Jack wasn't like that. He genuinely liked me and wanted to help me with my broadcasting career.

He was doing play-by-play for Saint Louis University basketball games and wanted me to come and do color analysis with him. There was a point that he thought basketball on the radio was boring. So we started taking turns doing the play-by-play. When St. Louis had the ball, Jack was talking and when the opponent had the ball, I was talking.

There was one game in which there was a loose ball after a rebound and neither of us knew who should be talking. There was silence for about 10 seconds and then we both just started laughing. So needless to say, our innovative idea ended there. The 10 or so games that I did with him doing SLU games gave me valuable experience and helped me get where I am today.

A few years later there were some people with the St. Louis Hawks organization who remembered hearing those broadcasts and gave me the chance to do their games. When they moved to Atlanta, I went with the team and it helped me get the job with the Braves.

I remember another time when I was producing one of Jack's talk shows and I screwed up. But throughout, Jack was ad-libbing, which he could do as well as anyone, and things went smoother than they should have. But it was obvious that I had made a major mistake.

Right after the show ended, Bob Hyland, the vice president of CBS Radio, called me down to his office. Jack said I wasn't going without him. We went in and Jack tried to take all of the blame. I wouldn't let him do that. After awhile, Bob told me to get out of the office and Jack said that was probably the best thing Bob had said all day.

Jack was always looking out for my best interests and someone I was proud to have as a friend. In addition, he and Dad formed what I believe was the greatest announcing duo in sports history. They worked so well together. Dad was the voice of the guy sitting in the bleachers with his shirt off and Jack was the emcee for the guy dressed in a dinner jacket. They worked so well together and played off of each other so smoothly. That combination formed something like a symphony. It was as pleasant as Perlman playing the violin.

I remember one time in spring training they showed up, probably after a good night out together and were still in good spirits. The White Sox had a catcher named Jerry McNertney. When he came up to bat the first time, one of them said his name in a peculiar way and there was laughter throughout the booth.

The next time he came up they couldn't even say his name. So when McNertney came up for his third at-bat, they announced that a new catcher had entered the game. That wasn't the case. McNertney played the entire game.

HE'S BEEN TO THE COUNTY FAIR ONCE, THE STATE FAIR TWICE AND NEVER HEARD A BETTER ANNOUNCER

BILL BROWN

Bill Brown, originally from Western Missouri, has been the play-by-play voice of the Houston Astros for the last 15 years.

I grew up in Sedalia, Missouri, listening to Jack Buck. I didn't know him until I became a big league broadcaster. I met him in the Seventies because I was doing the Reds games then on TV. I didn't get to know him too well, but we had quite a few contacts, and I got to know him better and better along the way. He was just an incredibly nice guy. It sort of reinforced the reason I went into baseball broadcasting.

I found that knowing Jack was an incredible experience. I've heard these stories from other people in the media who traveled with us. Alyson Footer who works for MLB.com, she's in her thirties and hasn't been in this business very long, but she was talking with me about how well he treated her. He'd sit down and have a cheeseburger with her in the pressroom there in St. Louis. He was just totally unassuming. It didn't matter who you were. You didn't have to have stature to be his friend. He was just really a nice guy.

Jack Buck had a major impact on my getting into broadcasting. As a kid, most of my friends liked Harry Caray better than Jack. They were on the air together at that time. I went against the grain. I preferred Jack's style. Harry, of course, was more bombastic and more emotional. He was more the showman than Jack. To me, Jack was the eyes and ears of the fan. He was a reporter. I thought he could certainly milk the emotion as well as any broadcaster and highlight the high points of the game as well as anyone I've heard. There's something about Harry that appealed to a lot of people in those days and of course later on when he was with the Cubs. He was always a very,

very popular type broadcaster—I think because he was willing to wear his emotions on his sleeve and he was willing to get down on players and bury them so to speak when they weren't playing well. But Jack was always more detached and more reserved and less opinionated. I went to Journalism School at the University of Missouri so with the journalistic background and that type of training, it just appealed to me more to have someone there who was reporting rather than someone who was emotionally involved in it as well. So I just preferred Jack's style all the way down the road. As the years went by for me, and I became closer to getting into this job, it reinforced what I wanted to do—to listen to him.

Earlier this year when we were in St. Louis, Jack and I had a very interesting conversation. We were having a cheeseburger in the pressroom there in St. Louis. He asked me if I was close to the players on the Astros and did I really get to know them well and spend a lot of time with them. I said, "Well, no, I really don't. That doesn't work well for me. I'd rather be a little distant from them because up in the booth you have to make judgments sometimes and if the guy's not playing and you're supposed to be his friend, that may not wear well on the friendship. I just don't like that fit for what we do." Certainly if people can do it, then that's no problem with me. I know some players better than others.

His point was that he had the same relationship with them. He liked to be friendly, but not a great friend to them in terms of, "Hey, I want this from you." It's just not a comfortable fit. He told me a story about his relationship with a couple of players. He said he had made Milt Thompson mad at him. When Thompson was playing left field with the Cardinals, Jack said something about him not having a good arm, and Milt took offense to that. But they talked it out, and they reached an understanding. Then Dave Parker was upset at him one time because of something Jack had said about Dave on the air, and Dave's mother heard it and took exception to it. Well Dave, of course, never heard the remark himself. They were able to work it out. He said to Dave, "Well, let's do an interview then." Dave said, "All right." They did an interview, and they actually talked about it on the interview—the fact that Dave's mother was upset about some remark Jack made about it. I thought, "Well, that's unique. That's something I wouldn't have done." Yet it showed to me that Jack was trying to get the point across to these guys, "Look, I know this is your profession. I know it's important to you and your family, but maybe you're making too much out of this. We can all live with what happened here, let's just all get along." That, to me, was one of the endearing qualities of Jack Buck, the fact that this is not brain surgery here. Yes, people get upset by remarks the broadcasters make, but they shouldn't let it ruin their day."

I felt that Jack had a lot more courage than I would have had under the circumstances of his illness. Quite frankly, I would not have been able to do that, at that age. Well, I don't plan to be broadcasting at that age unless I'm destitute and somebody wants me to work. Jack handled it with such grace and dignity and made fun of himself. I wouldn't have been able to do that. I thought he had tremendous courage being able to appear, not only on the air, but on the field with the poem he delivered on the field after September 11th. That's something very, very few people would be able to do with Parkinson's. Here again, he was trying to teach everybody something. I think that something was—If you still have a gift that you can give, you've still been blessed with something that you can pass along to help someone else, even though you're not one hundred percent physically, you can still have abilities. I really thought that was a very courageous thing he did—to continue working when he didn't have to. It showed me something. It really did.

CHARLEY IS SUFFERING FROM POST-ESPY SYNDROME

CHARLEY STEINER

Charley Steiner is the play-by-play voice of the New York Yankees with John Sterling. Steiner was born in New York City, graduated from Bradley University in Peoria and started his career at KSTT (now KJOC) in Davenport, Iowa. Wayne Larrivee, Travis Seibert, and Milo Hamilton also started at KSTT. Steiner was a SportsCenter *host at ESPN, a job he got with the help of his pharmacist.*

I certainly can recall the first time I met Jack. I probably was a sophomore in college at Bradley. I went down to Cardinal games quite often. Growing up in New York you'd inevitably see the Cardinals and the Mets. As a kid, like all prospective announcers, I used to listen to out-of-town games late at night. I listened to Jack and Harry on the radio, one of those old clock radios—only AM, and turn it and twist it to pick up KMOX. I always thought he was a great broadcaster. I had a press pass because I worked at my college radio station. That was a pretty good deal. I remember being in the men's room and there at the next urinal was Jack Buck. I thought, "This is pretty cool." I never shared that story with Jack, but years later, when I first started doing the games for ESPN, he obviously knew me better through my stuff on *SportsCenter* than my play-by-play stuff. But he had heard me a couple of times on ESPN radio. He came over and was uncommonly gracious. Said some wonderful things that gave me a lot of confidence as I was embarking in an area of my career that at that point I was unsure as to whether or not I was going to be good enough to do it. Those kinds of words were just like hope. "Maybe I can play in the big leagues."

Jack was a guy who I felt was a giant of our business just because he was so effortless. He would come over to me and initiate conversations about my career, not about his. I thought, "Well, gol-lee. Hey, this is pretty cool." Of course I find out as I get to know him better and better over the years that that's the way he was with everybody.

So on the one hand, "Jack Buck must think I'm pretty good—but then again he must think everybody's pretty good." That was what he was all about. He was uncommonly gracious.

Then as the years went on, he was one of the few guys who understood what it was like to broadcast for a local team, and broadcast for a network, as I ended up doing. I do the playoffs and the All-Star game and cover the World Series. I remember him telling me, "If you ever get a chance to broadcast a good home team in a good town, it'll be so much better for your life and lifestyle because you travel with the club, and you have home stands." I remember when I took the job with the Yankees that was one of the things I remembered. How many people in the profession could actually give me that advice having lived it? Jack was one. Jack and Vin Scully said the same thing to me a few years ago. Again, I was very lucky that I was able to land a job with the Yankees. They were so right. Now I have home stands as opposed to just traveling from one town to the next to do a game, then moving on to the next one.

I was there in St. Louis, and called the sixty-first home run. I don't remember exactly what Jack did that night. I'm not even sure—maybe Shannon did sixty-one. But again, it was just that sense of, "Here I am playing on the stage that Jack played on." But the years before, the thing I remember about the Gibson home run, to this day I will always remember, how poetic it was. "Five to four, I don't believe what I just saw." It was poetic. When everybody talks about that call and that moment, somewhere in his head in some crevice of that wonderful brain was poetry. It was clean. It was crisp and it was poetic. That's the thing about that one call that stands out. And those wonderful pipes that resonated. In our business, either you're lucky enough to have a voice or not, and he was blessed with a fast ball. A lot of guys in my business have a fast ball, they just don't know how to use it quite as well as he did.

I saw Jack for the last time late last season a couple of times. It was sad and yet remarkably courageous and brave. There he was having a terrible time with the Parkinson's and if it bothered him, he certainly wasn't letting on because he would come over as he always did, "Well, how are you, my boy?" By that point, I had begun to strike up a pretty good friendship with Joe because I would see him when we were doing a Sunday night game, inevitably Fox would be in town on a Saturday. So Joe and I became pretty friendly, too. I remember saying to Joe how remarkable I thought Jack was that if it fazed him, he certainly wasn't letting on that it did. And he would make jokes about the shaking. Somebody else had a bad case of the shakes, and I don't remember who it was. Jack said to him, "This is the S.O.B. I caught it from."

At that point, we would just talk. I remember being in someone's office and Jack was in there. We were on the road somewhere, maybe Colorado. Just three guys sitting around and it was one of those times where I just felt like Forrest Gump. He was always funny and charming, and that was the thing. I'm sure in the privacy of his own home, with his own family, it may have gotten to him, but he certainly never let on in any public setting that it was getting to him. Clearly he was straining at the mike and doing the best he could, but he was still great. He was still Jack. The thing that I admired about Jack—he was a broadcaster. He could broadcast anything. He was a great football announcer. He was a morning host at KMOX also. He'd be able to do morning drive, and then do baseball and then do all the other things that he did. He could communicate. He had a rare gift. As a broadcaster he was twenty-five years older than I am, so before the beginning of my career, when I twisted that little AM radio late at night to listen to KMOX, he was one of those guys that I patterned myself after.

On June 18th, we were still in New York, the last game of the series, and John Sterling and I are on the air, and our producer said that Jack Buck had just died. The game had ended and we were just about to begin the post-game show where we go through the highlights, out-of-town scores and have ample reason for thousands of dollars of commercials. That's the only reason there are pre-game shows and post-game shows. I said to John, "We've got to talk about this." We spent about ten minutes on the air talking about Jack that night. We just went off on our own just telling Jack Buck stories.

WIT HAPPENS
JON MILLER

Jon Miller is the voice of the San Francisco Giants and ESPN baseball. Along with Roy Firestone, he is the top sports mimic in the country.

I was always in the American League and Jack was in the National League until I went to the Giants. Sometime after the end of the 1983 baseball season, he called me at my home in Baltimore, and wanted to know if I was interested in coming and doing Cardinals' games with him. He worked with Mike Shannon at that time, and they were starting a new cable network. He would be doing all the Cardinal games that would be on this new cable network after they got it kicked off. They were going to need someone to do these games on the radio when he was over on TV. Then he would go away and do football games on the weekends, and I guess Monday Night Football and all the other things he did as well. I actually ended up going to St. Louis and talking to the people at the radio station. It was a thrill to get a call from him. There was the voice. Anyway I ended up staying in Baltimore. I had only done one year there and it had gone real well, so why would I leave, but it was pretty tempting. I probably wouldn't have had that much of a future in St. Louis. That was really the first time I had talked with him.

The last time I saw Jack was in St. Louis on September 7 of last year. We did a game on ESPN on a Friday night there—a Dodger-Cardinal game. I didn't realize it was the last time I was going to see him. He had a little radio show before the game, and he had a little studio in the bowels of the stadium. I was walking by, and Jack popped up out of this studio and asked if I could go on with him for a couple of minutes. I went in, and, all in fun, I did a Vin Scully impression and a Jack Buck impression and he was a great audience. He would laugh and laugh. He always wanted me to do it. Then he asked me what I thought about several things and then asked how Vin Scully would do this on the radio and "How about me? How would I play it there?" So it was all in fun, and he got such a kick out of it.

Then the next time I saw him, it was on television, like all the rest of us, on September 17th, the first game back after September 11th. He had that inspiring poem that he had written. Here he was with Parkinson's and very ill and yet he summoned all of his experience and all of his will to get out there in public and recite that poem. To me it showed another side of Jack that maybe was not known that well nationally. It was known in St. Louis, but not so well nationally—that Jack was so much more than a sports broadcaster. Here we were attacked, and we were bruised and frightened, and Jack inspired us. I thought it was pretty remarkable. That would be his lasting memory—legacy—for all of us.

When Jack was doing the CBS games, when they got the contract after NBC, he came to Baltimore for a Saturday afternoon game, and he called earlier in the week to the people who ran the CBS radio and TV affiliates in Baltimore. He wanted to come in for the game and if they had any sponsors or clients that would like to go to lunch with Jack that he would be happy to do that. They were kind of shocked by that. I asked him about it when I saw him at the ballpark before the game. He said, "Well, hey, we're all in this business together to try to make sense of it, so I had the time and to me it's part of the job. That's the way it was at KMOX." One of the things I didn't like about the job that KMOX proposed to me back after the 1983 season—they were talking about that I would do some talk shows in the off-season and maybe a hockey game here and there and different events. I kind of was into the notion of when the baseball season ended that I had the time off unless I chose to do something else. I remember asking Jack about it. Jack said the same thing then, "Well, we all work for the station, and it's in all of our best interests to do whatever we can to make the station a success."

SIGN OF THE CROSS
RANDY CROSS

Randy Cross is no stranger to excellence. The two-time All-American at UCLA played on the 1976 Rose Bowl champion Bruin team before helping the San Francisco 49ers earn three Super Bowl titles (1982, 1985 and 1989) as a center and guard. Following his 13-year NFL career, Cross joined the CBS Sports team as a game analyst. He was thrust unexpectedly into the radio booth during Super

Credit: CBS Photo Archive *Bowl XXIV for a little more than a quarter, working with Jack Buck. Cross spent the last two seasons as an analyst on CBS' The NFL Today studio show. This year he'll be back in the broadcast booth, teaming with Kevin Harlan.*

Jack and I worked together almost half of Super Bowl XXIV in New Orleans in 1990 because Hank Stram had laryngitis. That was my first year in broadcasting. I was supposed to do eight games that year but ended up doing about fourteen. Getting the opportunity to work with Jack during that Super Bowl, however, was out of the complete blue sky.

I had been out with some friends late the night before. I got a phone call at 8 or 8:30 the next morning. I picked up and the voice on the other end said, "Hey, Randy, this is Frank Murphy, president of CBS Radio. I wanted to know if you want to do the radio with us for the Super Bowl." He went through his whole spiel before I said, "Yea, that's pretty funny," and I hung up on him. About a minute later, the phone rang again. "Randy, this is really Frank Murphy. Do not hang up on me."

I was on the pre-game show and did some stuff during halftime. I was pretty sure I wasn't going to have to do any of the game. They were going to go with Hank and his laryngitis. I was out in the hallway during the third quarter, deciding what I wanted to do, when Neil Pilson came walking toward me. He asked me what I was doing out walking around. I told him I was just killing time since I wasn't going to do anything on the air during the game. He said, "Come with me; you're going on the air."

I went in there and sat down. It was between series. Jack was still smoking back then, and he had this ashtray full of butts. He looked over at me and said, "Don't worry, kid, the game's worthless. We're going to have fun." By that time, I think the score was 34-7.

There are play-by-play announcers who are worried about how they sound, and how they're going to be perceived, and how they're going to be remembered. Then there are guys who are more worried about how the guy next to him is going to sound, and how he's going to be perceived, and how he's going to be remembered. Jack was one of those guys. Jack was the poster guy for that. Like so many great announcers, he's in a dying breed of selfless front men. The broadcast wasn't about him.

Even as a player, sitting in one of their production meetings, I'd sometimes have a hard time concentrating on questions. I remember him asking me a question, and I'm listening to him talk, thinking, "Man, does this guy have a great voice, or what?" Then he'd stare at me, and I'd realized that I forgot the question. The same thing happened with me and Vin Scully. But when I heard their voices, I just got wrapped up in hearing them.

I listened to Monday Night Football religiously. Some of my favorite broadcast memories are listening to Jack and Hank. It was funny because Hank would say something like, "It's a one-back field, and it looks like a sweep to the right." Jack would then describe the play, "The handoff and the ball goes left." They wouldn't say anything else, but it was hilarious. Jack was such a nice guy, but he would occasionally put someone in their place.

People don't remember that he called that famous Joe Montana to Dwight Clark pass on the radio side. One of the great TV questions is who was doing the TV game? Everybody assumes it was John Madden and **Pat Summerall**, because they did the Super Bowl, but it was Vin Scully and Hank Stram.

I had retired from football the year before working that Super Bowl with Jack. The most impressive thing to me—although it might not be impressive to other people—is that working with Jack, and listening to him, made me forget about what I had been dwelling on for the previous two-and-a-half to three quarters, which was, "You big idiot, why did you retire? The 49ers are going to win it again." I forgot all about that. Suddenly, I was listening to the game and I was a part of it. It was a great experience.

Jack Buck was one of the few people in that business, especially in football during the later parts of my career, who if you saw him, you knew you were playing in a big game. That might sound unusual to the people in the St. Louis area who listened to Jack for a hundred and sixty-two games during the baseball season. As a football player, though, if you saw Jack Buck at a game, you knew you were playing on Monday night, or in the playoffs or in the Super Bowl. His name and his voice were associated with those types of games.

John Madden lost his long-time partner after Super Bowl XXXVI when Pat Summerall retired. Pat Summerall's real first name is George. He is called Pat because when he was a kicker with the New York Giants football team, the newspapers would print: "P.A.T.—Summerall." P.A.T. stood for "Point After Touchdown." Summerall played minor league baseball against Mickey Mantle.

In late 1953, the Cardinals chose Jack Buck over Chick Hearn from Peoria because Buck had done excellent Budweiser commercials that summer while broadcasting the Rochester Red Wings, the Cardinals' AAA team in New York.

CAUSE OF DEATH—LIFE

TREY WINGO

Although Trey Wingo grew up on the East Coast, and currently works as an ESPN anchor/ reporter out of the network's Bristol, Connecticut headquarters, St. Louis is like a second home. Wingo spent six years at KSDK television, St. Louis' NBC affiliate, and the city was the birthplace of his two children.

I don't believe there's ever been an announcer in any city who was more closely associated with the heart and soul of that city itself than Jack Buck. Jack Buck was St. Louis. Jack Buck was the Cardinals. For everything else he did—including Monday Night Football, the World Series, college football and college basketball—he was the voice of the Cardinals and really a spokesman for the city of St. Louis. I don't think I've seen a situation like that anywhere else.

The first time I met Jack was at a Cardinal game in 1992. I had moved to St. Louis in November of 1991 and I was at the stadium doing a live broadcast for the station where I was working when he walked by. I was getting excited because here comes Jack Buck. He comes up to me and says, "Hey, Trey, welcome to town." Here I was this punk reporter for a local NBC affiliate, and he knew who I was. That has stuck with me ever since, and will stick with me forever.

That was a great experience. In St. Louis, the Cardinals are everything. If you don't do the Cardinals right, you're in big trouble. With Jack coming up and introducing himself, I felt like I had just been given a hall pass. Jack Buck went out of his way to make me feel welcome before anybody else did. That's the best start to covering the Cardinals that anyone could ever imagine. I loved it.

Jack did CBS World Series games up until the 1992 season, until, for whatever reason, they decided not to renew his contract. Every year in St. Louis there is a baseball symposium. He was up there speaking, and everybody was asking about losing the World Series gig. He talked about how it wasn't a problem and how he's done Cardinal World Series before, but then he added, "The only thing that bothered me was losing all the m...m... m... money." That brought the house down.

Jack was one of the most gregarious people I have ever met. He felt comfortable when you felt comfortable, and he went out of his way to make sure you were comfortable.

The last time I saw Jack was before I moved away in 1997. The last time I spoke to him, however, was two days after his speech when the baseball players came back after attacks of September 11. I called him at his house. I told him, "Mr. Buck, I thought that was the greatest thing ever, and everybody here loved it. Once again, you perfectly put together what most of us were thinking." He said, "Thanks, kid, I appreciate it. You're doing great at ESPN, and we're all proud of you here." It was a great moment, and I'm so glad I made that phone call because it was the last time I spoke to him.

When I wrote the obit for him on ESPN—as hard as that was, I was honored to do it—the first thing I told everyone is that we had to end it with his speech from that night.

BUFFALO: SOUTH OF HEAVEN, WEST OF H.E. DOUBLE HOCKEY STICKS!
PAUL MAGUIRE

A former pro player with Buffalo and San Diego, Paul Maguire may have built a bigger name for himself as a television analyst. The longtime NBC analyst, worked with Jack Buck during Buck's last game on the network. Currently, Maguire is one of ESPN's top football analysts.

Jack's last game at NBC, Cleveland hosting Houston, we were partnered together. Neither team was going to the playoffs. The ground was frozen. Actually, there was a freezing rain, they put the tarp down and it froze to the field, so they used a bulldozer to get it up, but they couldn't get all the tarp out of the end zone. It was a mess.

At Cleveland's old stadium, our studio was in one of the owner's boxes. There was the inside part, where you could slide the doors and keep warm, and then we were set up on the bleacher seats in front of the box. It was so cold that day that Jack and I had snot hanging out of our noses the entire game—it was one of those days when you just couldn't help it. I thought we were going to freeze to death.

We finally reached the two-minute warning. Now, keep in mind that I have never had any aspirations to be a play-by-play guy; it's easy to do color, so I enjoy it. Jack stood up, put his hand on my shoulder and said, "Good luck. It's been really nice working with you. I'll see ya." And he headed inside. I'm thinking, "What am I going to do!" I couldn't believe it. It could've been 50-below, it wouldn't have made any difference, because I was so shocked. I was staggering, trying to figure out what I was going to say for the final two minutes of the game. Even though the two-minute warning break is about four minutes long, there wasn't enough time. I started repeating the score to myself, so I would at least get that right. All of a sudden, I hear in my headset, "Back in 30." Now, I'm really starting to panic. I looked around, but nobody was there. Then the producer said, "Back in 15." Then, "10, 9, 8…" I kept repeating the score in my head. Jack sat back down and asked me, "You nervous?"

Luckily I hit the choke button on my microphone, because I had a couple fun words for Jack. Come to find out, he had been hiding behind the glass doors inside the booth. People who are in this business for the first time will understand what I went through.

Among so many other things, Jack also taught me that the only mistake you ever make is an uncorrected mistake. It doesn't matter if you make the mistake in the first quarter and correct it in the fourth quarter, at least you corrected it. There are too many people who will latch on to what an announcer says as being right. Well, if it's not right, correct it. If you learn that lesson, you can go back and correct anything, and not worry about whether or not you make a mistake.

One of the things I realized from Jack, is that it's just a game. I played this game for eleven years, and that's all it is…it's a game. There's nothing monumental about what we did in the booth. It's like people sitting in a bar, eavesdropping on our conversation about the game. When we decide to make people think about all the homework we did, then we've defeated the purpose. As a color guy, I don't really have anything to say until the teams do something on the field. The stories that Jack told came from homework. As announcers we sometimes tend to think that what we're doing is monumental, but it's not. Once the game is over, the first thing a coach will do—win or lose—is tell his team to forget about it, because they have to get ready for next week.

Most importantly, Jack taught me how to take time for people. We were always late getting to the booth, which irritated the producers, because he stopped and said hello to people. I think his outlook on life was that if you're going to stop me and ask me something, obviously it must be important, so I'll stop and answer it.

JACK, WHAT #%$*@# IS THIS SEVEN-SECOND-DELAY BUTTON USED FOR?
HOWARD DENEROFF

Even though he was raised in Queens, New York, as a Mets fan, Howard Deneroff chose to listen to Jack Buck during the 1986 World Series, instead of the Mets broadcast. Deneroff is a Coordinating Producer with Westwood One/CBS Radio Sports.

I got thrown out of English class because of Jack Buck! He was calling the game that included his famous call of the Kirk Gibson home run. I was in a night English class, with an earpiece so I could listen to the game. The professor caught me with the radio and told me I had to turn it off. I said I was listening to the World Series. Evidently, he wasn't a baseball fan. I told him I wasn't missing the World Series, so he said I might as well leave. I walked out, and listened to Jack the rest of the time. Eventually, I dropped the English class.

The first time I dealt with Jack was in September of 1989. **Brent Musberger** was hosting the studio show I met Brent first and once I got over the shock of that, I had to get on the line and talk to Jack and Hank. Even though I was only a production assistant, I felt at that moment that I had made it. If nothing else, I had worked on a Monday Night Football broadcast with Brent, Jack and Hank.

When I met Jack in person the first thing I did was take out the camera. I had to have a picture with him. That picture, which also includes Hank, has not come off my bulletin board in thirteen years. I

> Brent Musberger was the home plate umpire when Tim McCarver made his pro-baseball debut for Keokuk (IA) in the Midwest League in 1959.

was with him a ton of times since then, but I never felt the need to take another picture. He also autographed his picture that was in one of my books about announcers. I was like a kid the first time I met Jack.

Jack and Hank worked together for eighteen years. Obviously, I didn't hear every broadcast to know all their funny moments, but one that is typical Jack and Hank was during a Monday night game in Seattle. That was when Bo Jackson was with the Raiders, and he had the 91-yard touchdown run. They described the play along the lines of "… he's going 91 yards for the touchdown, and he's still running. He's into the tunnel. He's boarded the bus. He's on his way to the airport. He's probably flying the plane by himself. **Bo Jackson** does everything." It was something along those lines. Again, it wasn't a hilarious moment, but it was typical fun between Jack and Hank.

Another thing that happened a couple times a year between them that was funny, was when Jack would ask Hank what he thought a team was going to do on the next play. "They're going to run to the right," Hank would say. Then Jack would describe the play, "…throwing left." It was obvious that Jack was teasing Hank a little. They had a loose broadcast.

There was never an ounce of "I'm Jack Buck and you work for me." His humble attitude almost looked like I was the announcer and he was the production assistant. He was just an incredible guy.

That's not saying the rest of the guys are terrible people—I can name many on-air people who are great, from Greg Gumbel to **Matt Millen**—but they are few and far between, especially considering

> In 1986, Matt Millen, currently president of the Detroit Lions, punched Pat Sullivan, the Pats' general manager, in a tunnel at the LA Coliseum. Sullivan had yelled at Howie Long of the Raiders. Pat Sullivan said that Millen hit him with his helmet. Matt Millen said his fist got hit by Sullivan's face.

> Bo Jackson's real name is Vincent Edward Jackson. He was named after Vince Edwards who was the star of his mom's favorite TV show, "Ben Casey."

Jack's stature. When I first met him he had been in the business nearly 50 years, and he treated me as if I had been in the business for 50 years. He treated me as if I were a longtime member of the regular crew. It was a pleasure.

I saw him last year when we were in St. Louis for a football game. We were staying in Clayton, and went to a restaurant across the street. He tapped me on the shoulder and said, "Nice of you to call me. You come to town and you don't even have the decency to call me?" He was giving me a good Jack Buck teasing, but I felt awful. We ended up having dinner together.

Even though this was only a month or so before he went into the hospital, so he couldn't have felt a hundred percent, he still held court at our table. There were several of us at the table, and Jack was telling stories, having a great time. Everyone at the table was spellbound. He was still sharp as a tack.

Famous Calls

On Mark McGwire's 60th home run, reaching the mark set by Babe Ruth, Sept. 5, 1998:

"Wake up, Babe Ruth! There's company coming!"

WE DIDN'T KNOW ANYTHING ABOUT HORSES—WE KNEW THEY HAD FOUR LEGS, GIVE MILK—THAT'S ABOUT IT

PAT McGRATH

Pat McGrath is a longtime radio and television sports statistician, who grew up in the Chicago area. From 1983 until they stopped working together in 1996, McGrath was the booth statistician for Jack Buck and Hank Stram during CBS Radio's coverage of the NFL.

I was fortunate enough to work with Jack Buck and Hank Stram for the better part of twelve years as a booth statistician. For a lot of guys in my business, the ultimate would have been to work with Pat Summerall and **John Madden**. But I always wanted to work with Jack and Hank, and I was fortunate to have that dream come true.

A nicer and more wonderful man you could have never met. The people with whom I work now are good, but Jack Buck was one in a million.

What you saw was what you got with Jack. It didn't matter if it was a celebrity, a bank president, the guy who ran the elevator at the ballpark, an usher, or a guy who ran the food line in the pressroom, Jack was so kind and so generous and giving to all of them. You watched how the man conducted himself, and you learned life's lessons.

I grew up in Chicago, where KMOX comes in fairly clear. You don't need the hands of a safe-cracker to pick it up. So, I listened to Jack growing up. It was fortunate that I happened to be working the

When former Olympic gold medal figure skater Peggy Fleming was stranded in New York following the September 11th attacks, she hitched a ride to her San Francisco home with John Madden on the Madden Cruiser, the custom bus that Madden travels in because of his fear of flying.

television side of things at CBS, and in early 1983, I was working in the graphics truck on a game that Jack and Hank happened to be doing. They didn't have a regular statistician on Monday nights; they just picked up people in the various cities. We were able to work something out to where I traveled with them, working with them until they finished up in early 1996.

When I first met him, I was struck at how unassuming he was. You just revere someone like that. I couldn't help but think, "Am I really working a Super Bowl with Jack Buck?" It doesn't matter if you're doing a Green Bay-Tampa Bay game to two percent of the country, or doing the Super Bowl, Jack taught me to give my best effort, no matter what.

There was a Super Bowl where Hank came down with laryngitis that week. He gave about sixty-two speeches that week...he's a one-man speech-making machine during the week of the Super Bowl. As the game went on, Hank's voice got worse and worse. It was tough on Jack because he was calling the game and serving as half-analyst. Hank was not his usual verbose self; he kept things to a minimum.

When the San Francisco 49ers took a 41-10 lead in the third quarter, our guy scribbled a note that read, "Your voice sounds really bad," and passed it to Hank. Jack looked at it and kind of winked at me. Hank took the message, wadded it up and threw it under the table. The 49ers went down and scored again to make the score 48-10, and another note was passed to Hank that read, "Your voice sounds really, really bad." This one was written in big, bold print. Hank wadded it up and tossed it under the table. The 49ers scored again to make it a 55-10 game, and Hank was yanked. Jack joked that at least Stram was pulled the same time as Joe Montana.

Even when games got out of hand, Jack always had a sense of humor. When we did the 49ers and the San Diego Chargers in Super Bowl XXIX, the game was out of hand pretty early. In fact, San Francisco led 42-18 in the third quarter. The Chargers scored a late touchdown in the game, and Hank made a comment like, "It doesn't really matter if they go for two on this." Jack, with a glint in his eye said, "Well, the 49ers really don't care what the score is," he paused, then added, "but I know some people who do."

Jack enjoyed going to the racetrack. I spent a lot of my free time in Southern California during the summer. So, when the Cardinals were going to be in California for a series, I called Jack and suggested we go up to **Del Mar Race Track**.

That summer in Del Mar, they had what they called the Fantasy Race Call. You'd pay twenty dollars, and they'd take you to the booth, up on the roof next to Trevor Denman, who calls the race on the public address system. They would give you a headset, a pair of binoculars, and they put a tape in the VCR. After the race, you have a tape of yourself calling the race. Some baseball teams do the same type of thing.

I signed myself up for the second race the day that Jack and I were going to be there. I picked up Jack from the hotel. As we were driving to the track, I tossed him the program and said, "Start studying the horses for the second race." He paused, and then said to me, "Kid, how about I study them for the first race?" I said, "No, I want you to study them for the second race because you're calling the race." He wanted to know what I meant, so I explained the deal to him. Then he said, "Kid, you forgot one thing, didn't you?" I said, "What's that?" In true Jack form he replied, "I'm color-blind." Yep, it's probably a little difficult to call a race if you're color-blind.

This specific race was a turf race where, at that track, the horses come directly out the chute at you, as opposed to running straight from the gate on the side. So, being color-blind and the only way he could pick up the numbers was right above the horses' eyeholes, it could make things difficult.

He called the race, and he did a pretty good job for someone who had never done it before. As the horses turned for home he called it, "Folks, this is going to be a heck of a finish." It turned out to be a four-horse photo finish. I gave him the signal that the number-one horse won, and instead of saying the horse, he named the jockey, "Laffit Pincay sticks his nose out in front, bringing about a lousy daily-double of eight and one." The way he said it, he obviously didn't win.

> The Del Mar Race Track was founded by Pat O'Brien, and Bing Crosby in 1936. Crosby once had a song about Del Mar called "Where the Turf Meets the Surf."

He tossed me the tape and said, "You can burn this thing now, because I don't want anybody ever to see it." We walked over next door to meet Trevor Denman, who's probably the preeminent race caller in America, and Jack invited him to come to the ballpark that night to call a couple innings. Trevor had an engagement and couldn't do it. Jack said, "He's a lot smarter than I am; he didn't get sucked into it."

I held onto the tape for a number of years. I hadn't seen Jack in about four years. We would talk a couple or three times a year. Last June, the Broadcast Museum in Chicago had a tribute for him, so I planned to see him then. I told Carole about the tape. She told me that Jack probably would love to see a copy of it. After seven years, I finally went out and had a duplicate made of the tape, and sent it down to him shortly before Thanksgiving. He finally got to see it. I saw Carole and Joe at Jack's memorial service, and I know he got a kick out of watching that.

Things kind of went full circle from Jack pulling a little something on Joe, to having something done to him. That was a special day. Every once in a while I show that tape to friends.

I'd ride in the car with Jack and Hank to the stadium on Monday nights, and they very rarely, if at all, discussed what they were going to talk about during the game. They wanted it to be fresh and spontaneous. About fifteen minutes before they came on, they'd do an insert into the pre-game show with Jim Hunter or Greg Gumbel back then. That's about the only time Jack and Hank talked about the game before about ten minutes before the hour. Jack always wanted it to be fresh and not rehearsed.

Jack was on the committee that made the nominations and voted on the Pro Football Hall of Fame. That always occurred during Super Bowl weekend. I remember how passionate he was about lobbying for Jackie Smith and Dan Dierdorf to be elected. Dierdorf was elected in the last year that Jack was on the committee. I dropped Jack and Carole off at the hotel the day that it was announced, and then Jack literally ran into Dan in the lobby. Jack was so incredibly happy for Dan, which Dan talked about at Jack's memorial service.

THE HAPPY HUNGARIAN
AL HRABOSKY

A broadcaster with Fox Sports Net, Hrabosky moved into the booth after a 13-year major league career pitching for the Cardinals, Royals and Braves. He has worked Cardinals' games since 1985.

When I wanted to get into broadcasting one of the first people I called was Jack Buck to learn how to get into it and who I needed to talk to. I don't know if there's any young broadcaster in St. Louis who hasn't gotten some input and help from Jack in pursuing a broadcasting career.

In many ways he kind of established for young broadcasters what they need to do in the community and how they need to get involved with all the charitable organizations and civic groups and just be available for the different banquets that are very instrumental in the community.

I can remember one time being on a private jet and we were going with Stan Musial and Lou Brock, Andy Van Slyke, Bob Forsch, myself and Jack. Jack was kidding, "if this plane goes down it will be the biggest funeral ever in St. Louis," and yet, we had the biggest funeral ever in St. Louis for just one person on that plane.

FIRST-TIME, LONG-TIME BUCK FAN
MIKE CLAIBORNE

Mike Claiborne is a program director and on-air talent at KFNS Sports Talk Radio in St. Louis and a weekend host on the Sporting News Radio Network.

The first time I met Jack I was sitting in the sports office at KMOX, and he just strolled in. He extended his hand and said, "And you are?" I introduced myself, and he said, "I'm Jack Buck." I said, "Yeah, I know." He was cool. It wasn't anything earth shattering. He was just very cordial.

One year we were doing a high-school all-star game called the Shoot-Out. It was my first real assignment with the station, and they said, "You're going to do it with Jack." I had basically over-prepared. He sat down and started telling jokes and stories about when he was doing St. Louis University basketball, and he got me really, really loose. We're doing the game. Kenny Anderson, who later went to **Georgia Tech** and who's now with the Seattle Supersonics, was the marquee player. He had done nothing the first few minutes. Jack looked at me and said, "You've got all these notes about this guy. It doesn't appear he's really that good." I said, "Well, just sit back and wait. You just never know." And about twenty-seven points later, he just kinda looked at me and said, "You still didn't get a chance to use those notes 'cause the guy was that good." He really made a joke of it to the point where we both got a good laugh out of it. Jack was a guy who kept it loose and kept it fair. He just made sure he could draw out of his partner.

I do a talk show here now, but after his death, we didn't take callers that day. We just had other people on who knew him and let them share their thoughts and their stories about him.

> There are only five Division One schools without University in their names: Boston College, Georgia Tech, the Naval Academy, the Air Force Academy, and the U. S. Military Academy (West Point).

HOCKEY WOULD BE MORE FUN IF THE PUCK WAS TRANSPARENT

PETE WEBER

Pete Weber is the play-by-play voice of the Nashville Predators in the NHL. He also once worked for WGIL Radio in Galesburg, IL.

The first time I met Jack Buck was when I was working at WGIL in Galesburg. As a Cardinals fan, I went to a game in St. Louis. I walked up and introduced myself to him. It must have been 1969 or 1970.

I sent him a letter when his book, *That's a Winner*, came out. At the time I was making a switch from doing baseball to doing hockey on a full-time basis. He sent me a nice note back almost as if he were thanking me for writing him. Here I was thankful just to know that one of the gods of this business was responding to me.

Part of my baseball upbringing also involved doing Rochester Red Wings games. I used to try to get around the old-timers who had worked with him there to get as many stories as I could of his one season doing the Rochester Red Wings. He was held in such reverence there, and that's an earnest reverence, because nobody knows he's sick or anything like that. That's just a great deal of respect for the individual that everybody there had for him.

The whole reason I ever got involved in this business to begin with was as a kid growing up in Galesburg either listening to KMOX or trying to pick it up on WMBD. Later when I went to WGIL, we carried the Cardinal network and listened to Harry Caray and Jack Buck do the games. The first draw to me, without any question, was Harry

Caray, but then after a while it got through my thick head that guy sitting there with him is very talented in and of himself. I truly enjoyed listening to him and I remember him doing the AFL games back in the early sixties. I've always been one of those guys who rooted for the renegade league. When he was doing the AFL he wasn't afraid to try things like the "At Your Service" program which he pioneered on KMOX radio, getting away from sports that one year the Cardinals were stupid enough to have him out of the broadcast booth. Although he didn't enjoy talking about it, he did a great job when NBC developed its wrap-around program called *Grandstand* in the mid-Seventies. Ultimately that fell to Lee Leonard and Bryant Gumbel, but Jack was the guy who got it started. NBC knew this was a very well rounded man who could talk about virtually anything. The best part about Jack was he just never, ever took himself seriously. He wanted people to know he enjoyed what he was doing and felt fortunate to be able to do it.

My enduring memories of him are really going to be the 1963 and 1964 Cardinals. I was twelve and thirteen then. I grew up in a house where my father was a Cubs fan, and I could never figure out why anybody would want to follow them. At that point, it had only been ten-fifteen years since they'd been in the World Series. Well, we've stretched that matter on! He and Harry covering that 1963 race that was taken care of when the Dodgers came in late in the year and swept them at Busch Stadium. But then in 1964, that miracle comeback and the miraculous fold, too, by the Philadelphia Phillies. Those are my memories of him.

Jack Buck was definitely Mr. St. Louis. The best story I heard in the immediate aftermath of his death was the fan who walked up to a guy from KMOX outside Busch Stadium and handed in his walkman or his transistor radio to the guy that was there. He said, "Here, I've used this for years to listen to Jack Buck. I don't need this anymore."

LET'S GO TO THE VIDEO

GEORGE MICHAEL

George Michael is the star of the long-running popular, nationally syndicated "George Michael's Sports Machine." Michael was raised in Mehlville, Missouri and credits his tremendous success to Jack Buck

W e fast forward to the spring of 1973, and Bill White is working with me at Channel 6, WFIL in Philadelphia. Bill had been with the Cardinals and then with the Philadelphia Phillies. I wanted to do play-by-play in baseball. At the time I was working also as a rock-and-roll disk jockey. I had done rock-and-roll and had gotten Disk Jockey of the Year and all that stuff.

But I knew that I wanted to do sports—that's all I cared about. I said to Bill White, "I need a break, and I don't know how to get it. Being successful, I don't want to have to go to Elmira, New York and do Class D baseball." I felt I had already spent a fair amount of time paying my dues. What we did was we set up a microphone in Shibe Park in Philadelphia, and I did a dummy game between the Cardinals and the **Phillies**. I did all nine innings. Bill listened to the tape. We edited it down to about an hour. He said, "Now I want you to get together with Jack Buck."

The Cardinals came to town in the spring of 1973, and Bill set it up for me. Jack said, "Hey, I know George. Have him come on over." I went over there, and I was scared to death. I brought my tape with me.

> P.K. Wrigley and Milton Hershey were bitter business rivals. When Wrigley bought the Chicago Cubs, Hershey tried to buy the Philadelphia Phillies...and sell chocolate gum. Hershey failed in both efforts.

Well now, you figure he's gonna give me two minutes, and get the heck out of here 'cause I'm interfering with his day. I go into the room. He orders lunch. He had coffee. He said, "Let's listen to it." He listened to the whole tape—it ran almost an hour. He said, "How many other people have heard this tape?" I said, "Only Bill White." He said, "Well, you can do this today. What you may not know in homework, you'll learn. Here are the few things you've got to change. Don't say a ground ball to Belanger. Say a ground ball to short, Belanger up with it. Don't say a drive to Don Baylor. Give the position first." He told me certain things about enthusiasm, not to be afraid. He took me through every single thing that I had on the tape, and he gave me very high grades. He said, "Now what you've got to do is build up the nerve to leave that rock-and-roll and go into sports because you can do it. So, do it."

I sent the tape to Jerry Hoffberger, who owned the Baltimore Orioles. I figured nothing would ever happen. I get a call in April of 1974, and it's from Hoffberger. He said, "We'd like to have you come do our games on vacation relief for Chuck Thompson and Bill O'Donnell. They're gone around thirty games a year, and we'd like to have you do it. " Well, I don't know s—from Shinola about the Orioles or the American League. I'm a National League guy, but this is a chance to do a World Champion team. I call Jack Buck and say, "Jack, I don't know. Should I turn it down?" He said, "Heck no. Do your homework. Study the media guide. Read *The Sporting News*. Get their press releases. You can do this." He tells me a couple of things to remember—"Don't try to get ahead of the play"—his rule number one. "Don't anticipate 'because you'll end up apologizing. Remember the ball goes to the position, player's name second. If somebody does something great, don't be afraid to say it." I said, "I've got a problem, Jack." He said, "What's the problem?" I said, "Well, we're divided by a thin glass. They're gonna be playing the White Sox, and next door is going to be Harry Caray." He said, "Just don't listen." I said, "But people say I sound like Harry." He said, "Don't worry about it."

I went down there, and on June 10, 1974, I did the first game. I was scared to death. But Don Baylor hit a game-winning home run in the tenth inning. For whatever reason, I called it a Bohemian blast, and the Orioles were owned by National Beer. Jerry Hoffberger runs in and wants to sign me to a long-term contract. I'm thinking about Jack Buck. "This guy told me what to do and how to do it."

I worked with the Orioles that summer of 1974. I sent Jack a tape. He pointed out a few things. He was my critic, my guide. I didn't see him or hear from him for a while. I was in St. Louis a couple of times, and we saw each other on the field. What amazed me was that instead of my having to say, "Hey, that's Jack Buck." He would come over and say, "Hey George." And he was terrific.

> **Because Jack Buck went out of his way to be nice to me, we have the largest intern department... and I take time with every intern.**

You have guys come to you all the time and say, "Hey, man, will you listen to my tape?" You try to encourage them. You try to point some things out, but you don't know if they're going to go anywhere. Most of the time, you're just being polite. You don't want to say, "Man, you stink." Even though Jack had told me all this, I always worried about whether or not I was good enough. Well, I ended up going to New York and worked up there for six years. I knew I was going to leave to go to a full-time sports job. When I came here, I sent him a note and thanked him for his help. I thanked him several times, but I wrote him a long letter about two and a half years ago and just laid it all out to him—that I really had been very grateful, and the effect that he had in this. Because Jack Buck went out of his way to be nice to me, we have the largest intern department of any TV station in the country, and I take time with every intern. I put them on the air doing in-studio work, let them do stuff, see themselves on tape, and every time I do it, I always say, "This is for you, Jack Buck." He took time that was beyond just, "Sure, I'll listen to your tape." He went way out of his way. Whenever I'd see Jack Buck, it would always be, "Don't forget. You owe your career to me. Pick up my tab." But then, bingo, the tab would be picked up. I will never be able to say thank you enough. I'm grateful that I did write him. It was before he got really sick. He was special. And, the guy was a great announcer

The last time I saw Jack was three years ago down in St. Pete. We saw each other in the piano bar at the Don Cesar hotel. Once again, as he had said to me twenty times, he said, "You owe that career to me. Don't forget it now." I wrote him saying, "I owe what I've got in my career to you." He'd say, "You owe that career to me. When you get the big paycheck, be sure to send me some." Then he bought a CD for me of the guy who played piano there. This guy was phenomenal. He had put out a CD and Jack bought a CD for me and said, "Enjoy the memories." That was the last time I talked to him.

Jack Buck was a friend who took time to help. He was a star who took time to help a guy with a Beatle-looking haircut, a rock-and-roll disk jockey, saying, "You can do it. You've got to get the courage to do it." There just aren't enough people like him. Most guys are so involved in their own careers, they don't have time for anybody. This guy went out of his way.

There's no blueprint on how to do a memorial service like the Cardinals put on. Whatever you do, you do with the best of intentions and anyone who criticizes it or complains—hey, go fly a kite. There was only one Jack Buck. Personally, I thought it was great that they did what they did so everybody could express their emotions or grief or feelings. Can you really ask more than that? The fact that ten thousand people showed up—that is incredible. It touched us so deeply because there are no more Jack Bucks. We've got Vin Scully left and Ernie Harwell's gonna retire.

What people forget is that in St. Louis, baseball is everything. Because the Cardinals are everything. That's where we're from. That's what it is. That's what we live with. I grew up in Mehlville, and we lived and died by the Cardinals. The people who put the ceremony together—I don't know how you could do it better. It gave everybody the ability to go and express their emotions. The Cardinal baseball announcer is a part of everybody's life. It's not like the announcers we've got now. There are a hundred sportscasters. I know that in the industry where I'm considered like the last of these local TV giants, I understand that. When I started, everybody was. Jack Buck was one of the icons. I give my due to Vin Scully because Vin has been there since forever, but for the Midwest, hey, it was Jack Brickhouse—but I don't think Jack Brickhouse ever came close to being what Jack Buck was.

Jack Buck was a part of people's lives. When Jack spoke they trusted him. The difference between Jack and Harry Caray was Jack never got on individual players. He would tell you if the guy was in an 0 for 13 slump, but he wouldn't say it in a way that made you want to boo him. I remember what Harry Caray did to Kenny Boyer, "Captain Kenny. O for 14!" That's just not necessary. "Brooks Lawrence, hasn't won a game since forever." Things like that. Jack would say, "Brooks Lawrence. He's been struggling of late, working on his curve ball." Or whatever, it was said in a positive way, and the players appreciated it. Players don't know how good they had it with Jack Buck.

For a new ballpark in St. Louis, I would think they would name a section or a garden or something like that for Jack. The truth is that stadiums cost so much. You've got to get back that money somehow, that if Anheuser-Busch would put up millions for naming rights, then it's got to be. Sure it would be great to call it **Buck Stadium**, but you've got to remember forty years from now you're still stuck with Buck Stadium and no money coming in. And forty years from now, you're going to have a different set of problems. It would be ideal to do that, and it's a beautiful thought, but business-wise it can't happen.

The impact he had on me was that, number one, I'll always help everybody else; and number two, I'll keep both feet on the ground and remember I'm only here for a short time. So make sure it's good. Make sure it's good.

> Bob Murphy has been the Voice of the New York Mets for 40 years. His brother, Jack, was a sportswriter in San Diego. The latter was so influential in bringing major league baseball to San Diego in 1969 that the city named the park for him: Jack Murphy Stadium.

FURTHERMORE, HANK FEELS THE WASHINGTON GENERALS ARE DUE
HANK STRAM

Hank Stram was Jack Buck's broad-casting partner on Monday Night Foot-ball for CBS Radio for seventeen years. Stram, the winningest coach in AFL history has gained fame in recent years by correctly predicting the Super Bowl winner twenty-seven years in a row.
His seventy-six-step formula had the Patriots winning Super Bowl XXXVI

W e got to be great friends during the days of the American Football League when Jack was broadcasting games for ABC. When we were the **Dallas Texans** (later the Kansas City Chiefs) in the American Football League, Jack broadcast almost all of our games. We had a great relationship that started there. So, when we started working together, we had a great rapport in the booth. We had a lot of fun, and enjoyed each other very much.

Many years ago, I got a call from CBS asking if I was interested in doing Monday Night Football. I told them that I thought it'd be great. I told them that I was currently working with Curt Gowdy on television and asked who I'd be working with on radio. They said it would be Jack Buck. We became partners, and worked together for the next 17 years.

It was a great relationship. There was no pride of authorship. We were great friends. We just went into the booth each week and did our thing. Jack never met a stranger. He liked everybody; and they liked him.

In the first year of the AFL, there were 600 fans at a Los Angeles Chargers (later San Diego) home game against the Dallas Texans. Chargers' owner Barron Hilton wanted to refund their money, lock the gates, sit at mid-field by himself while Lamar Hunt, the Texans owner, sat alone across the field. Hunt nixed the idea. The Chargers were named after Hilton's credit card company, Carte Blanche.

Jack liked peanut butter, so I called him Skippy. When I called him that, though, he got a little "irrigated," as my mother would say. We were in Cleveland doing a national game on television. One of the engineers was around us while we were talking. After Jack walked away, the engineer said to me, "Coach, Jack seemed to be very upset when you called him Skippy. Now I have to go down and interview him." I said that it was a term of endearment. "Jack loves it when you call him Skippy," I told the engineer. "So when you go down to interview him, be sure to call him Skippy. He'll think you really like him." After the interview, the engineer ran up to our booth and told me, "Coach, I did what you told me...I called him Skippy. Boy, was he mad. He really let me have it." I told him, "Well, you must have presented it in the wrong way, because normally when you call him Skippy, he knows it's a term of endearment. You must have blown the whole deal." The engineer replied, "One thing's for sure; I'll never talk to you about what to call Jack again. I'm sure not going to be up in the box anymore to talk to him, because he was really upset."

> **"Jack loves it when you call him Skippy," I told the engineer. "So when you go down to interview him, be sure to call him Skippy...**

Skippy liked Snickers candy bars. He brought a brown paper bag to every game, full of Snickers. I'd sneak around, waiting for him to go someplace so I could suck up a few of those Snickers. One day he walks into the booth and with that low voice of his says, "Here you are, Coach, here are some goodies for you." When he left, I grabbed what I thought was a Snickers, but it was a piece of the equipment for the telephone! I picked it up thinking it was a candy bar, and I was going to suck it up like my last supper, but the next thing I knew it felt like all my teeth were gone. Jack had taken that metal piece and wrapped it up in Snickers paper. He was upstairs laughing. As my mother would say, I was very "irrigated" about that.

Jack had a big heart. He was an easy rider. He was a big spender and a big tipper. Most of the people in the broadcasting business throw tips around like they're manhole covers…not Jack. He would give a waitress a 50-dollar bill.

He was always well prepared and he knew I was well prepared. We didn't talk about the teams during the week. Our broadcasts were smooth as could be. He was very easy to work with, and he had great timing.

I have so many people come up and tell me how much they enjoyed listening to us broadcast games. Then, they ask me why we stopped doing the broadcasts. It's simple: we got bounced out. We were going along at a great pace, then one day they told us that we were finished. We weren't surprised by the move; we were shocked. Bob Kipperman called me during the off-season and wanted to meet me for lunch in New Orleans, which is near my home. Bob and I were getting ready to have lunch. He told me that new people were taking over CBS Radio, and that Jack and I would no longer do Monday Night Football games. After I got up from falling out of the chair in total shock, I asked him if anybody else knew about it. He said, "Nobody knows about it. You're the only one." After he left I got a call from Bill Sevara, who was our engineer, saying how he heard that Jack and I had been fired. He said they told him a few days ago.

We really had a great time together. I look back to those days and think about how fantastic it was. We never had anything but fun all those years. We just walked in there one day, pushed the button, and had a great 17 years.

WE'RE DOWN TO OUR LAST BUCK
JOE BUCK

The apple didn't fall far from the tree in the case of Joe Buck. In a summer in which Joe Buck lost his father and grandmother within several weeks, he was kind enough to share some of his views on his illustrious father.

I'll never forget my first play-by-play broadcast…my dad left me in the booth by myself. I was supposed to go to prom that week. A girl had asked me and then, about a week and a half out, she canceled on me, so to sort of soften the blow, my dad took me with him to New York for my birthday. I was in the back of the booth, kind of listening, kind of not. In the fifth inning, without any warning whatsoever he said, "Now to take you through the fifth inning, here's my son, the birthday boy, Joe Buck." I looked down there and probably turned white as a ghost. I ran down there, I was begging him not to do that. To me it wasn't that crazy because he'd done something like this on my sixteenth birthday where he had me on the air for a minute, but when he did this he said "to take us through the inning." I thought, "There's no way I'm going to be able to do this" because I hadn't been paying that much attention to the game. As I looked down, I was saying "No, please" and he tapped Mike on the shoulder and he and Mike got up and left, so I ran down there and did it.

It was probably the most boring inning in the history of radio baseball play-by-play but I got through it. Nothing really happened, it was a 1-2-3, inning, and when I got back and sat down next to the engineer, Colin Jarrette, who was from Trinidad. I said "I was pretty good, huh?" I was feeling pretty good about myself. In his very distinctive and distinguished voice, he said, "It lacked description." So that brought me back down to earth, realizing that if you are going to do radio play-by-play one thing you probably want to be good at is describing things. I evidently failed in his eyes.

Mike and my dad came back in and they were kind of laughing at me, but my dad told the story a thousand times after that about how he wouldn't have done it if he didn't think that I was able to handle it. The reason he thought I was able to handle it was that I would do games into a tape recorder in the booth in St. Louis and then we would listen to the tapes on the way home, after games. This was from the time I was thirteen when I did about ten games into the tape recorder that summer, then another ten when I was fourteen, maybe ten or twelve when I was fifteen all the way to when I was eighteen. They knew I at least had the mechanics of it down. He wasn't trying to embarrass me or do anything but give me a shot at something not a lot of kids get to do on their eighteenth birthday.

My dad was always behind me every step of my career. I remember after game six of the first World Series I broadcast in 1996, I was thinking of him the whole time I was looking at the camera when I was signing off. I called home after the game and asked "what did you think?" and he said "When did it come on?" And I thought "Yeah, right, you were listening to every word, watching every play every second." He liked to act like it was no big deal but I knew it meant a lot to him. I found out later my parents had tears in their eyes that night.

I always wanted to be an announcer. Well at first I wanted to be a baseball player, like most kids. When reality hit there, I had no desire to do anything else. I think I probably recognized that it was something that I wanted to do from the time I was five or six on. I didn't want to be a policeman, a fireman, or a lawyer or a doctor; I wanted to be my dad.

I was doing Triple A when I was nineteen. I was at Louisville, and I knew the only reason they had hired me was I was Jack Buck's son. My dad had always told the story that both he and I first learned the meaning of the word "subsidize" because that was what he was doing for me, he was subsidizing my income because I was making all of $200 a month.

I think if it hadn't of worked out he would not have let me get to the next level with the Cardinals. I might have tried Triple A for a few more years and he would have pulled me aside and said "Hey, this isn't for you." He had seven other kids and it wasn't as if we all ended up calling baseball games on the radio. He knew I loved the game and I was around him a lot. He took me on road trips when I was eight or nine years old. I was in Philadelphia, Pittsburgh and Houston as a little kid running around, hanging around ball players, and being with him. I was on the team charter flights, and the team bus. It was just something I'd been around my whole life. I was afforded that luxury because he and I got along so well together. I didn't give him any trouble. I wasn't the typical little ten-year-old who was getting in to everything. I respected what he did and I didn't want to bother him. I just wanted to be with him and I knew that if I was a whiny little ten-year-old kid he'd probably leave me at home. Consequently, I wasn't a whiny little kid and was probably hanging around adults more when I was ten than most twenty-year-olds do.

> **I just wanted to be with him and I knew that if I was a whiny little ten-year-old kid he'd probably leave me at home.**

I never really got into any trouble as a kid. The most trouble I got into was fighting with my sister Julie, and we got a "bad report" from our baby sitter one night when my parents came in from having dinner. Day after day I fought with my little sister—you know, just bugging her like kids do. One night he came in after they had begged me not to bother her and I'd done it anyway. We got a bad report and he woke me up and asked "Did you get a bad report tonight?" and I said "Yeah" and he flipped my bed over! He reached down and grabbed my mattress and flipped me over! After that, I wasn't bad anymore.

He said "Don't act like that any more" and we laughed about it later. Everything was done with his sense of humor. He never really truly got mad. I'd say the maddest he ever got with me was when he was on a long road trip and I was seventeen years old. My best friend and I talked my mom into trading my Bronco in for a sports car. Here's how spoiled I was—my parents gave me a Bronco for my sixteenth birthday and I traded it in for a Mazda RX7. It was going to be my big surprise to show my dad when he got home from the road trip. He got home Sunday night real late, and I was waiting up for him because I couldn't wait to show it to him. He knew nothing about it. He came home and went through the garage and saw the thing. He walked in and said "Who's living with us? Mario Andretti!" My mom started to explain and then I came downstairs and said "Dad did you see my new car, Mom got that for me!"

He didn't smile or speak for about two days. He just hated it. He hated the fact that I had it. It was kind of a little snotty car to have. Here I was, I talked my mom into dumping the car that he and my mom had got me. It all happened without him knowing anything about it and it just bothered him that it happened.

The funny thing was, I got into this little "fender-bender" accident coming home from baseball practice one day, and he said "I knew that nothing good would ever come out of you having this car!" and I said "Dad it was nothing, I just lost control when I was coming around the corner and I hit a little wall and there was a little dent in it." And he said "Yeah, I'm getting rid of this thing, you never should have had this thing in the first place!" This was in the afternoon. He was leaving for the ballpark that day and as he was getting in his car and backing up out of the garage he just smashed into my car. It was totally by accident. He pulled up and the look on his face when he got out of his car was priceless. He hated the car from the beginning, and now he hits that car with his car because he couldn't see it behind him. That was it. That car was gone shortly after that.

I didn't know Chip Caray as a kid. I never really realized he spent so much time in St. Louis as a kid until we talked about it later. There was a chance there for a while that we would wind up working together in St. Louis. He would do the television while I the radio. It ended up that I went over and did more TV and he went to Seattle at that point. He ended up back in Chicago. He and I never really spent much time together until he went on one road trip with the Cardinals and was doing kind of an on-air audition. We hung around a little. I've only known him and admired him from afar.

When I went to college, I chose Indiana because it was on a list of schools with good English and Communications departments. It wasn't Missouri and it wasn't Syracuse. Everybody I've heard of from Bob Costas on down went to Syracuse. Missouri was a place everybody went to also. I just wanted to go out of state, I wanted to go away to school, but I didn't want to be so far away I couldn't get home. I got there and looked around the campus and just fell in love with it and ended up going there. My parents would come and visit me there. I got to show off my dad at the old fraternity house and it was fun.

Very few people know how much my dad had to put up with in the hospital. I saw a picture today when my sister, Julie, brought her newborn in to meet him for the first time. It was about two or three weeks before he died. Seeing the image of him in that bed looking the way he looked was just tough to take. It just brought it all back. For seven months he had one thing after another hit him and he just kept going. I don't know how he did it. The doctors don't know how he did it. Only because of his determination did they even think he had a prayer of getting through any of it. Even early on in the process. Then more things came up, and then more complications, and then radical surgeries with the Parkinson's operation. His attitude through it all was amazing. I would spend night after night with him in the hospital.

Those were some of the best talks we ever had, better than the road trips, better than any time we spent together here at home, at his house, or with me growing up. Just seeing him and his attitude in that situation.

He said to me one night before I left for Spring Training, "I hope my laying in the hospital, going through this, teaches you something. You should realize by looking at me in this position that in one way or another we will all end up in this situation. It might be quick, it might be long, but this should teach you to have fun and live your life." We were just in the process of putting money down on a house. He said, "Buy your house, enjoy your kids, enjoy what you are able to do because you don't know how long it's going to last." To get that from him was something different than things we ever discussed.

He always tried to keep me from getting too excited about myself and keep me from biting off more than I could chew. When we were buying our second house when my first child was born, he thought it was too big. He came over and looked through it. Instead of saying, "It's a great house" he just said "Well, who the heck is going to live with you, the Rams?" He would just kind of low-key everything. He would keep me grounded. His praise was probably the most important thing that I could get in my career but he

> I wish I had known him when he was a younger guy...

didn't heap it on me. He just said, "That was a great job Buck, you did us proud, keep your head up, and keep on going." Little shots of encouragement and praise went a long, long way. When he said I did all right I didn't care what anybody else thought of the performance I had.

When he was lying there in the hospital bed and facing the Parkinson's surgery, he was about as sick as anybody could be. To get through a major operation like that was incredible. He was so excited because it was a success. That was an example of how tough this guy was.

I wish I had known him when he was a younger guy, I saw pictures of him in his army uniform, and when he was starting out broadcasting. Just seeing a picture of a vibrant young guy, I didn't get a chance to see much of that. I know how he ended up. To see what he went through and how he endured it was phenomenal. I will never ever complain about anything that happens to me physically or anything in my life, healthwise after seeing his attitude going through that.

He would tell people in interviews how proud of me he was. He would say to me, "You're the best, you're the best." That's really all he would do. He was thrilled. In his mind I was better than him, in my mind I'll never be as good as him, and I think it's great that way.

How will I ever live up to the man? I'm gonna have to carry a lot of $100 bills around I guess. It was amazing. It never ended. He was truly a guy who never forgot from where he came. Because of that he was willing and really could never wait to throw it around and spread it around when he got the opportunity. There were people in his life along the way who made an impression on him by being generous. I think he wanted to be that person for a lot of people when he became an older person. He certainly succeeded in that regard.

Just the other day I was in Baskin-Robbins with my kids and my wife, and some of the Ladue firefighters were in there getting ice cream for their station. Their ice cream was put on the counter. They put their money up and I reached in, grabbed my money and gave them back theirs, and paid for their ice cream. They gave my kids a tour of the firehouse and I bought them dinner that night. My wife turned to me and said "That was a Jack Buck thing to do, right there." And it was, and that was totally why I did it and I plan on doing more of that.

There are interns, people who had a short time at KMOX who have come out of the woodwork since he passed away talking about him giving them $100 or buying them dinner one night when they were out. It's just amazing the stories of how generous he was.

One of the most important things he did in his career was one of the last things he did in his career.

One of the most important things he did in his career was one of the last things he did in his career. It was writing that poem after September 11th. He spent a lifetime building up that kind of credibility and that kind of presence. When he delivered that poem on September 17th and stood out on that field the first night back—it was a weird night at the ballpark. I was there doing the game on TV. It was the very first major league game after the tragedy. Everybody was scared to death about what's happening, it was like the world was coming to an end. People were thinking "Should we even be in a ballpark playing baseball?" When he stepped out there on the field and read that poem, it didn't matter if you were a player, a firefighter, a fan, a non-fan. You didn't have to be a baseball fan to appreciate what that meant. It was a big moment in the country's recovery when sports resumed. One of the most important moments when baseball came back was that speech on the field. When he said it was okay to be there it felt like it was okay to be there. The pressure was off; it was time to get back to playing baseball and doing what we do, as awful as September 11th was.

I saw him as he was headed down to read the poem, and said "You're gonna cry, aren't you?" He said, "I will not cry." I said "Dad, you cry at everything, you're gonna cry." He said "I will not cry" and looked me in the eye and didn't blink. I said, "All right, I'll bet you." Well he went down there and did it and he didn't cry. He came back up to the booth and said, "Until you said that to me I thought I was gonna break down, and when you challenged me I made up my mind that I wasn't gonna cry."

He was touched by so many things in his life. One time he joked that he was known to cry at the sight of a good card trick! That's just the kind of guy he was. When he delivered that poem, I was just waiting for him to well up and not be able to continue but he was just strong as could be. Even with the Parkinson's and in some respects as informed as he was, he just nailed that thing. It was a big, big moment.

I've been working at the network level since 1994, and I have never one time had to worry about what was to follow when someone said, "I worked with your dad." He worked with a lot of people, and he worked with a lot of people I work with now and when they say "I worked with your dad" I know what's coming. They don't even have to finish the sentence. Every one of them says "He was one of the nicest, most selfless people I've ever worked with in this business and I enjoyed every minute of it." I mean to a man, to a woman, everybody says that about him. So whenever anybody's writing a book about him or has a comment about him I don't worry about it because he was as consistent a guy as I've ever heard about.

He was consistent away from the public eye. He was as consistent when people weren't watching as he was when they were. He was a Depression-era kid who had a work ethic and it was ingrained in him when he was a young man. It never left him. He never got too big for the situation he was in and he never took for granted that he was making money and he was doing something that people would kill to do. He approached everything like that. That's really what kept him this warm, generous person that we all knew.

So many people can't do that. They can't take what they do and set it aside from the person they are. It becomes who they are and it becomes a public perception that becomes larger than life. People become hard to take, and he was not one of those people.

All I heard were stories that he must have had a unique childhood—not unique to the time, but certainly different from the way the children grow up these days. I've been reading his book lately. Though his mother was tough, you can see from those quotes in the book how much respect and how much love he had for his mom, and how much he loved being around his dad. I think he and I were similar in that way. I think he enjoyed being around his father and he admired him and so did I. I enjoyed being around my dad and I admired him. I couldn't get enough of him.

My oldest daughter will be able to remember him, she's six. One time, when she was two and a half, maybe three years old, my dad had been babysitting her. My wife, Ann, and I came in the back door and as we walked in my dad was on all fours in the kitchen. Ann and I looked at each other. We thought he'd had a heart attack or something. I thought he was on the floor having pains or something and here he was going around on all fours barking like a dog and he was doing it to make my daughter laugh. My mom walked in right behind us and she said "He never did that with you!" He just enjoyed his grandkids and he enjoyed the younger kids more later in life than when I was little.

I don't know anybody who worked as hard as he worked and had the kind of schedule he had. It was just ridiculous how much he worked and he wasn't making a ton of money at that time either. He had to do all those jobs to support and feed all of us.

We had a lot of time together, but he would just go out of his way to make it. If it was getting off a red-eye and sitting with us at breakfast before we went to school and getting his work done and sitting down at dinner at night, he'd make that happen. Or we'd take our show on the road. We'd take trips together. I was probably in every major league ballpark since I was thirteen. He and I went everywhere—I'd go to Vegas with him, I'd go to L.A. with him. Whatever he did, I did. If he was playing blackjack, I'd be playing video games, and we'd meet at two in the morning and go to bed and get up the next day and fly home.

My friends loved my dad. They loved being around him. My dad had nicknames for all my friends and they loved the fact that Jack Buck knew who they were and could joke with them about things. My dad knew me so well that I think he trusted my judgement with who I brought around the house. He was interested in what they were doing. He remembered my friends names. They loved him. When he died, I heard from friends I hadn't heard from for years. People were just pouring out their hearts to me about how much my dad meant to them when they were growing up.

He knew everybody. People would come up to him and he knew their father or he knew their brother. And people who worked at the brewery for a long time. If their dad had worked at the brewery he would remember them. The next time he saw them he would remember them and talk to them and pick up where they had left off. I don't have that trait. I didn't inherit that from him.

> **I had a great dad.**
> **I loved my dad.**
> **I miss my dad.**

There was really a deep love for each other between Mike Shannon and my father. Like any relationship, they had their ups and downs, but when he was sick, Mike really helped take care of him in the booth. He took the pressure off him and made sure he was okay, and when he passed away, it really hit Mike hard. I was there and I know how much love there was between them. They were a good team.

I had a great dad. I loved my dad. I miss my dad.

Appendix

Christine Buck's Eulogy

Joe Buck's Eulogy

A Poem by Jack Buck

Timeline

Cubs Singers

"He left a trail of love and laughter wherever he went"

Christine Buck's eulogy to her father

Good morning, I'm Christine Buck, I'm number three. There are eight, you know, I'm number three.

Nobody can prepare you for the death of a parent, regardless of the circumstances. The truth is, we know we're lucky, because so many people understand the depth of our loss. It's also their loss. The phrase "Random Acts of Kindness," should have been invented for him. He understood something a lot of people never understand. The more you give, the more you get back, and he gave of himself in countless ways everyday. Our dad's philosophy was simple. It's either right or wrong. Good or bad. You take this road or that road. He always said, "I like people. It's as simple as that. I like people to like me and I work at it."

He had an incredible sense of humor, and it was just that, a sense. Like hearing or smelling or touching. It was just who he was. He was aging, but he never grew old. He was always charming and he could be disarming. Sometimes it happened to him. He recalled once when an attractive woman looked at him and said, "What did you used to do?" And as he said, "That'll take you down a peg." Once while golfing, he looked at the caddie and said, "You are, without a doubt, the worst caddie I've ever seen." And he said, "Oh, Mr. Buck, that would be too big of a coincidence."

He was always in the moment and not just when he was doing play-by-play. He was a fantastic master of ceremonies. He would prepare for a speaking engagement all the time. He had scraps of paper sticking in his pocket. He said, "The cleaners know more about my business than I do."

But, you know, he never really got it. He never understood what he meant to this community. He used to say, "I'm a modest man with much to be modest about." We would beg to differ. He rarely had a private persona. What you saw was what you got. He left a trail of love and laughter wherever he went.

Our father never walked. He strolled. His advice to a reporter once was, "Kid, never run to your mike." Time was always of essence. He wouldn't say, "Meet me at 5 o'clock or fiveish—5:03."

He raised the bar on a lot of things. Watching him struggle with his health and watching him struggle in the hospital, raised the bar on what we can complain about. He certainly raised the bar on tipping. We went to a carwash once and the manager said to my sisters and I, "Your father tipped every guy in here $100 once." I looked around, there were 25 guys, you know. He raised the bar on being polite with good manners. He raised the bar on how to be classy and humorous and caring. He raised the bar on how to live life to its fullest. Don't waste time, don't forget people less fortunate than you. The love and support of this community has helped our family celebrate his life. And thank you for that. Thank you for understanding what a gem he was. The world was definitely a better place because of him.

We have to pick up the slack now. Give more to charities. Remember the veterans, people with cystic fibrosis and Parkinson's. If we all do Random Acts of Kindness, we might all be able to fill the void he left just a little bit. On behalf of my family, thank you St. Louis. We said how we shared him, but the truth is, he wouldn't have it any other way. And I want to read to you something that epitomizes what he means to his fans. And this is from one of his fans, an anonymous letter that was left in front of his statue.

"Goodbye, old friend, it's time to say farewell. You were always there in both good times and in bad. It seems you always knew just what to say and, most times, you would say what I felt. You were my eyes when I could not see and my voice when I could not speak.

You have lived a good life and fought the tough fight. It is now time for you to rest, old friend. We spent many years together, and although we never met, you were a constant friend. On that I could depend. God has blessed your life, and now it's time to be by his side. Go crazy, heaven, go crazy."

I hope that person's listening. We love you, Dad, and we miss you. Goodbye.

"He had a gift, and he made anyone he met feel special"

Joe Buck's eulogy to his father

Good morning. I guess I'm number seven. It's an awful feeling to sit down there and realize your eulogy is not as good as the one you just heard. But we'll give it a shot.

First I would like to thank Rev. Rodney Stortz and Twin Oaks Presbyterian for the job they have done handling all of this. The music already has been hard to take, sitting here in the front row it has been absolutely gorgeous.

There's no doubt that these past seven months, which have been excruciating for my father and for his family and friends, have been for a reason. To me, the Lord wanted to give us all a transition period from life with this wonderful man to life without him. It was a tough road. Tough for him to experience, I'm sure, and tough for us to watch.

The fact that he fought so hard right until the end did not surprise anyone who knew him. Seemingly everyday there was something new staring him right in the face, and he stared right back. He didn't ever say, "Why me," instead he put his fist forward and said, "Let her rip." That was Jack Buck.

Over the past six or seven years, his health was declining, whether it was Parkinson's or diabetes or bouts of vertigo, he always seemed to be tested. The test was, will you let this ailment stop you from doing your work? Will you let this disease and its symptoms change your attitude? The answer from him was always no.

It didn't bother him that Parkinson's made him shake so bad sometimes that it took him 10 times as long as it once did to sign an autograph. Or made it difficult to hold a microphone steady enough to conduct an interview before a ballgame. "Let other people worry about the shaking," he would say.

He would take insulin shots before every game. He did in final years, with Cardinal trainer Barry Weinberg administering the brief pain while having to hear another joke that had either already been delivered at a banquet or was about to be.

Sometimes his vertigo was so bad that he had to sit in the players' lounge, eat a snack, usually peanut butter and crackers, talk to George Kissel, a longtime Cardinal instructor, listen to whatever rap music he was subjected to on the clubhouse stereo, let the symptoms subside, and then head up to the booth to tell the world about Cardinal baseball.

He loved the Cardinals. He loved staying young by talking to the current players. He loved the life, he loved the travel, and the experiences that it brought him and the people that he met.

He knew that he had a responsibility to a listening audience to be fair, accurate and, most of all, entertaining. He was all that, night after night, year after year, and as Tony La Russa said, he never went into a slump. I got the chance to see it all firsthand. Not only as a kid but as a broadcast partner.

As a kid, I would trail after him following the game and hold his beer while he signed autographs for fans on his way to the car. I got so close to him on that walk so I could let everyone know that that was my dad. As an adult, I tried to get that close to him again when we were in the booth so I could learn from him.

That's my relationship with him. One of literally millions that he had in his life. You see, I don't believe I'm anymore qualified to stand up here today than anyone out there in the audience. He had the unbelievable ability to connect with everyone he came across. Social status meant nothing to him. Race, who cares? In fact, it was those people who others might consider beneath them that he went out of his way to befriend and help if he could.

The name Tommy Hanlon comes to mind, a young man my dad ran across who had some challenges in life and took the bus to work at the ballpark every day. Naturally, like all Hall of Fame announcers, my father would pick him up and take him home from time to time.

Someone who had grown up in Tommy's neighborhood called in to KMOX the other day and said one afternoon all the kids in the street were standing by as my dad pulled up in his car. My father rolled down his window and said to the boys, "You take care of my Tommy, OK."

That was Jack Buck. I didn't know about that story until I heard it on the radio two days ago. He would never brag about it, he just did it. There are so many stories like that.

My relationship with him was different than what he had with anyone of my brothers or sisters or the grandchildren, it was certainly different than the one he had with my mother. It was not that it was better or worse, it was just different. Unique. He had a gift, and he made anyone he met feel special.

He had some sayings that I will never forget.

> *"Worry, I'll tell you when to worry."*

> *"Don't holler till you hurt."*

> *"And things turn out best for those who make the best of the way things turn out."*

Well I believe we are making the best of the way things turned out. This celebration of his life has been so moving and so helpful. All of the cards during his fight and after will never be forgotten. Our family cannot thank you enough. It has been replayed many times recently, my father saying at a banquet that my mom once asked him what he would say if he met the Lord. And his response was, "Why have you been so good to me?" Well, after that exchange which I'm sure has already taken place, is there any doubt that the Lord said, "Well done, my good and faithful servant."

I will miss the style and elegance he had about him, I will miss the way people were drawn to him when he entered a room, I will miss that voice. And I will miss those words put together as only he could. His philosophy of life, and I quote, "There are many laughs and tons and tons of strife, I've been able to minimize it and state my philosophy of life. Simply put, you'll choose a road, the one you'll travel on. You go and go and go and go and pretty soon you're gone." Just like him, understated as always, humble as always, we know it's not true. He may be gone, but he will never be forgotten.

A Poem by Jack Buck

Since this nation was founded, under God
More than 200 years ago
We have the bastion of freedom
The light that keeps the free world aglow
We do not covet the possessions of others
We are blessed with the bounty we share

We have rushed to help other nations, anything,
anytime, anywhere

War is just not our nature
We won't start, but we will end the fight
If we are involved we shall be resolved
To protect what we know is right

We have been challenged by a cowardly foe
Who strikes and then hides from our view

With one voice we say, "There is no choice today,
There is only one thing to do"
Everyone is saying the same thing and praying
That we end these senseless moments we are living

As our fathers did before, we shall win this unwanted war
And our children will enjoy the future we'll be giving.

—by Jack Buck, written after the tragic events of September 11, 2001

Jack Buck Timeline: 1924-2002

Aug. 21, 1924	Born in Holyoke, Mass., to Earle and Kathleen Buck, the third of their seven children.
1939	Family moves to Cleveland.
January, 1941	Graduates from Lakewood (Ohio) High School.
June, 1943	Drafted into Army during World War II.
February, 1945	Deployed to Europe for combat.
March 15, 1945	Wounded in action (arm, leg injuries) in Remagen, Germany. Receives a Purple Heart.
1946	Enrolls at Ohio State University.
1948	Marries Alyce Larson. They have six children (Beverly; Jack Jr., Christine; Bonnie; Betsy and Danny) before divorcing in 1969.
December 1949	Graduates from Ohio State University.
1950-51	Broadcasts minor-league baseball on radio in Columbus, Ohio. Also broadcasts Ohio State football and basketball.
1952	Works as television sportscaster in Cleveland.
1953	Broadcasts NBA and minor-league baseball on radio in Rochester, N.Y.
1954	Hired, with Milo Hamilton, to broadcast Cardinals baseball alongside Harry Caray.
December 1959	Fired by Cardinals.
1960	Broadcasts St. Louis Hawks NBA games and is hired full time by KMOX (1120 AM). Broadcasts baseball nationally for ABC-TV. Also does bowling, college basketball, pro bowling and American Football League broadcasts. Becomes a host of KMOX's "At Your Service" shows, billed as the nation's first radio call-in programming.

Winter 1961	Rehired to work on Cardinals broadcasts.
September 1963	Moves from broadcasting AFL games on ABC-TV to NFL contests on CBS-TV.
October 1965	Broadcasts live from the top of the Gateway Arch the day it is completed.
October 1967	Buck, Jay Randolph and Gus Kyle form the radio play-by-play team for the Blues' inaugural season. Buck and Randolph give way to Dan Kelly and Kyle the following year.
December 1967	Is one of CBS-TV broadcasters of famous "Ice Bowl Game," Green Bay's 21-17 victory at home over Dallas for the NFL title, in a game played when the temperature at kickoff time was 13 degrees below zero.
March 1969	Marries Carole Lintzenich. They have two children (Joe, Julie).
April 1970	Becomes No. 1 man in Cardinals radio booth after Caray is fired in the off-season; Does play-by-play of Super Bowl on CBS-TV.
April 1972	Mike Shannon joins Buck in the Cards' booth, beginning what is one of the longest-running pairings in sports broadcasting history.
September 1975	Becomes host of *Grandstand*, a new NBC studio show, and announces he will relinquish his Cardinals broadcast duties in 1976.
Winter 1976	Bob Starr, the voice of the football Cardinals, is named to replace Buck in the baseball broadcast booth. But Buck is fired from *Grandstand* in March and is back behind the Cards' microphone for about 30 games.
April 1977	Returns full time to broadcasting the Cardinals, with Starr assuming a secondary role until leaving in 1980 to broadcast California Angels games.
September 1978	Becomes the radio play-by-play voice of *Monday Night Football* and the Super Bowl, working with analyst Hank Stram. Their run lasts for 16 of the next 18 seasons, being broken only by a two-year period (1985-'86) in which CBS Radio loses the broadcast rights to NBC.

October 1985   Utters his most famous call in broadcasting the Cardinals, as Ozzie Smith's improbable home run wins Game 5 of the National League Championship Series.

"Smith corks one into right, down the line. It may go...Go crazy, folks. Go crazy! It's a home run and the Cardinals have won the game 3-2 on a home run by the Wizard. Go crazy!"

July 1987   Is inducted into broadcasters' portion of baseball's Hall of Fame.

October 1988   Has his most-famous call nationally, in describing injured Dodger Kirk Gibson's limping to the plate as a pinch-hitter then belting a two-run homer before limping around the bases to win Game 1 of the World Series.

"Gibson swings and a fly ball to deep right field," Buck says on CBS Radio, the anticipation in his voice growing. *"This is going to be a home run! Unbelievable! A home run for Gibson and the Dodgers have won the game 5-4! I don't believe what I just saw!"*

April 1990   Is hired to be the play-by-play announcer for CBS' coverage of its No. 2 baseball game each week. But he is elevated to the top spot after Brent Musburger is fired two weeks before CBS' first telecast. He continues his Cards duties.

December 1992   Is fired from his CBS post after network officials say he never adapted to the trend in TV sportscasting that has the play-by-play announcer being a set-up man for the analyst (in this case Tim McCarver).

April 1995   Goes into semi-retirement; broadcasts only home games unless there is a special circumstance.

August 1995   Is voted into Radio Hall of Fame, joining a group including Jack Benny, Dick Clark, Paul Harvey, Bob Hope, Larry King, Rush Limbaugh, Groucho Marx, Arthur Godfrey, Lowell Thomas, Edward R. Murrow and Orson Welles.

January 1996   Broadcasts his 17th Super Bowl, most at the time of any announcer. One was on CBS-TV, the others on CBS Radio.

March 1997	Publishes autobiography, *That's a Winner*, which is what he says when he broadcast the final out of a Cardinals victory.
April 2000	Receives Lifetime Achievement Award at the sports Emmys ceremonies in New York.
Winter 2001-Spring 2002	Undergoes five surgeries in a span of about 5½ months, including three major ones. He has an operation in December to treat cancer, one in January to remove an intestinal blockage and one in March to implant sensors in his brain and chest to help control Parkinson's disease.
June 18, 2002	Dies in St. Louis at age 77.

Chicago Cubs All-Time Seventh Inning Stretch Guest Conductors 1998-2002

Actors/Actresses

Ann-Margret	2001
Tom Arnold	2002
Bea Arthur	2001
James Belushi	1999
Tom Bosley	2000
Kyle Chandler	1999
Joan Cusack	1998
John Cusack	1999
Barbara Eden	2000
Jeff Foxworthy	1998
Dennis Franz	1998
Mel Gibson	2000
Cuba Gooding, Jr.	1999
David Alan Grier	1999
Bonnie Hunt	1999
John Leguizamo	2002
Jay Leno	1998
Jonathan Lipnicki	2000
Bernie Mac	2002
John Mahoney	1999
Joe Mantegna	1998, 2002
Jerry Mathers	1998
Laurie Metcalf	1999
Bill Murray	1998
Chris O'Donnell	1998
Bronson Pinchot	2001
Harold Ramis	1999
Mickey Rooney	2001
Marion Ross	2000
Alan Ruck	2001
Gary Sandy	2001
Gary Sinise	2000
Vince Vaughn	1999
Dawn Wells	2002
Robert Wuhl	2000

Music

Frankie Avalon	1998
The B-52s	2000
Lance Bass, 'N SYNC	2001
Chuck Berry	2001
Big Head Todd & the Monsters	2002
The Buckinghams	2000
Michael Bolton	2000
Meredith Brooks	2002
Jimmy Buffett	1998, 1999
Cheap Trick	1998
Chicago	1999
Billy Corgan, Smashing Pumpkins	1998
Deborah Cox	1999
Charlie Daniels	2000
Dennis DeYoung, Styx	2000
Joey Fatone, 'N SYNC	2001
Faze 4	2001
Peter Frampton	2002
The Grand Ole Opry	2000
Buddy Guy	1998, 1999
Mickey Hart, Grateful Dead	2000
Hootie and the Blowfish	1999
KC & The Sunshine Band	2000
Cyndi Lauper	1999
Richard Marx	1999
Martina McBride	1998
Tony Orlando	2000, 2002
Radio City Rockettes	2000
Kenny Rogers	1999
Koko Taylor	1998
Eddie Vedder, Pearl Jam	1998
Mary Wilson—Supremes	2001

Well-Known Faces

Barney the Dinosaur	2001
Bozo the Clown	2001
Budweiser Whassup Guys	2000
Dick Clark	2000, 2001
David Copperfield	2000
Mark Cuban	2002
Roger Ebert	2001
Susan Hawk, Survivor I	2001
Bill Kurtis	2000, 2002
Bill O'Reilly, The O'Reilly Factor	2001
Pat Sajak	1999
Cael Sanderson	2002

Macho Man Randy Savage	1999
Donald Trump	2000
Governor Jesse Ventura	2000
Vanna White	2002

Olympians

Bonnie Blair	1998
Nicole Bobek	2000
Josh Davis	2000
Jennifer Gutierrez	2000
Nancy Kerrigan	1999
Karch Kiraly	1999
Frank Klopas	1999

Hockey

Chicago Wolves	2000
Chris Chelios	1998, 2000, 2001, 2002
Keith Magnuson	1998
Steve Maltais	2000
Stan Mikita	1998
Loren Molleken	1999
Ed Olczyk	2000
Dennis Savard	2001
Alpo Suhonen	2000
Brian Sutter	2001
Doug Wilson	2002

Baseball

Ernie Banks	1998, 1999, 2000, 2001, 2002
Glenn Beckert	1999, 2001
Mike Bielecki	2000, 2001
Bill Buckner	2002
Don Cardwell	2002
Joe Carter	2001
Jody Davis	2001
Andre Dawson	1998, 1999, 2000
Bobby Dernier	2000
Carlton Fisk	2000
Gary Gaetti	2001
Ken Holtzman	2001
Randy Hundley	1998
Fergie Jenkins	2001
Tommy Lasorda	1999, 2002
Vance Law	2001, 2002
Vernon Law	2002
Bill Madlock	2000
Minnie Minoso	1998

Paul Molitor	1999
Mickey Morandini	2001
Keith Moreland	2002
Joe Morgan	1998
Stan Musial	1998, 2000
Andy Pafko	2000
Tony Perez	2000
Jimmy Piersall	1998
Rick Reuschel	2002
Ryne Sandberg	1998, 1999, 2000, 2001
Scott Sanderson	1998
Ron Santo	1998, 1999, 2000, 2001, 2002
Ozzie Smith	1999
Tim Stoddard	2001
Steve Stone	1998, 1999, 2000
Rick Sutcliffe	1998, 2000, 2001, 2002
Bruce Sutter	2001
Billy Williams	1998, 2002

Basketball

Elton Brand	2000
Cory Carr	1999
Tyson Chandler	2001
Terry Cummings	2000
Eddy Curry	2001
Bryce Drew	2001
Michael Finley	1999
Ron Harper	1999
Steve Kerr	1998
Bob Love	1998
Corey Maggette	1999
Tracy McGrady	2000
Scottie Pippen	1998
Jalen Rose	2002
Norm Van Lier	2001
Antoine Walker	2001
Bill Wennington	1999

Basketball Coaches

Steve Alford (Iowa)	2001
Mike Brey (Notre Dame)	2001
Jim Calhoun (UConn)	1999
Jimmy Collins (UIC)	1998
Tom Crean (Marquette)	2002
Pat Kennedy (DePaul)	1999
Lon Krueger (Illinois)	1999
Mike Krzyzewski (Duke)	1998

Dave Leitao (DePaul) 2002
Jim Les (Bradley) 2002
Rick Majerus (Utah) 1999
Ray Meyer (DePaul) 1999
Bill Self (Illinois) 2001

Boxing

Muhammad Ali 1999
George Foreman 1999
Joe Frazier 2000

Football

Damien Anderson 2001
Drew Brees 2000
Dick Butkus 2000
Kevin Butler 2002
Marc Colombo 2002
Roosevelt Colvin 2002
Gary Fencik 2000
Jim Flanigan 1999
Dan Hampton 1999, 2002
Paul Hornung 2001, 2002
Erik Kramer 1999
Jim McMahon 1998
Steve McMichael 2001
Cade McNown 2000
R. W. McQuarters 2002
Walter Payton 1999
Jake Plummer 2000
Simeon Rice 2001
Marcus Robinson 2000, 2001
Mike Singletary 1999
Roger Staubach 2000
Brian Urlacher 2000, 2001
Tom Waddle 1998
Otis Wilson 1999

Football Coaches

Barry Alvarez (Wisconsin) 1999
Gary Barnett (Northwestern) 1998
Mike Ditka (Bears) 1998, 1999, 2000, 2002
Dick Jauron (Bears) 1999, 2000
Marv Levy (Bills) 1998, 2001
Bob Stoops (Oklahoma) 2002
Hank Stram 2000
Joe Tiller (Purdue) 2001
Ron Turner (Illinois) 1999, 2002

Randy Walker (Northwestern) 2002
Tyrone Willingham (Notre Dame) 2002

Special Guests

American Girl Theater Actresses
(American Girl Day) 2002
Barbie 1999
Tae Bo's Billy Blanks 1999
Dutchie Caray 2000
Ryan Clifford 2000
Private Jeremy Crandall 2001
Downers Grove South HS
Football Champs 2002
Comedian Tom Dreesen 1998, 2001
Elgin Children's Chorus 1999
Francis Cardinal George 1998
Bob Grimm
(IL Teacher of the year) 2002
Arne Harris Family 2002
Hinsdale Central HS Girls
Basketball Champs 2002
Ken Hubbs' Family 2002
Illinois Barber Shop Quartet 1999
Astronaut Dr. Mae Jemison 2000
Deloris Jordan 1999
Astronaut Captain James A. Lovell 1999
Maine South HS Football Champs 2001
The Roger Maris Family 1998
Wayne Messmer 1998, 1999, 2000
New Trier HS Baseball Champs 2000
New Trier HS Ice
Hockey Champs 2000, 2002
Connie Payton 2000
Pleasant Plaines HS
Baseball Champs 2000
Organist Gary Pressy 1999
Rent Cast Members 1999
Kate Shindle, Miss America 1998
Scott Turow 2002
Paul Vallas 2000
Pete Vonachen 1998
West Aurora HS Boys
Basketball Champs 2000
Westinghouse HS Boys
Basketball Champs 2002
Westlawn Little League
Baseball Champs 1999
Ronnie "Woo Woo" Wickers 2001
Wrigley Field Ground Crew 2000

Broadcasters & Journalists

Chris Berman (ESPN)	1999
Lou Boudreau (Cubs)	1998
Thom Brennaman (Diamondbacks)	2000
Jack Brickhouse (Cubs)	1999
Jack Buck (Cardinals)	2001
John Callaway (WTTW)	1999
Chip Caray (Cubs)	1998,1999, 2000, 2001, 2002
Rob Dibble (ESPN)	2000
John Drury (ABC-7)	2002
Gail Fisher (Fox Sports Net)	2000
Pat Foley (Blackhawks)	2000, 2002
Eric Goodman (Fox Sports Net)	2000
Arne Harris (WGN Sports)	1998, 2000
Ernie Harwell (Tigers)	1998
Jerome Holtzman (*Chicago Tribune*)	1998
Pat Hughes (Cubs)	1998, 1999, 2000, 2002
Walter Jacobson (Fox-32)	1999
Harry Kalas (Phillies)	1999, 2002
Dave Kaplan (WGN)	1998
Kathy & Judy (WGN)	2000
Vince Lloyd (Cubs)	2000
Steve Lyons (Fox)	1998
Jon Miller (ESPN)	1999
Joe Nuxhall (Reds)	1998
Spike O'Dell (WGN-Radio)	1999
Dave Otto (Cubs)	2000, 2001
Dan Patrick (ESPN)	1999, 2000, 2001
Allison Payne (WGN-TV)	1998
Digger Phelps (ESPN)	1998, 1999, 2000, 2001
Dan Roan (WGN-TV)	1998
John Rooney (ESPN-1000)	2002
Steve Sanders (WGN-TV)	1998
Stuart Scott (ESPN)	1999
Vin Scully (Dodgers)	1998
Bob Sirott (Fox-32)	1999
Tom Skilling (WGN-TV)	1999
Bob Uecker (Brewers)	1998,1999, 2000, 2001
Dick Vitale (ABC/ESPN)	1998
WGN Morning Crew	2000

Last Call

We hope you have enjoyed this tribute to Jack Buck. The author is preparing a new book for Redbird fans and you could be part of it.

The book *For Cardinal Fans Only*, subtitled *St. Louis Cardinals Fandemonium* is scheduled for release soon as part of an 81-book series on sports fans. *For Cardinals Fans Only* will be stories from Redbird backers relating their funniest, neatest or most poignant tale about going to a Cardinal game in St. Louis, on the road or Spring Training, listening to a game on the radio or watching on TV.

Send your story to *For Cardinal Fans Only*, 2662 Metro Blvd., St. Louis, MO 63043.

For information on ordering more copies of *Remembering Jack Buck* or any of the author's other best-selling books, go to www.fandemonium.net or call 602-738-5889.

Belated presstime thanks to Mr. Charles Brown for his extraordinary assistance, as well as Mr. Bill Vollmar, Catherine Tierney, Roger Wissman, and handsome Ricky Harrold.

Publisher's Note: The page count expanded from 255 to 288 to reflect the number of full page photos in this book.